Gender Matters

Gender Matters

Rereading Michelle Z. Rosaldo

Edited by

Alejandro Lugo and Bill Maurer

Ann Arbor

THE UNIVERSITY OF MICHIGAN PRESS

2003   2002   2001   2000   4   3   2   1

A CIP catalog record for this book is available from the British Library.

Library of Congress Cataloging-in-Publication Data

Gender matters : rereading Michelle Z. Rosaldo / edited by
    Alejandro Lugo and Bill Maurer.
        p.   cm.
      ISBN 0-472-11046-2 (alk. paper)
      ISBN 0-472-08618-9 (pbk. : alk. paper)
      1. Rosaldo, Michelle Zimbalist—Views on sex role.   2. Sex role.
    3. Feminist theory.   4. Feminist anthropology.   I. Lugo, Alejandro,
    1962–   II. Maurer, Bill, 1968–
    HQ1075   .G43   1999
    305.3—dc21   99-6290
                                                                CIP

To Our Teachers

Contents

Preface and Acknowledgments

The idea of revisiting Michelle Z. Rosaldo's feminist work was born in the classroom. After receiving undergraduate anthropological training in the "four-field" approach at New Mexico State University, I went to the University of Wisconsin in the fall of 1985 to continue my education in sociocultural anthropology. I was exposed to feminism for the first time at Madison through the courses offered by Maria Lepowsky and Ann Stoler in anthropology and through a seminar on Latin American feminism taught by Florencia Mallon in history. In the fall of 1986 I sat in Ann Stoler's class, "Women, Work, and Social Change," and discussed theoretical selections from both *Woman, Culture, and Society* (1974) and *Toward an Anthropology of Women* (1975), including Michelle Rosaldo's influential essay "Woman Culture and Society: A Theoretical Overview," along with a few of its subsequent critiques (particularly that her proposition was too universalist and dichotomous).

It was not that I disagreed with pointing out the limitations in dichotomous thought; particularly as years went by I became much more concerned with another problem: that there seemed to be too much agreement among many critics (as I elaborate in my own essay in this volume) about the political and theoretical weaknesses in Rosaldo's feminist framework. Thus, not having completely agreed with fundamental criticisms of Michelle Rosaldo's early work, I was perplexed by the welcome reception given in class to Temma Kaplan's (now classic) essay "Female Consciousness and Collective Action: The Case of Barcelona, 1910–1918," a sophisticated study of the radical and revolutionary possibilities embedded in "women as life givers and as life-sustainers." To me, as a student at the time, Kaplan's discussion of "female consciousness" had a striking resemblance to one of Michelle Rosaldo's hopes for social transformation vis-à-vis and despite domestic/public narratives. At that time, I also thought that Rosaldo was much more concerned with what happens and what does not happen after the revolution: do discourses about the domestic and public continue once the dust settles? I felt intellectually unable to propose to my classmates, and to my professor, an alternative reading of the essay on Barcelona by connecting it to Michelle Rosaldo's 1974 propositions; I reluctantly, though respectfully, decided to agree back then with the critiques launched at Rosaldo's work. After all, I was a neophyte; I had just been introduced to feminist thought.

In that same class we also read Fernandez-Kelly's pioneering work on Mexican maquiladoras, *For We Are Sold, I and My People,* one of the first feminist critiques, within and from anthropology, of the global assembly line. With an additional seminar on "Colonial Cultures" taught by Ann Stoler and with my growing theoretical and ethnographic interest on the U.S.-Mexico border, in the summer of 1987 I carried out preliminary fieldwork at the U.S.-Mexico borderlands among male and female factory workers. In the fall of 1988 I left for Stanford to work with Jane Collier, Sylvia Yanagisako, and Renato Rosaldo, who, since the mid-1980s, had been theorizing the border experience through his notion of cultural borderlands. Once at Stanford I took a seminar on the "Cultural Construction of Gender," taught by Janice Stockard. In that course I wrote a research essay—a fledgling version of my own chapter in this volume—that focused on the reconsideration of Michelle Rosaldo's early ideas.

After I began reconsidering Rosaldo's work, I noticed that, while there were several volumes and special issues in journals dedicated to her, there had never been a session organized or a book published addressing Rosaldo's intellectual contributions either to feminism or to anthropology. In the fall of 1991 I attended the American Anthropological Association (AAA) meetings in Chicago. It had been ten years since Michelle Rosaldo's accidental death in the Philippines. But, to my surprise, I looked in vain in the AAA program for a session in memory of such a pioneering anthropologist: the meetings went by without a tribute to one of the female scholars who had helped institutionalize feminist anthropology in the United States.

In the spring of 1992, while teaching my first seminar on gender at Bryn Mawr and with the intellectual encouragement of Jane Atkinson, Judith Shapiro, and Jane Collier, I put together a session in memory of Michelle Rosaldo ("Papers in Honor and Memory of Michelle Z. Rosaldo: Toward New and Different Readings of Her Feminist Work"). The session took place at the 1992 AAA meetings in San Francisco. Louise Lamphere chaired the panel; Anna L. Tsing and June Nash served as discussants; Jane F. Collier, Christine E. Gray, Carol P. MacCormack, Jane M. Atkinson, and I delivered essays reassessing Michelle Rosaldo's legacy.

This is how the idea that emerged in Ann Stoler's class came to develop into a session at the AAA meetings several years later. Since that time the session has gradually been transformed into a book project. Some of the original participants (Jane Collier, Christine Gray, Louise Lamphere, Carol MacCormack, and myself) provide here substantially revised versions of the original essays presented in the session (Lamphere turned her introductory statements into a prologue). Sadly, Carol MacCormack, one of the original participants in the panel, unexpectedly suffered a stroke, and, to the discipline's and to feminism's loss, she passed away in May 1997. Thus, Carol MacCormack will not be able to continue the dialogue with future generations, though she left for us the last version of her essay, in which she abides by her criticism of Michelle Rosaldo's feminist work.

Miguel Díaz Barriga, Matthew Gutmann, Bill Maurer, and Ana María Alonso were all invited at different times after 1992 to write additional essays that would help broaden the parameters of the book. I invited Díaz Barriga, Gutmann, and Maurer because I knew that they had ethnographic material on gender relations and because it seemed to me that they were three additional male anthropologists who were willing to address the feminist question, either from the angle of social movements, from the study of masculinities, or from a focus on sexuality, respectively. Besides his essay on sexuality in feminist anthropology, Bill Maurer also contributes his fine editorial, ethnographic, and theoretical skills to the coeditorship of the volume as a whole. Without Bill's help as my coeditor (since 1994), I am not sure I would have gotten this far. This edited volume is a product of our combined human efforts and of our intellectual partnership.

Finally, Ana María Alonso agreed to write the afterword. I thought that Alonso could offer her sophisticated insights on recent developments in feminist anthropology, which now encompasses not only studies of women but also studies of masculinity—as her own work on northern Mexico shows.

In retrospect, I can say that from the beginning it was never easy to find enough anthropologists for the session or for the volume; most people either did not have time to collaborate or simply were not willing to reconsider Michelle Rosaldo's work.

My persistence with this feminist project through the years would not have been possible without three sets of people. First, I would like to thank the many students—female and male—who took my courses on gender (and who inspired me to continue) at Bryn Mawr, the University of Texas at El Paso, and, more recently, at the University of Illinois at Urbana-Champaign. I am especially grateful to Elea Aguirre, Genevieve Bell, Charles Cuauhtemoc Chase-Venegas, Margarita Chavez-Chamorro, Angelina Cotler, James Gilmore, Martha Gonzalez-Cortez, Mary Holbrock, Michelle Johnson, Stephanie Johnston, Kevin Karpiak, Guisela Latorre, Marie Leger, Kathy Litherland, Walter Little, Ladonna Martin-Frost, Zulma Mendez, Betty Padilla, Sarah Philips, Angelica Rivera, Maria Tapias, and M. J. Walker.

Second, I am deeply thankful to my feminist teachers and to my feminist colleagues and friends, male and female, most of them already mentioned in the previous paragraphs. Especially, I offer my deepest gratitude to Jane Collier, Louise Lamphere, Bill Maurer, and Renato Rosaldo, who in their own distinctive ways stood as friendly pillars faithfully supporting, though not always uncritically, the intellectual and political project I had in mind. At Illinois I would like to thank Nancy Abelmann, Janet Keller, Cameron MacCarthy, Andy Orta, and, especially, Brenda Farnell, Alma Gottlieb, Phil Graham, Bill Kelleher, Sonya Michel, Arlene Torres, Angharad Valdivia, and Charles Varela.

One of my hopes is that the reader will find in these essays a spirit of intellectual engagement similar to the one with which Ann Stoler teaches and writes her anthropology. I am grateful to Professor Stoler for stimulating what led, in the end, to this volume. In spite of the generous input that came from teachers, students, and colleagues throughout the years, I am fully responsible for any error found in my own interpretation of Michelle Rosaldo's texts and ideas.

Third, and last, this feminist project is carried out in large part *en agradecimiento* and for the love of the main women *dentro de mi familia* who have shaped and continue to influence my gendered existence: on the one hand, the seven women who "raised" me (my grandmother, the late Rosalía Reyes, my mother, Vicenta Juárez de Lugo, and, out of nine siblings, my five sisters—all older than me—Cruz, Luz Elena, Rosa María, Lidia, and Guadalupe); and, on the other, my two lovely daughters, Rosalía and Elena, and my wife, Martina Miranda-Lugo.

During the years this book was in the making, I have struggled, as most people do, with questions and issues of gender politics in my own life. I have come to feel more or less comfortable with my role as a teacher, a colleague, a father, a brother, and a son. With regard to my role as a husband, Martina is the only one who is best able to judge, in our everyday life, my own inconsistencies, my best intentions, and the extent to which I practice, hopefully for the better, what I believe so much in preaching. With profound gratitude and love I dedicate my project to her.

The initial professionalization of my original idea would not have been possible without Ellen Lewin and the Association for Feminist Anthropology. I am sincerely thankful to both Professor Lewin and the AFA for opening a space for my session in San Francisco in 1992. In this context I will always be indebted to the original participants: Jane Atkinson, Jane Collier, Christine Gray, Louise Lamphere, the late Carol MacCormack, June Nash, and Anna Tsing. I also want to thank all the contributors, not only for unconditionally helping with the volume but especially for their patience, particularly through the ups and downs and throughout the last five years since I started the editorial journey. Finally, I am deeply grateful to two anonymous University of Michigan Press reviewers and to Susan B. Whitlock, editor, for their rigor and simultaneous enthusiasm for the volume from beginning to end. I hope that the final result does justice to the legacy of Michelle Zimbalist Rosaldo.

Alejandro Lugo

Prologue: Rereading and Remembering Michelle Rosaldo

Louise Lamphere

In the past ten years feminist anthropologists have done a great deal to reclaim our early foremothers. Beginning with *Women Anthropologists: A Biographical Dictionary* (Gacs et al. 1988), we have discovered more about the lives of women anthropologists including those who studied women even during the nineteenth century. We now have biographies (in some cases more than one) and articles on many of the most important female anthropologists—Alice Fletcher, Elsie Clews Parsons, Ruth Benedict, Margaret Mead—as well as a sense of how minority women, archaeologists, and women who worked in museums and laboratories contributed to the discipline (Parezo 1993; Bolles 1997). The importance of women to the writing of ethnography has been explored, and the contributions of women who began to write in the 1950s and 1960s have been analyzed (Behar and Gordon 1995). With this volume we begin to look at the anthropology of feminists in my own generation, those who came of age professionally in the 1970s. Michelle Rosaldo, perhaps because she died so young, but also because she was one of anthropology's most important feminist theorists, is a particularly appropriate focus for our attention at the end of the 1990s. The twenty-five years since the beginnings of what was to become *Woman, Culture and Society* give us sufficient distance to appraise her work and to value her legacy. A generation of anthropologists has been trained in the intervening time. Those now entering graduate school and the profession were likely to have been only babies when Shelly and I worked on this collection. Our children were not yet born, and mothering was a somewhat abstract possibility.[1] Our training in social anthropology, ethnoscience, and the works of Durkheim, Weber, Geertz, and Lévi-Strauss is much different than the blend of Marxism, interpretive anthropology, history, and postmodernism that informs much of the discipline today.

Time brings changes in anthropological theory, a shift in the topics that seem important to study, and even a transformation of the gender, class, and racial/ethnic characteristics of anthropologists. Thus, as Kamala Visweswaran points out, "different historical moments engender different strategies of reading" (1997:597). We have seen this in Barbara Babcock's reinterpretation of Ruth Benedict's work. Feminists of my generation were taught to critique Benedict's approach to the study of culture and personality, seeing her descriptions of the Zuni Apollonian, Plains Dionysian, and Kwakiutl Megalomaniac patterns as simplified caricatures or "psychological types" writ large. Instead, Babcock has emphasized Benedict as a precursor of interpretive anthropological practice and even postmodernism (Babcock 1995:105, 123). With her training in literary criticism and her sensibilities as a poet, Benedict read cultures as "texts" organized around "tropes" long before terms like *root metaphors, key symbols,* and *master tropes* became common terms in anthropological analysis. As Babcock says, she taught us "not only to read cultures as texts but also to read texts as cultural documents" (119). Likewise, Elsie Clews Parsons was rarely read outside of those interested in southwestern religion and folktales. She was known as a folklorist and eclectic. Her early feminist writing was erased from the anthropological canon. More recently, the insights she provided on her own upper-class institutions have been emphasized (Deacon 1997), the dialogic nature of her prose has been noted (Lamphere 1995; Babcock 1991), and her continued interest in gender and women's roles in her research in the Southwest and Mexico has come to the fore. Such new interpretations of feminist anthropological work stem from the recent emphasis in cultural anthropology on historical context, examining anthropological theories as emerging in particular historical periods and reflecting the class, race, and gender positions of theorists.

This leads me to place Shelly's research and writing in the context of her background, her training at Harvard, her involvement with the feminist movement, and her years at Stanford. In many ways Shelly's and my experiences in the 1960s and 1970s were parallel, especially in terms of the intertwining of feminism and anthropology, our efforts to transform the academy, and our desire to put a personal politics into practice through constructing a dual-career family, participating in a communal household, and sharing parenting and housework by integrating men into the domestic sphere.

Shelly Zimbalist was raised in a Jewish upper-middle-class family in a Long Island suburb, where she attended Great Neck South high school.

She entered Harvard as a freshman in 1962, the same year I came as a graduate student. I first met her in a small seminar on economic anthropology taught by Frank Cancian during the spring of 1964. Karen Brodkin (Sacks), Pam Lambert, Shelly, and I were the only four students I can remember who met in a small informal seminar room at 9 Bow Street, the three-story house that was the home of the Social Anthropology Program before William James Hall was opened in 1965 to house all four segments of the Social Relations Department. Shelly was only a sophomore, but she had taken a freshman seminar from Evon Z. Vogt ("Vogtie") and conducted fieldwork during the summer of 1963 on the Chiapas project. She returned to Chiapas in the summer of 1964 and also conducted field research in Spain during the summer of 1965. She majored in history and literature at Harvard, writing her honors thesis on the poetry of W. B. Yeats. Her major gave her a grounding in literary criticism and a sense of how to write prose that was much more nuanced and layered than my own.

Shelly and Renato began dating in the fall of 1964, when Renato became a newly enrolled graduate student in social anthropology in the Department of Social Relations and a tutor in Leverett House. They were married in June 1966, when Shelly also graduated from Radcliffe. In the fall Shelly entered the social anthropology graduate program at the same time that Renato was beginning his third year of study. She and Renato decided to do field research in the Philippines, choosing to study the Ilongots, an "exotic" and remote culture in northern Luzon, Philippines, rather than continuing to work in Chiapas. Like many young graduate students, it seemed important to conduct research in a faraway place among "primitive" peoples, in their case examining the lives of swidden agriculturalists who also practiced head-hunting.

Shelly and Renato were in the Philippines between the summer of 1967 and the summer of 1969. During this period I had finished my dissertation on Navajo kinship and cooperation, had taken a year's job at the University of Rochester, and then had been hired as an assistant professor at Brown University in Providence, Rhode Island. By the fall of 1969, when I saw Renato and Shelly in Cambridge, the world had changed. Both Martin Luther King and Robert Kennedy had been assassinated, the antiwar movement had grown, and the Harvard Strike the previous spring had brought radical politics to campus. In 1966 the antiwar and civil rights movements had engaged only a few white students on northeastern campuses. Within the next three years there was a radical shift that politicized students and brought them into a mass movement against the war in Vietnam.

Beginning in 1967 and 1968, women's groups emerged from various New Left organizations, primarily in large cities like Chicago and New York, many in reaction to what was viewed as male domination in these organizations. In Boston, Bread and Roses, a socialist feminist organization, issued a position paper in June 1969 (Hole and Levine 1971:411) and formed over twenty-five small groups in which women participated in discussions and "consciousness-raising." This term originated with the New York Redstockings group to express the importance of sharing personal experiences in small groups in order to understand the political nature of women's oppression. "The personal is political" became an early motto of the movement. In October 1969 Shelly joined a Bread and Roses group that included a number of Radcliffe graduates and friends (including Judy Herman, Susan Carey, and Gail Parker). This set of close friends became her way into politics. Nancy Chodorow, another friend of Shelly's from undergraduate days, was a member of a different Bread and Roses group. From this early beginning in an activist socialist feminist organization, Shelly and Nancy developed their feminist ideas in tandem over the next several years, often through correspondence. Nancy's participation in 1971–72 in a small group that discussed mother-daughter relationships, her training in the sociology doctoral program at Brandeis, and her exposure to object relations theory not only shaped Nancy's approach to a theory of gender personality development but also had an important impact on Shelly's own conceptualization of sexual asymmetry.

In August 1970 Shelly and Renato moved to Palo Alto, where Renato had accepted a position as an assistant professor in the Department of Anthropology. There they joined George and Jane Collier, who had also been Harvard students, although Jane was completing her Ph.D. degree at Tulane and parenting (with George's help) two young children. Renato and George held the tenure-track positions, while Jane and Shelly, both finishing their degrees, were "faculty wives."

During this year Shelly participated in a consciousness-raising group and also began, with Jane and a number of graduate students, to articulate ways in which feminism might reform how anthropologists thought about women and men in other cultures. The most concrete result of this was a course during the spring quarter 1971 on "Women in Cross-Cultural Perspective" (taught by Jane Collier, Julia Howell, Kim Kramer, Janet Shepherd Fjellman, Ellen Lewin, and Shelly).

Embracing Feminism

The early 1970s were a time when those of us who participated in the broader women's movement through consciousness-raising groups, testifying at hearings on abortion rights, participating in rallies and marches, attending conferences or other movement activities, began to integrate our feminism into the academic fields in which we had been trained. For Shelly this first meant participating in the 1971 course and then helping to organize a symposium at the American Anthropological Association (AAA) meeting in November 1971 in New York City. This was an association meeting full of controversy. The discipline had been rocked by the revelation that anthropologists had participated in counterinsurgency activities in Thailand. I still remember a packed ballroom where, at the AAA Council of Fellows meeting, a report of a committee to investigate these alleged activities (chaired by Margaret Mead) was resoundingly turned down for not condemning clandestine research (Wakin 1992:211–13).

It was in this atmosphere that feminist papers were first appearing on the program in significant numbers. Shelly had mailed me a copy of the lectures from the spring 1971 class, and we were already talking about a book, so I attended the Stanford session at the November American Anthropological Association meeting with anticipation and was impressed with the quality of the material. Before I returned to London, where I was spending a year's leave, Shelly and I decided to put together a collection of essays on the new cross-cultural research on women. We wrote to thirty-five women who had given talks on women at the anthropology meetings or who had participated in the Stanford course. By February we had received enough replies to draft an outline of a collection with over twenty contributions to submit to presses. Looking back over our correspondence, both of us seemed uncertain about how to proceed, nervous about turning contributors down and yet increasingly aware that the book was unfocused and too long. As Shelly wrote on February 1, 1972: "Wow! My desk is a mess, and things feel incredibly complicated. At the same time, I feel very excited by the kinds of responses we've had."

We were both extremely naive about how to handle contacts with presses and how to shape what was soon becoming an unwieldy volume. In turning our book prospectus down, an editor from Harper and Row wrote to Shelly, in January 1972, that "the outline is excellent but that a book based on papers given at a symposium has a limited appeal in the paperback market." Shelly voiced a series of worries, "One is the sheer number of our contributors . . . And, related to that—some of our contributors seem to be of 'uncertain' quality; does that mean that we'll edit like hell, or reserve the right to decide on seeing the papers that some people won't be included . . . Have you thought about when and how we'll be 'hard-nosed'; it really scares me, but I think we may well want to have some freedom in accepting papers, and I think we should get together on how we'll proceed."

Shelly turned for advice to Monica Wilson, a senior female anthropologist, who was at the Center for Advanced Study at Stanford that year. During a conversation with Shelly at a party Wilson suggested paring the book down drastically and eliminating papers on "'big societies," that is, complex societies such as the United States and Taiwan. In writing to me about this exchange, Shelly suggested we might have to cut some of the papers: "When I get confused I get mainly very very anxious, so I would really appreciate knowing what you think as soon as possible . . . Again, I'm sorry to be flashing an SOS with the request that YOU make some difficult decisions. But when local feedback is all of the kind that says, 'God girl, you've sure taken on a mouthful' and stops there—I don't know where else to turn."

I was much less willing to make such hard decisions. In a letter to Shelly I said: "I can see that matters concerning the book are getting a bit more complex. I know that 22 people is really too many, but I also don't see how we can cut anyone out at this point. I'd say the thing to do is (1) to be nasty about the September 1st deadline . . . and (2) ask people to rewrite if the paper is poor and perhaps in that way we cut the number of articles down." Eventually, we had to "bite the bullet." Although some authors eliminated themselves, we had to tell others that their pieces would not fit in the book or that the outside reader recommended against inclusion. I suspect Shelly was more comfortable about this than I was—a commentary on our different personalities and approaches to scholarship. Shelly was always highly critical and demanding of herself and others when it came to judging the quality of an argument or the use of theory. While I tend to dislike conflict and wish to "patch things over," Shelly was less tolerant of insufficiently worked out analyses. For her (and here I think she was correct), as painful as eliminating several articles was, it made for a better and more coherent book.

For six months we had been trying to find an established press that would consider publishing the collection. The breakthrough came when Shelly talked to Jess Bell and Bill Carver at Stanford University Press in

May 1972. They were interested but wanted us to cut several authors and have the remaining ones submit longer abstracts. Shelly quickly wrote most of those on our list (several had dropped out by this time), assembled the abstracts, and returned a packet to the press in July. Then began a long year of working with authors, who turned in drafts by the end of the summer. I traveled to Palo Alto in August 1972; I remember sharing Renato and Shelly's small house for several days as Shelly and I pored over drafts. We discussed the essays together and then divided them up, each of us working individually with authors, usually writing a long letter with comments and suggestions (in the days before computers and e-mail, a time-consuming task). I traveled to California again in January 1973 (for another long working session in the dreary winter rainy season). By this time we were close to assembling the whole manuscript, which was submitted to the press during the spring and sent to an outside reader. In those days there were hardly any senior women who had published on women or gender, and so our outside reader was male. The reader and our editors at Stanford urged us to drop several essays. We agreed in three cases but went on to push for continued revisions for three others. In at least one case our extensive rewriting was met with serious objections by the author, and she eventually produced her own set of revisions, which were acceptable to the Stanford editor. In a second case both the Stanford editor and I "cut and pasted" until we had something with which all three of us were satisfied. During this period Shelly drafted the introduction from notes she had made, and I added suggestions, rewording, and revisions. At last, at the end of the summer in 1973, the book went into production, with the last two or three essays straggling in. By the time it appeared in April 1974, Shelly was already in the Philippines on her second field trip there.

It was not until a year or two later that we both realized that the book was making an important impact on both anthropology and feminism as practiced in other disciplines. We began conversations with our coauthors about what to do with the profits over the years. We shared our ideas over the phone and sometimes sent checks to the volume's participants and at other times contributed to a fund for Guatemalan children in memory of Lois Paul (one of our contributors, who had died in 1976) and to a variety of feminist organizations.

During the years between 1970 and 1974 Renato and Shelly were attempting to forge a dual-career marriage, a difficult proposition when couples were rarely hired in the same program. At Harvard, in the generation preceding us, Bea Whiting, Florence Kluckhohn, and others had only held lectureships and research associate positions, while their husbands enjoyed full professor status. At Stanford Louise Spindler was a lecturer while her husband, George, was a full professor, and Margery Wolf and Lois Paul both conducted joint research with their husbands in Taiwan and Guatemala, respectively, but remained in the status of faculty wives. There was not much precedent for "dual-career equal partnerships" in academe.

In 1970–71 Shelly completed her dissertation, and during the following year she was a member of the Committee on Linguistics, teaching courses but still not a full-time faculty member. Other jobs in the Bay area had not materialized, and she started thinking seriously of applying for a position on the East Coast. Even looking for a job three thousand miles away from one's husband or partner was an unusual occurrence in the early 1970s. In addition, a woman had to rely on a personal network of patrons and their close colleagues. In the days before advertisements and affirmative action jobs were found by word of mouth, usually though full professors (male) recommending their students to department chairs who called on the phone. In December 1971, just after the AAA meetings (and an interview in New York), Shelly received a job offer from Columbia. She wrote in a hasty letter:

> [Robert] Murphy called on Tuesday to offer me (you're wonderful, your work is excellent, just what we want . . . an incredible high!) a job at Columbia. [Ben] Paul [chair of the Stanford Anthropology Department] now speaks (ironically, admitted) of 'if we can convince you to stay' and [Charles] Frake says he promises to buy a big sailboat and let us use it if I turn down Columbia. So, things look like they'll work at Stanford; and after a year of self-doubt, anxiety, and feeling that THEY are all against me, I feel reasonably relaxed, confident, and pleasantly alive.

By December 30, 1971, the Stanford Department had voted half-time appointments for both Shelly and Jane Collier. Renato asked the university if they could split the one and a half positions into two three-quarters positions, and they agreed. Eventually, Shelly came to feel that the arrangement was exploitative: "Both Renato and I put in full-time labor for three quarters pay . . . instead of four full-catalogue courses a year we do three apiece. Apart from that we work a full load. That extra course is a bonus. It gives me flexibility that I like . . . I don't know if I'll continue to feel that way. I might sell an extra quarter time to someone else so as to feel less exploited." In working out a stance as a partner (rather than wife) in a dual-career couple, Shelly pushed for a vision of her life in which she was not confined to a domestic sphere nor a subordinate to her husband in the public sphere. As Lugo and Maurer point out in their introduction, these are interventions that embodied the notion of gender as performativity. They were part of her feminist theorizing and also part of the way she thought about her partnership with Renato: "We have very separate intellectual styles. Given the same data and similar theoretical orientations, we would still write very different papers. Our colleagues see us as two and a half people, not as one and a half. We are both strong individuals and our 'togetherness' seems to add to our presence" (Stanford University *Campus Report,* May 25, 1977).

From January to December 1974 Shelly and Renato returned to the Philippines for a second field trip to the Ilongot, one that was to shape Shelly's book *Knowledge and Passion* (1980a). Over the next seven years Shelly's personal and intellectual effort went into building a collective household (in which her children could be an integral part) and changing the university through increasing the presence of academic feminism. In 1974 Renato and Shelly purchased a collective house with two other Stanford couples. Their year at Princeton at the Institute for Advanced Studies in 1975–76 provided Shelly with time to get started on the book and to solidify important intellectual relationships with Clifford Geertz and Ellen and William Sewell.

Shelly wrote to me in March 1976 from Princeton that she was pregnant: "Starting to get fat with baby is making that seem realer." After much soul-searching and negotiating, they turned down two job offers from the new department at Johns Hopkins, since Stanford had offered Renato tenure in order to keep them. "We decided that if Stanford could give Renato tenure we'd just as soon have our baby in good weather with the company of good friends."

After the Princeton year the house on Embarcadero became their home, and a number of young Stanford faculty shared their collective lives over the years in which Sam (born September 21, 1976) was an infant and toddler and Manuel (born July 28, 1980) came into the world. By 1978 Shelly and Renato were able to negotiate full-time appointments, adding one-quarter time to each position. Shelly received tenure in 1979. Over the Christmas / New Year's break in 1980–81 Shelly mockingly described herself as "the Kompleat Mother—I'm breast feeding Manny on the floor of

Gymnastics West where Sam is having a gymnastics lesson." At the same time she was dashing off a note to me about what to do with the 1980 book royalties.

In the late 1970s Shelly put a great deal of effort into teaching feminist anthropology. She and Jane Collier continued to teach the course that had been offered collectively in 1971 under the same title, "Women in Cross-Cultural Perspective." They also cotaught several graduate seminars (one on gender relations among Australian Aborigines, another on women in chiefdoms) in which they jointly worked through some of their important theoretical ideas. Much of Shelly's *Signs* article on "The Use and Abuse of Anthropology" (1980b) and her joint article with Jane (Collier and Rosaldo 1981), were a result of this collaboration.

Shelly was also involved in the creation of a program in Feminist Studies at Stanford. She began meeting with a group of Stanford faculty, including Nan Keohane, Barbara Gelpi, Myra Strober, and Estelle Friedman, at the newly formed Center for Research on Women (now the Institute for Research on Women and Gender). Estelle and Shelly cochaired the committee, and Estelle remembers that Shelly did much of the administrative work to get the undergraduate major approved. The name of the program, Feminist Studies (rather than Women's Studies), is a tribute to Shelly's insistence that the undergraduate major take this much more controversial name since it focused on a critical analysis of gender and its intersections with other forms of hierarchy. Estelle remembers how much Shelly's appreciation for complexity enriched the field of feminist scholarship. She was able to go deeper and further into an analysis than others around her and find the language that articulated the intricate relationships between gender and other social categories.

Michelle Rosaldo as Theorist

Although Shelly drew a great deal from anthropological theory in formulating her ideas about gender asymmetry and the dichotomy between public and private spheres, her own experience in the women's liberation movement and her attempts to integrate her personal and professional life (rather than to be pushed into a domestic sphere) undoubtedly played a role in how she thought about women's position theoretically. For most of us in the early 1970s there was no separation between our discipline (anthropology), our participation in the women's movement, and our personal choices about partnerships (with males or females) and raising children. Rather, we attempted to bring the same principles that integrated social critique, a commitment to egalitarianism, and the struggle for change to bear in all areas of our lives.

Shelly was a subtle and brilliant thinker. Although critics have often labeled her work as fitting into a neat category—structuralist, interpretivist, symbolic—her arguments are actually less easy to characterize. It was during our collaboration in 1972–73 that I began to see how different Shelly's intellectual style was from mine. I would often write "plain Jane" straightforward sentences, which Shelly would reword, adding clauses, qualifying, and making the meaning more nuanced. It is her prose that makes it possible to see connections that Alejandro Lugo and Bill Maurer make to Foucault's work on power, to recent analyses of the imposition of Enlightenment categories on colonized peoples, to current interest in the anthropology of the self, and even to the reflexivity emphasized in so much contemporary ethnographic writing. One of the important contributions of several authors in this collection is their interest in going beyond the early critiques of Rosaldo's use of the public/domestic dichotomy as too simple, rigid, and circular to be useful in our understanding of gender relations. Instead, these authors argue, Rosaldo's analysis helps us see the particular force of these categories in many societies, including our own, and to emphasize a performative perspective.

A few examples from Shelly's texts will suggest how nonreductive and complex her arguments were. In discussing domestic and public orientations in the "Woman, Culture and Society: A Theoretical Overview," Shelly says she is providing "the basis of a structural framework necessary to identify and explore the place of male and female in psychological, culture, social and economic aspects of human life." This is a framework for exploring and thinking about a complex set of relations—not a rigid set of categories. Shelly goes on to argue that "the opposition does not *determine* cultural stereotypes or asymmetries in the evaluations of the sexes, but rather underlies them." Again, as Lugo and Maurer point out in their introduction, Shelly is here rejecting a simplistic causal model and instead positing a cultural logic that has a kind of performative force (indicated by Shelly's use of the term *evaluation*) that seems very similar to Judith Butler's analysis of gender relations (1990, 1997).

In her 1980 *Signs* article Shelly staked out a position that clarified how she saw sexual asymmetry and the usefulness of the domestic/public dichotomy. Then she went on to break new ground in understanding the historical lineage from which the domestic/public concepts emerged and to call for a new approach rooted in practice or performance, in which cultural meaning (or what would today be called discourse) still had an important role. "It now appears to me that woman's place in human social life is not in any direct sense a product of the things she does (or even less a function of what, biologically, she is) but of the meaning her activities acquire through concrete social interactions. And the significances women assign to the activities of their lives are things that we can only grasp through an analysis of the relationships that women forge, the social contexts they (along with men) create—and within which they are defined" (1980b:400).

In her book *Knowledge and Passion* we see the working out of this performative perspective. Throughout her analysis Shelly attempts to explicate Ilongot concepts—in an almost Benedict-like fashion—through contrasts with her own thoughts and perceptions of incidents in the field. She talks of "following the Ilongot," explaining, first, words for feelings and then the social and practical situations to which emotional idioms were applied (Rosaldo 1980a:223). In rereading the book, I was struck by the postmodern-like stance Shelly took even in the late 1970s. Her sentences were always qualified, placing herself as well as her consultants in a dialogue. Her prose was shifting and contextual, giving us a sense of multiplicity rather than unity and always pointing up the contrast between the anthropologist and her subjects. For example, she discusses how Ilongot children reacted to a tape of Joan Baez "singing in a tremolo that for Ilongots recalled the quivering tension of such songs as stir men's hearts to kill—about a soldier going off to war." But, rather than see the similarities in our reaction and those of the Ilongot to the song, Shelly emphasized the differences: "Baez's song protested against war and invoked mourning, whereas for Ilongots her quivering voice was like a fluttering bangle or a twisting heart" (222).

Feminist Anthropology since 1974 and Michelle Rosaldo's Legacy

Since 1981 anthropology and feminist theory have been transformed in a number of ways that seem to veer away from Shelly's contributions. First, postmodernist theorists (using the work of Derrida, Lacan, and Foucault) attacked the validity of Enlightenment concepts and emphasized the importance of discourse (deconstructing the fundamental categories used by social science). Anthropologists, however, have drawn much more on Foucault than on Derrida or Lacan, partly because of their firm commitment to an analysis of power and the grounding of discourses in concrete practices. Second, the analysis of texts and ethnographic writing has led to a critique of objectivist description and forced feminist anthropologists and others to position themselves within their texts, to take reflexivity seriously, and to invent new ways of writing more dialogically. Third, and perhaps most important, the critiques of anthropology as a colonial discipline and of feminism as a white woman's movement have shifted the focus of feminist work so that it includes the voices of U.S. women of color and women throughout the Third World.

It might seem that feminist anthropology of the 1990s is all about situated knowledges, diaologic texts, "women's voices," and "performativity." Yet there is another strain that has developed through socialist feminist analysis, the study of gender and colonialism, and the continued importance of concepts of class and power in gender relationships. There is a continuity here that is rooted in the analysis of materiality and meaning, which were issues that very much occupied Shelly's interest. Many of the essays in this volume draw on socialist feminist and Marxist traditions that, unlike Christine Gray's reading of the literature, have found much to gain through an analysis of the impact of colonialism and the new global economy.

The mark of a great scholar is his or her impact on the thinking of others. Since Shelly died when she was only thirty-seven years old, her potential influence over students in the 1980s and 1990s was lost. We can only surmise that she would have taken the insights of postmodernism, the writings of women of color, and the attention to textuality and turned them from fresh insights into feminist predicaments. That her work can be reread in the 1990s and remains an inspiration to younger scholars is a testament to her skill as a thinker and her insights as a feminist anthropologist.

NOTE

1. Several of the contributors to *Woman, Culture and Society,* however, were mothers and may have brought that experience to their analyses.

REFERENCES

Babcock, Barbara
    1995   "'Not in the Absolute Singular': Rereading Ruth Benedict." In *Women Writing Culture,* ed. Ruth Behar and Deborah A. Gordon, 104–30. Berkeley: University of California Press.

Behar, Ruth, and Deborah A. Gordon
    1995   *Women Writing Culture.* Berkeley: University of California Press.
    1996   *The Vulnerable Observer: Anthropology That Breaks Your Heart.* Boston: Beacon Press.
Bolles, Lynn
    1997   "Women Ancestors: A History of Black Feminist Anthropology." Paper presented in a session on "The Poetics and Politics of Black Feminist Anthropology," American Anthropological Association, Washington, D.C., November 19–23.
Butler, Judith
    1990   *Gender Trouble: Feminism and the Subversion of Identity.* New York: Routledge.
    1997   "Critically Queer." In *Playing with Fire: Queer Politics, Queer Theories,* ed. Shane Phelan, 11–29. New York: Routledge.
Collier, Jane F., and Michelle Z. Rosaldo
    1981   "Politics and Gender in 'Simple' Societies." In *Sexual Meanings,* ed. Sherry Ortner and Harriet Whitehead, 275–329. New York: Cambridge University Press.
Deacon, Desley
    1997   *Elsie Clews Parsons: Inventing Modern Life.* Chicago: University of Chicago Press.
Gacs, Ute, Aisha Khan, Jerrie McIntyre, and Ruth Weinberg
    1988   *Women Anthropologists: A Biographical Dictionary.* New York: Greenwood Press.
Hole, Judith, and Ellen Levine
    1971   *The Rebirth of Feminism.* New York: Quadrangle Books.
Lamphere, Louise
    1995   "Feminist Anthropology: The Legacy of Elsie Clews Parsons." In *Women Writing Culture,* ed. Ruth Behar and Deborah A. Gordon, 85–103. Berkeley: University of California Press.
Parezo, Nancy J.
    1993   *Hidden Scholars: Women Anthropologists and the Native American Southwest.* Albuquerque: University of New Mexico Press.
Rosaldo, Michelle
    1974   "Woman, Culture and Society: A Theoretical Overview." In *Woman, Culture and Society,* ed. Michelle Zimbalist Rosaldo and Louise Lamphere, 17–42. Stanford: Stanford University Press.
    1980a   *Knowledge and Passion: Ilongot Notions of Self and Social Life.* Cambridge: Cambridge University Press.
    1980b   "The Use and Abuse of Anthropology: Reflections on Feminist and Cross-Cultural Understanding." *Signs* 5 (3): 389–416.
Visweswaran, Kamala
    1997   "Histories of Feminist Ethnography." *Annual Review of Anthropology* 26:591–621. Palo Alto: Annual Review Press.

Wakin, Eric
  1992 *Anthropology Goes to War: Professional Ethics and Counterinsurgency in Thailand.* Madison University of Wisconsin Center for Southeast Asian Studies, Monograph no. 9.

The Legacy of Michelle Rosaldo: Politics and Gender in Modern Societies

Alejandro Lugo and Bill Maurer

For the past twenty years the work of Michelle Z. Rosaldo has had a profound impact on feminism and anthropology, both among scholars who knew and worked closely with Rosaldo, and continued her research agenda after her death in 1981, and those, like the editors of this volume, who never knew Rosaldo but who find her work provocative and, in our own cases, were led to graduate work in feminist theory and anthropology in part because of her interventions. For both of the editors reading Rosaldo's lead essay in *Woman, Culture and Society* (Rosaldo and Lamphere 1974) was a defining moment in our anthropological educations and in our development as persons; it led us to rethink our position as gendered (male) subjects, to bring feminist analysis "home" to our everyday lives, and, ultimately, to become graduate students at Stanford University, where we studied with some of Rosaldo's colleagues and coauthors.

Some of the contributors to this volume are anthropologists who knew and worked with Rosaldo (Lamphere, Collier, and MacCormack as colleagues and Gray as a student of hers) and some who had not but had relied heavily on her thinking (Díaz Barriga, Gutmann, Lugo, and Maurer). Four of these scholars (Díaz Barriga, Gutmann, Lugo, and Maurer) are younger male ethnographers who were trained in the tradition of feminist anthropology during the 1980s and received their Ph.D. degrees in the 1990s under female feminist anthropologists of Michelle Rosaldo's generation. The intellectual combination of different genders and generations in the volume permits us, as editors, to make necessary connections between Michelle Rosaldo's varied positionalities, as the remarkable young scholar that she herself was and as a feminist theorist who persuasively noted that "the tendency to ignore imbalances in order to permit a grasp of women's lives has led too many scholars to forget that men and women ultimately live together in the world and, so, that we will never understand the lives that women lead without relating them to men" (1980a:396).

In this sociological and theoretical sense the volume as a whole—and specifically the essays by Díaz Barriga, Gutmann, Lugo, and Maurer—shows how the anthropological study of "masculinity," "femininity," and gender (meaning both women and men) has been inspired by the work of Michelle Rosaldo. At the same time, and perhaps most important, the volume tries, from different gender, generational, and intellectual perspectives, to push the field of feminist anthropology forward by reconsidering several of Michelle Rosaldo's lasting influences. The most important of these, ultimately, is best captured in Rosaldo's own words, in which she stated not only that gender matters but that genders matter: "If men . . . appear to be the actors who create the social world, our task is neither to accept this fact as adequate in sociological terms nor to attempt, by stressing female action, to deny it. Instead, we must begin to analyze the social processes that give appearances like these their sense, to ask just how it comes about—*in a world where people of both sexes make choices that count*—that men come to be seen as the creators of collective good and the preeminent force in local politics" (1980a:414–15; emph. added).

We should state at the outset what this book is and is not about: it is more a productive than a critical retrospective of Michelle Rosaldo' work; although it is not an uncritical commemoration, this book celebrates Michelle Rosaldo's significant role, especially as the young theorist and ethnographer that she was, in helping shape the kind of anthropological enterprise that we practice today, in the late 1990s (and intend to be, we argue, for many generations to come). To that end the volume will provide an in-depth analysis of Rosaldo's many contributions to anthropology and feminism. Yet this volume is not "the next step" in feminist anthropology: rather, we hope that a rereading of Rosaldo's ideas and arguments, and their reconsideration vis-à-vis recent, exciting ethnographic work, will further enrich this vital branch of our field and help confirm its proper location at the center of the center of anthropological inquiry.

As editors, we hope to make a case for a general reconsideration of Rosaldo's key theoretical ideas, especially those surrounding the public/domestic dichotomy, the self and emotion, social personhood, and critiques of essentialism in studies of gender and society. Each of the essays takes one or more of these analytically and politically useful insights from Rosaldo's work and sets it in motion for new intellectual and political practices. The authors do not always share the same perspective on

Rosaldo's work, and they do not necessarily agree with one another on Rosaldo's legacy. But, together, they point to exciting syntheses of old and new feminist analysis and to new directions for feminist research and politics. We attempt to spell out some of these directions in this introduction.

We have organized this introduction in terms of what we see as Rosaldo's major theoretical contributions to anthropology: her elaboration of the public/domestic analytical dichotomy for the analysis of gender cross-culturally; her intervention in the positivist agenda of cognitive and psychological anthropology; and her attention to the social bases of emotion and feeling. Each of Rosaldo's contributions pointed toward and, we believe, can be used to push forward three recent analytical innovations in anthropology: an analysis of the biopolitics of populations; a consideration of the performative practices that constitute social subjects; and a questioning of the interiority presumed to inhere in socially produced individuals. Finally, we believe Rosaldo's theoretical insights help us move beyond the quandaries of identity politics in useful and politically important ways.

From the Public/Domestic Dichotomy
to the Biopolitics of Populations

The elaboration of the public/domestic analytic dichotomy to explain women's subordination has arguably been Michelle Rosaldo's most significant contribution to feminist anthropology. In her elemental feminist essay "Woman, Culture, and Society: A Theoretical Overview" Rosaldo proposed that "an opposition between 'domestic' and 'public' provides the basis of a structural framework necessary to identify and explore the place of male and female in psychological, cultural, social, and economic aspects of human life" (1974:23). More specifically, she stated:

> "Domestic," as used here, refers to those minimal institutions and modes of activity that are organized immediately around one or more mothers and their children; "public" refers to activities, institutions, and forms of association that link, rank, organize or subsume particular mother-child groups. Though this opposition will be more or less salient in different social and ideological systems, it does provide a universal framework for conceptualizing the activities of the sexes. The opposition does not *determine* cultural stereotypes or asymmetries in the evaluation of the sexes, but rather underlies them, to support a very

general (and, for women, often demeaning) identification of women with domestic life and of men with public life. These identifications, themselves neither necessary nor desirable, can all be tied to the role of women in child rearing; by examining their multiple ramifications, one can begin to understand the nature of female subordination and the ways it may be overcome. (23–24)

For Michelle Rosaldo what was "perhaps most striking and surprising is the fact that male, as opposed to female, activities are always recognized as predominantly important, and cultural systems give authority and value to the roles and activities of men" (19).

In the years following the publication of her essay anthropologists divested the cultural analysis from her theoretical framework and reduced it to positivist interpretations of domestic and public "spaces" (e.g., from the domestic kitchen to the public plaza or marketplace, respectively). Consequently, anthropologists went about attempting to draw the boundaries between the public and the private in particular societies, delineating how women's work in the "domestic" had "public" ramifications, arguing that women did have public roles or authority, after all, and pointing out the limitations of the public/domestic dichotomy in societies that seemed not to have such clearly demarcated domains. When brought to "the field," the dichotomy, not surprisingly, seemed to soften with use, and many began to view it less as an ethnographic certitude and more as a simple yet powerful imposition of Western categories on diverse cultural realities.

As emerges in several of the essays here (Collier, Lugo, Maurer, and Díaz Barriga), however, the recognition of the public/domestic dichotomy as an imposition of Western categories does not strip it of its usefulness and, in fact, is itself an important intervention in understanding the legacy of Enlightenment political philosophy and practice as it has impacted the world, both colonial and postcolonial. Studies of colonialism have demonstrated how colonial officials actively enforced public and private on colonized populations (e.g., Comaroff and Comaroff 1991; Chatterjee 1993; Lazarus-Black 1994; Stoler 1995), generating a whole series of resistances against and capitulations to a bourgeois order spread through imperial ventures, war, and commerce. In fact, Michelle Rosaldo had much to say about the Victorian tenets that have given ideological support and constitution to gender relations during these imperial and colonial ventures since the turn of the century. As she wrote, "The turn-of-the-century social theorists [Durkheim, Spencer, Engels, Simmel, Malinowski, Radcliffe-

Brown, among others] whose writings are the basis of most modern social thinking tended without exception to assume that women's place was in the home. In fact, the Victorian doctrine of separate male and female spheres was, I would suggest, quite central to their sociology" (1980a:401).

Many anthropologists are now engaged in a critical reassessment of the imposition and spread of Enlightenment categories, their internal contradictions and their constitutive force in colonial and postcolonial worlds (Handler and Segal 1990; Fitzpatrick 1992; Strathern 1992; Thomas 1994; Collier, Maurer, and Suarez-Navaz 1995; Young 1995; Coombe 1997). In this context, in 1980 Michelle Rosaldo articulated the need for understanding the domestic/public dichotomy as a problematic Victorian ideology. As she stated very clearly:

> My stress on the Victorians derives, first of all, from a conviction that they are our most relevant predecessors in this regard, and second, from an intuition that the Victorian dichotomies—in their appeal to maternity and biology—were in fact, significantly different from what came before [since the time of the Greeks]. Once it is realized that domestic/public constitutes an ideological rather than an objective and necessary set of terms, we can, of course, begin to explore the differences in formulations which may appear initially to be "more of the same." (1980a:402 n. 20)

Through Michelle Rosaldo's insights about the ideological, biological, and political aspects of Victorian institutions in the metropole, and especially considering the dispersion of British, French, and American colonialisms during the late nineteenth century and during most of the twentieth century, we have come to acknowledge a vital theoretical connection between the work of Michelle Rosaldo and that of Michel Foucault (1977, 1978). For instance, the public/domestic dichotomy, as an Enlightenment imposition and as a Victorian ideology, produces new social categories and social realities in the act of being enforced through colonial and capitalist regulations of populations. In parallel manner Foucault's notion of biopower brings together the public world of the state, of regulation, of social order writ large, with the domestic in an exploration of the power of the state to call forth subjects and the power of subjects to recreate their subjectification by and for the state (Foucault 1977, 1978; Donzelot 1979). With regard to power, gender, and morality under the modern state Michelle Rosaldo noted about the Victorian legacy:

Victorian theory cast the sexes in dichotomous and contrastive terms, describing home and woman not primarily as they were but as they had to be, given an ideology that opposed natural, moral, and essentially unchanging private realms to the vagaries of a progressive masculine society. And, similarly, I would suggest that when modern theorists write that paternity is a variable and social fact whereas maternity is a relatively constant and unchanging one, constrained by nature . . . or perhaps, when they distinguish moral kinship from the bonds of selfish interest forged in economic life; or, then again, when they describe the differences between apparently formal and informal social roles and forms of power—they are the nineteenth century's unwitting heirs. (Rosaldo 1980a:404)

Following Foucault, anthropologists today are looking to the mutual implication of domination and resistance in everyday acts of statecraft, medicine, pleasure, and knowledge. Thus far, they have found that modern biopolitics of populations, key to the regulation and governance of citizens of states inspired by the social contract vision of "liberty, equality and fraternity," brings public and domestic together in a synergistic tension that preserves the fiction of separate spheres while maintaining their imbrication into each other (Horn 1994; Ginsberg and Rapp 1995; McClintock 1995). Foucault has contributed the important insight that power is productive, not only repressive (and that its repressions are always themselves productive). Thus, it now becomes a crucial analytical task to highlight the productive practices of power that make the illusion of separate spheres seem real and determinative of people's lives and subjectivities. This is, in the end, a self-reflexive task as well: for many people the doctrine of separate spheres seems to correspond to our everyday experiences, as we move in self-discipline from home to work and back again, enjoy our domestic pleasures "apart" from the eye of the state, and make our private consumer choices in a market supposedly "free."

From Positivism to Performativity

Rosaldo's interventions in psychological and cognitive anthropology had a lasting impact as well and contributed a great deal to anthropological interest in the "self" (Rosaldo 1983, 1984). As she put it, "My point is simple. Psychological idioms that we use in offering accounts of the activities of our peers—or our companions in the field—are at the same time 'ideological' or 'moral' notions. As ethnographers (and moral persons) we are compelled at once to use them and to suspect them" (135). Rosaldo took a long-standing problem in psychological anthropology, the distinction between "guilt" societies and "shame" societies, and completely revised the terms of the debate. Rather than assume that people in shame societies are constrained by social conventions to rein in their inner desires, while people in guilt societies self-monitor to control those inner passions (and feel bad when they fail), Rosaldo called for a critical examination of the "view of persons as embodiments of continuing and conflictual inner drives and needs"—part and parcel of Western psychological thinking—and thus a reassessment of the very different ways that different "selves" are created in different societies.

Like her discussion of public and domestic, however, her reanalysis of psychological anthropology was taken up in a positivist spirit by some of her colleagues and followers. What others picked up on was her comment that "the 'selves' that [feelings such as guilt or shame] help defend—and so, the way such feelings work—will differ with the culture and organization of particular societies" (Rosaldo 1983:136; qtd. in Levy's [1983:129] introduction to the special issue of *Ethos* in which Rosaldo's essay appears). Rather than question the very terms of analysis like the self, anthropologists and psychologists thus went about busily identifying different selves in the cultures of the world, even as they (rightly) sought to destabilize the analytical persistence of the autonomous cogito as a unit of analysis in Western social science. This research agenda was a kind of "butterfly collecting" that went on without much critical reflection on the very category of the self itself (e.g., Markus and Kitayama 1991). Rosaldo called attention to this problem in her final essay, worrying that a cross-cultural psychology may not be possible: "insofar as our psychology is wedded to our culture's terms in its accounts of people elsewhere in the world, it is unlikely to appreciate their deeds" (1984:150).

Recent anthropological and feminist theory echoes, in some respects, Rosaldo's initial concerns and calls attention not to the selves themselves as units of analysis but to the practices and technologies that constitute different ways of being (de Lauretis 1987; Battaglia 1995). This work demonstrates the reiterative and citational practices through which people continually reenvision and reify seemingly solid categories of self and social life, the practices that make "essences" seem so essential (Butler 1993; Morris 1995). Performativity theory shifts the discussion away from selves and forces us to question the discursive regimes under which it makes sense to "think" selves and "feel" selves (Díaz Barriga, Gutmann, Lugo, Maurer, this vol.; see also Lugo 1990; Borovoy 1994).

Moving beyond positivism also compels a questioning of other categories of analysis and social life, other apparently "real" objects and subjects, to investigate how such entities come to be so real and to have the force of objectivity behind them. Social studies of science and technology, for example, have explored certain entrenched categories of modernity and their performative reiterations (Strathern 1992; Latour 1993; Franklin 1995). For feminist anthropologists working from the legacy of *Woman, Culture, and Society* (Rosaldo and Lamphere 1974) and *Toward an Anthropology of Women* (Reiter [Rapp] 1975), foundational texts of the 1970s, such a rethinking of objectivism compels a rethinking of Marxism and materialism. What, for instance, are the limits of the discursive production of "land," "resources," "jobs," and the "workers" who make worlds and selves from them (MacCormack, Gray, Díaz Barriga, this vol.)? This kind of reflexive move also demands an accounting of the "objects" and "authors" of anthropological inquiry; how and what do we study, and what is the position of researcher and researched in their performance of clearly (and not-so-clearly) defined roles in the objectivity game (Gray, Gutmann, Maurer, this vol.; Bourdieu 1977)?

From Emotion and Feeling to the Question of Interiority

A third lasting influence of Rosaldo's work has been on the study of emotion and feeling, which, in anthropology and beyond, has been heavily indebted to her ethnography *Knowledge and Passion* (1980). Rosaldo drew attention to deeply held sentiments, apparently interior states of being, and opened up these "interiors" for critical analysis. Researchers picking up this thread of inquiry have truly gone to the heart of the matter, as it were, by interrogating not just the cultural construction of emotion or sentiment but the construction of interiority itself. They have asked under what discursive regimes of power it makes sense for people to imagine that they "have" interiors, selves that "feel" at a corporeal level. Work on emotion has been closely connected to work on the body (Scheper-Hughes and Lock 1987; Lutz 1988) and also to work on the performativity that grants the body its materiality and simultaneously creates the necessary fiction of interiors to bodies under certain regimes of power (Lugo, this vol.; Abu-Lughod and Lutz 1990; Butler 1993; Steedman 1995; Collier 1997).

Often politics repeat the claims of interiority and rely on coincidences of feeling or sentiment to generate attachment to causes or, alternately, disaffection. Highlighting that these are claims, historically and discursively situated and not universal or, at least, unproblematic, interrupts their endless repetition and reveals cracks and fissures in modern imaginings of the self, its "inner" workings, and its politics. To say that these are claims is not to suggest that they are "authored" by a prediscursive or autonomous subject. Rather, the claims are repetitions of existing norms such that these norms are stabilized (Laclau and Mouffe 1985; Hall 1995).

Beyond Identity and Sentiment

This deconstructive move brings us back again to the performativity of domestic and public and the stabilization of self and world by reiterative practices that conjure up essences and realities together with bourgeois individuals and their "free" choices. Opening up interiors opens up the whole realm of bourgeois politics and subjectivities. In this regard Rosaldo had been concerned with how feminists had challenged, mostly ineffectively, social science discourses about gendered personal identity. She wrote:

> one gets the feeling that feminist distress with the failure of social science to address issues of gender in the past feeds a sense that gender as a sociological issue is inherently different from other aspects of social organization with implications for personal identity, demanding some sort of nonconventional (and usually, psychologically oriented) account. My own sense, by contrast, is that our frustration stems, first, from the failure of sociological theory to relate gender in systematic ways to other kinds of inequality and, second, from the inadequacies of a utilitarian tradition [including much of Marxist social thought] that has made it extremely difficult to conceptualize the sociological significance of human consciousness, culture, or thought. (1980a:408 n. 38)

Feminist political theorist Joan Scott (1992) has crystallized a number of disparate concerns with the kind of identity politics and theoretical maneuver that preoccupied Michelle Rosaldo and that gained force in the 1980s. Scott highlighted the fact that the resources identity politics drew upon were in the main sentiment and affect based on a presumed commonality of experience among members of specific groups. Recognizing that groups and individuals only come into being through social practices and that the experiences particular to them are themselves products of social relations, Scott called for an analytical deconstruction of the category of experience itself as an Enlightenment construct based on Western understandings of self and society. Yet others have convincingly argued that to state that identity and experience are social constructions does not help account for their tangible reality, their lived force, in people's everyday lives. For this reason Paul Gilroy (1993) has called for a stance of "anti-anti-essentialism," by which he means a critical perspective on essentialism that at the same time does not dismiss the lived reality of categories and experiences deemed immutable or essential but, rather, tries to account for that reality in politically engaged terms.

Accounting for the "realness" of social constructions raises questions of agency and transcendence. If we acknowledge that social constructions are made real by our practices, do we concede that we can never overcome, say, racial or gender oppression? Recent feminist theory rejects this proposition and instead argues for a critical engagement with the practices that continually produce and reproduce the "realities" of the social world. From this position such theory puts forth the subversive potential of practices that mock, mimic, or in other ways transgress the social realities by performative iterations of other realities—the drag performance, for instance (Butler 1993). Donna Haraway (1991) reminds us that the realities we construct are themselves parts of our subjectivities and are open to disarticulation and rearticulation, and Allucquere Stone (1995) notes that such things as the apparently real facts of sex and the apparently "virtual" persona of cyberspace are both contingent articulations of self and social world. While we may not be able to "transcend" the inherited categories reiterated in social worlds impacted by capitalism, colonialism, and Enlightenment social theory, we may very well be able to introduce new variations on the theme that highlight the contingencies of our social world and denaturalize it (Visweswaran 1994).

Book Overview

In our estimation the anthropological issues and theoretical themes discussed here constitute Michelle Rosaldo's feminist legacy for the twenty-first century. The volume is organized into two main parts, "Domestic and Public Revisited" and "History, the State, and Class," which provide a forum for the presentation of ethnographic materials and theoretical engagements that challenge, expand, reflect on, or simply apply Michelle Rosaldo's own insights about feminism and anthropology and about social theory and society more generally.

In part 1, "Domestic and Public Revisited," the first four essays recapture one of Rosaldo's most criticized theoretical conceptualizations of gender relations: the domestic/public dichotomy. This section begins with a Marxist-feminist essay, "Land, Labor, and Gender," in which one of Rosaldo's well-known critics, the late Carol MacCormack, continues to argue that the "ranked dichotomy of domestic and public domains" does not constitute a "robust" feminist critique due to its static, universalizing, and, therefore, biological reductionist bent on its consequent analytical interpretation of gender relations.

By giving a feminist angle to the structural Marxist theories of Meillassoux and Terray and examining a sample of precapitalist and capitalist societies from Africa and Asia, MacCormack proposes, instead, to look at key elements in modes of production—in this case, at the multiple uses of land (both as subject and/or instrument of labor)—in order "to tease out some reasons why gender, age, and class exploitation may be greater in some social formations than in others." MacCormack argues that a Marxist emphasis on modes of production effectively transcends "the static process of putting people in categories" and, moreover, that a Marxist historical perspective on gender relations does show, for instance, how so-called domestic domains are in fact often constituted by external processes, such as the global economy.

The second essay in this section, "Destabilizing the Masculine, Refocusing 'Gender': Men and the Aura of Authority in Michelle Z. Rosaldo's Work," by Alejandro Lugo, challenges Rosaldo's critics (including herself in 1980) by trying to demonstrate that the universalism, essentialism, and biological reductionism seemingly embedded in the domestic/public dichotomy are, for the most part, products of selective misreadings of Michelle Rosaldo's 1974 theoretical and political position. Lugo argues that her critics ignored Rosaldo's recommendations for social transformations in our society (e.g., bringing men into household obligations) and in this process separated Rosaldo's own political strategy and practice from her theoretical interventions in trying to explain how and why the activities of both men and women were given different social values cross-culturally. Through ethnographic material collected at the U.S.-Mexico border among male and female maquiladora workers, Lugo suggests that the theoretical and empirical consequences of this misreading are many, particularly for feminist anthropology: for instance, Michelle Rosaldo's rigorous focus on the study of gender, of both men and women, was set aside; her early contribution—her preoccupation with men as gendered subjects—was left in the dust; and, finally, her theoretical and political concerns about what constituted the "sources of power" and the "aura of authority" in gender relations were, ironically, muted.

The third essay, by Bill Maurer, "Sexuality and Separate Spheres: Gender, Sexual Identity, and Work in Dominica and Beyond," theorizes the category of "sexuality" in relation to capitalism in the Caribbean. Through ethnographic revelations of how work and sexuality are defined by both men and women in creole-speaking Dominica, Maurer argues that the ideology of the domestic and public continues to produce sexual and gendered identities that are directly connected to a local discourse on "wage work." Maurer argues that, since women are not considered to be part of the labor market and thus do not work for wages, their economic and labor contributions (whether in the public or the domestic domains) are not considered, even by women themselves, to be work at all; this lack of public recognition in the realm of work is smoothly translated into a cultural acknowledgment regarding women's sexuality—that is, that women have no "sex," especially apart from their sexual and social relations with men. In this process Maurer shows that sexual and gender identities are themselves products of social relations but that (combining Michelle Rosaldo and Judith Butler), "whether or not markets actually determine people's social status, people who think in terms of market rationality act as if they do, and find it natural."

The last essay in the first section, Miguel Díaz Barriga's "The Domestic/Public in Mexico City: Notes on Theory, Social Movements, and the Essentializations of Everyday Life," tries to show, relatedly, that the ideology of the domestic and public continues to be quite dominant as a hegemonic construct, in this case, in Latin America, particularly affecting the nature and outcome of urban social movements. In fact, Díaz Barriga argues that it is not possible to theorize urban social movements in the Third World without confronting the pervasiveness of the discourse on public and domestic life and experience, either on the part of poor women or on the part of scholars studying the phenomenon. By examining poor women's narratives of their participation in grassroots organizing in Mexico City, Díaz Barriga suggests, following Michelle Rosaldo (1980), that "resistance to traditional gender relations not be seen simply as creating continuities between the domestic and public" but as a pragmatic attempt, on the part of the common folk, "to move away from the broader inequalities and essentializations of everyday life."

In part 2, "History, the State, Class," three contributors give rigorous scrutiny to issues and topics touched upon in the first section; in particular, Michelle Rosaldo's feminist legacy for the varied but strategic ways in which we, as scholars, can address our own cultural assumptions of what men and women are about. This includes the kinds of research questions we should ask when studying gender and, more concretely, how we address "unexpected" encounters with such themes as history, the state, and class in the varied contexts of modernity, nationalism, and (once again) capitalism.

Jane Collier's essay, "Victorian Visions," reflects on Michelle Rosaldo's feminist preoccupation with how such nineteenth-century social thinkers as Marx, Bachofen, Spencer, and Durkheim theorized marriage, sex, and the family under capitalism. The specific phase of modern capitalism during the late nineteenth-century produced politically unstable contexts and discourses that influenced what these men wrote and said about women, particularly within a context heavily characterized by a continually imminent "breakdown of morality in public life." In this essay Collier argues that Michelle Rosaldo was interested in these historical questions precisely to identify the "gaps in contemporary theory which can be traced to turn of the century assumptions" about women. Based on a series of course notes put together in 1978 for a seminar she taught with Michelle Rosaldo at Stanford, Collier shows how Rosaldo herself hoped to uncover the gender assumptions inherent in the subtle (and not so subtle) rhetorical strategies of social scientists and political debaters. Collier examines how these biased assumptions permeated such social and theoretical inventions as "the family," "marriage," "the public," and "the domestic" during the Victorian era. In this process Collier discusses the complex ways in which gender conceptions are in fact shaped by larger political issues and, more important, how capitalist discourse affects and effects "how we attempt to shape and make sense of our relations with others."

Matthew Gutmann's essay, "A (Short) Cultural History of Mexican Machos and Hombres," focuses on the history and nationalist problematic that led to changing male identities of working-class men in a barrio of Mexico City. By juxtaposing the *muchachos'* personal narratives about what it means to be a man with and against key anthropological and philosophical texts on Mexican men and Mexican identity (by Oscar Lewis, Americo Paredes, Octavio Paz, and Samuel Ramos), Gutmann provides an analysis of the political economy of machismo, its relatively recent invention in the twentieth century, and its unhappy rearticulation with a masculinity that is itself "a product of men and women's cultural efforts." Through an elaborate discussion of how we can best interpret gender relations that are constantly in flux, particularly in ethnographically challenging contemporary societies such as Mexico City, Gutmann reminds us, following Michelle Rosaldo, that there comes a time when "what is needed . . . is not so much data as questions"—new and different questions that can possibly be translated into new ways of studying and interpreting not only men as men and women as women but also "manliness" and "womanliness" as historically and culturally gendered categories of analysis.

In the final essay, "Myths of the Bourgeois Woman: Rethinking Race, Class, and Gender," Christine Gray theorizes the category of class through an in-depth analysis and criticism of the uncritical way in which the "bourgeois woman" is often lumped together with bourgeois men in most Marxist feminist critiques of "class" domination in capitalist societies. Gray specifically argues and tries to demonstrate through rich textual discussions that feminist scholars have not properly considered the vulnerability middle-class women experience whenever they challenge dominant discourses of femininity (in this case, particularly as this femininity is manifested in the ideologies and practices embedded in the doll Barbie). Gray observes that, for the most part, bourgeois men, and not bourgeois women, have been the privileged ones, specifically during the last two decades of the twentieth century; a time in which high numbers of middle-class women (including female academics) are getting divorced, are "opting" for having children, and, when possible, are giving preference to their own professional careers (instead of that of their husbands). Challenging what she views as an erasure of white middle-class women in the ethnographic and theoretical texts of such feminists as Emily Martin, Rayna Rapp, and Karen Sacks, Christine Gray argues that, until we rigorously unpack the thick relations between gender, class, and race in feminist analysis, feminist academics, and particularly feminist anthropologists, will continue to reproduce the domestic/public ideology that still pervades and, in fact, often sustains contemporary capitalist social relations. Gray suggests that the tensions currently being experienced by both poor women and by white middle-class women of any color and race can be better understood through Michelle Rosaldo's enduring critique of gender inequalities. As Gray herself notes:

In fact, once one recognizes that Rosaldo's work is an almost perfect theoretical rendition of capitalist gender ideologies and practices, it provides a useful perspective for exploring the subtleties of capitalist accumulation in non-Western societies, for ferreting out the symbolic structures that generate the myths and antagonisms of Western capitalism. How are Western ideologies of public/private space, and the idea of the bourgeois woman who "does it all" without messing up her hair, being imposed on non-Western societies?

Conclusion

As a whole, the essays in this volume variously explore the connections, ruptures, and continuities that characterize the four major shifts we identified early on as constituting the legacy of Michelle Zimbalist Rosaldo. First, they move us from simplistic discussions of the public/domestic dichotomy to a more productive and sophisticated conversation on the biopolitics of populations. That is, they connect Michelle Rosaldo with Michel Foucault, for, as we noted, the French philosopher's notion of biopower brings together the public (the world of the state, of capitalist regulation, of social order writ large) with the domestic (the world of the home, the family, reproduction, and sex). Second, the volume seeks to shift from a focus on positivist theoretical practice to Judith Butler's conceptualization of performativity, which should allow us to recognize, as Bill Maurer argues in his essay, that "practices, which call upon the persons to continually reiterate their supposedly inherent or natural attributes (including things like 'sex' or 'race'), in fact are constitutive performances, creating the materiality of individual identities in the act." Third, the essays make an analytical departure from sentimental notions of feeling and emotion to a conceptual (though not necessarily purely cerebral) discussion of the interiority of the person; that is, they call for a move toward *social* feeling, in which sentiments, emotions, and "feeling selves" are in themselves, following Michelle Rosaldo, products of social relations and of concrete social practices. We agree, as we think Michelle Rosaldo would, with social science philosopher Charles Varela when he states that

"I think," "I feel," "I intend," or "I will," are first person first order avowals that publicly express a mental state of a speaker and not a report of a mental state *in* the speaker. They are expressive indices of speech acts at a person-place and not descriptive revelations of a "hidden" self and its "hidden" states of mind. (1995:371)

Fourth, and finally, though related to the third proposition, the volume makes an inclusive (instead of excluding) theoretical motion to move beyond (though not exclude) "identity" into a more engaging sense of the *social person.* That is, it seeks to go beyond exclusive studies of "masculinity" and "femininity" and into more rigorous studies of gender, of both men and women, and last, but not least, to move beyond "domestic" and "public" and into a better understanding of the logic and performance of capitalism and its respective hegemonic constructions of social existence, particularly as the latter manifests itself in why, when, and how "we attempt to shape and make sense of our relations with others" (Collier, this vol.).

Michelle Rosaldo was not only a pioneering and sophisticated feminist scholar, but also a major theorist within the general field of anthropology and, more admirably, one of the best minds—indeed, a true philosopher—of the study of "social life." The ideas and ideals of Rosaldo's feminist interventions were profound. Destabilize public and domestic, and you destabilize patriarchy. Question the self, and you question being. Critique identity, and you unpack subjectivity. Explore emotions, and you explore the inner lives of human beings to reveal how they are constantly "becoming" in social worlds of their making but not their choosing. What are the implications of a move beyond public and domestic, beyond the self, beyond (but without excluding) sentimentalism and humanism? These are wide-open questions. It remains the task of feminist anthropology to work through them. This volume represents a number of interwoven attempts to do so.

REFERENCES

Abu-Lughod, Lila
1990 "The Romance of Resistance: Tracing Transformations of Power through Bedouin Women." *American Ethnologist* 17 (1): 44–55.
Abu-Lughod, Lila, and Catherine Lutz, eds.
1990 *Language and the Politics of Emotion.* Cambridge: Cambridge University Press.
Battaglia, Debborah, ed.
1995 *Rhetorics of Self-Making.* Berkeley: University of California Press.

Borovoy, Amy
  1994   "Good Wives and Mothers: The Production of Japanese Domesticity in a Global Economy." Ph.D. diss., Stanford University.
Bourdieu, Pierre
  1977   *Outline of a Theory of Practice.* Cambridge: Cambridge University Press.
Butler, Judith
  1993   *Bodies That Matter: On the Discursive Limits of "Sex."* New York: Routledge.
Chatterjee, Partha
  1993   *The Nation and Its Fragments: Colonial and Post-Colonial Histories.* Princeton: Princeton University Press.
Collier, Jane
  1997   *From Duty to Desire: Remaking Family in a Spanish Village.* Princeton: Princeton University Press.
Collier, Jane, Bill Maurer, and Liliana Suarez-Navaz
  1995   "Sanctioned Identities: Legal Constructions of Modern Personhood." *Identities* 2 (1–2): 1–27.
Comaroff, John, and Jean Comaroff
  1991   *Of Revelation and Revolution: Christianity, Colonialism and Consciousness in South Africa.* Chicago: University of Chicago Press.
Coombe, Rosemary
  1997   "Contingent Articulations: Toward a Critical Cultural Studies of Law." MS.
de Lauretis, Teresa
  1989   *Technologies of Gender: Essays on Theory, Film, and Fiction.* Bloomington: Indiana University Press.
Donzelot, Jacques
  1979   *The Policing of Families.* New York: Pantheon.
Fitzpatrick, Peter
  1992   *The Mythology of Modern Law.* New York: Routledge.
Foucault, Michel
  1977   *Discipline and Punish: The Birth of the Prison.* New York: Pantheon.
  1978   *The History of Sexuality,* vol.1. New York: Pantheon.
Franklin, Sarah
  1995   "Science as Culture, Cultures of Science." *Annual Review of Anthropology* 24:163–84.
Gilroy, Paul
  1993   *The Black Atlantic: Modenity and Double Consciousness.* Cambridge: Harvard University Press.
Ginsberg, Faye, and Rayna Rapp, eds.
  1995   *Conceiving the New World Order: The Global Politics of Reproduction.* Berkeley: University of California Press.
Hall, Stuart
  1995   "Fantasy, Identity, Politics." In *Cultural Remix: Theories and Politics of the Popular,* ed. Erica Carter, James Donald and Judith Squires, 63–69. London: Lawrence and Wishart.

Handler, Richard, and Daniel Segal
  1990 *Jane Austen and the Fiction of Culture: An Essay on the Narration of Social Relationships.* Tucson: University of Arizona Press.
Haraway, Donna
  1991 *Simians, Cyborgs, and Women: The Reinvention of Nature.* New York: Routledge.
Horn, David
  1994 *Social Bodies: Science, Reproduction and Italian Modernity.* Princeton: Princeton University Press.
Laclau, Ernesto, and Chantal Mouffe
  1985 *Hegemony and Socialist Strategy: Toward a Radical Democratic Politics.* London: Verso.
Latour, Bruno
  1993 *We Have Never Been Modern.* Cambridge: Harvard University Press.
Lazarus-Black, Mindie
  1994 *Legitimate Acts and Illegal Encounters: Law and Society in Antigua and Barbuda.* Washington, D.C.: Smithsonian Institution Press.
Lugo, Alejandro
  1990 "Cultural Production and Reproduction in Ciudad Juárez, Mexico: Tropes at Play among Maquiladora Workers." *Cultural Anthropology* 5 (2): 173–96.
Lutz, Catherine
  1988 *Unnatural Emotions: Everyday Sentiments on a Micronesian Atoll and Their Challenge to Western Theory.* Chicago: University of Chicago Press.
Markus, Hazel, and Shinobu Kitayama
  1991 "Culture and Self: Implications for Cognition, Emotion, and Motivation." *Psychological Review* 98 (2): 224–54.
McClintock, Anne
  1995 *Imperial Leather: Race, Gender, and Sexuality in the Colonial Context.* New York: Routledge.
Morris, Rosalind
  1995 "All Made Up: Performance Theory and the New Anthropology of Sex and Gender." *Annual Review of Anthropology* 24:567–92.
Reiter [Rapp], Rayna, ed.
  1975 *Toward an Anthropology of Women.* New York: Monthly Review Press.
Rosaldo, Michelle Z.
  1974 "Woman, Culture, and Society: A Theoretical Overview." In *Woman, Culture, and Society,* ed. Michelle Z. Rosaldo and Louise Lamphere, 17–42. Stanford: Stanford University Press.
  1980a "The Use and Abuse of Anthropology: Reflections on Feminism and Cross-cultural Understanding." *Signs* 5 (3): 389–417.
  1980b *Knowledge and Passion: Ilongot Notions of Self and Social Life.* Cambridge: Cambridge University Press.
  1983 "The Shame of Headhunters and the Autonomy of Self." *Ethos* 11: 135–51.

1984 "Toward an Anthropology of Self and Feeling." In *Culture Theory: Essays on Mind, Self and Emotion,* ed. R. Schweder and R. Levine, 137–57. Cambridge: Cambridge University Press.

Scheper-Hughes, Nancy, and Margaret Lock
1987 "The Mindful Body: A Prolegomenon to Future Work in Medical Anthropology." *Medical Anthropology Quarterly* 1:1–36.

Scott, Joan
1992 "Experience." In *Feminists Theorize the Political,* ed. Judith Butler and Joan Scott, 22–40. New York: Routledge.

Steedman, Caroline
1995 *Strange Dislocations: Childhood and the Idea of Human Interiority.* Cambridge: Harvard University Press.

Stoler, Ann
1995 *Race and the Education of Desire: Foucault's History of Sexuality and the Colonial Order of Things.* New York: Routledge.

Stone, Allucquere
1995 *The War of Desire and Technology at the Close of the Mechanical Age.* Cambridge: MIT Press.

Strathern, Marilyn
1992 *Reproducing the Future: Anthropology, Kinship, and the New Reproductive Technologies.* New York: Routledge.

Thomas, Nicholas
1994 *Colonialism's Culture: Anthropology, Travel and Government.* Cambridge: Cambridge University Press.

Varela, Charles R.
1995 "Ethogenic Theory and Psychoanalysis: The Unconscious as a Social Construction and a Failed Explanatory Concept." *Journal for the Theory of Social Behaviour* 25 (4): 363–85.

Visweswaran, Kamala
1994 *Fictions of Feminist Ethnography.* Minneapolis: University of Minnesota Press.

Young, Robert
1995 *Colonial Desire: Hybridity in Theory, Culture and Race.* New York: Routledge.

PART I

Domestic and Public Revisited

Land, Labor, and Gender

Carol MacCormack

Retrospective

In those heady days before *Woman, Culture and Society* had been published, the contributors to the book had forthright debates. I was not in harmony with Michelle Rosaldo's ranked dichotomy of domestic and public domains. I felt that such static labels were another aspect of what Edmund Leach had called butterfly collecting and would not help us find a robust feminist critique. Also, basing women's putative universal status on childbearing came rather too close to biological reductionism for me. As Rosaldo was careful to explain in 1980, however, what may seem a "natural" fact must be understood in social terms, the byproduct of institutional arrangements that could be changed (397).

On purely empirical grounds, by 1970 I had completed my first long period of fieldwork in coastal Sierra Leone, where significant numbers of women held overt political office at village and chiefdom levels and where aristocratic or especially adept women controlled land, labor, and something we might call capital in both a Firthian sense and a classical economic sense. Women also controlled overt religious offices with all the sanctioning power those offices legitimized. In coastal Sierra Leone there is a clear sexual division of labor, but there are roles for women and men in both domestic and public space. In mixed farming that includes rice farming women expend more labor time in production than do men. To a large extent women retain the product of their labor and dominate local markets. They are not particularly tied to their children in domestic space but travel long distances marketing or farming, with an infant on their back, or they leave children in extended households with co-wives and kin (MacCormack 1982).

At a superficial level this West African case study seemed not much different from Rosaldo's description of Ilongot society in the Philippines. She described those rural women as being active in the productive work of rice farming and in complex repertoires of magic and ritual. Women spoke out with confidence in public forums, boys were not socialized to dominate or denigrate women, nor did men as husbands demand submission from their wives. Both men and women did work in domestic space. Rosaldo also described men's hunting, however, and ranked the exchange of meat from hunting above domestic consumption of rice. Therefore, she ranked men above women. This set up a theoretical inconsistency with Sherry Ortner (1974), in the same volume, who ranked nature below culture, and therefore believed Ilongot men hunting in nature's wild should rank below women working with deliberately planted crops in ordered fields (see MacCormack and Strathern 1980, for fuller discussion on this use of ranked categories).

But that is now history in anthropology. If we might consider the thesis that a domestic versus public dichotomy is not a robust theoretical basis for explaining gender roles, in what framework might we reconsider the kinds of ethnographic cases presented by Rosaldo and others in the early days of the feminist critique in anthropology?

In conversations with Rosaldo I was aware of her command of Marxist theory, which indeed transcends the static process of putting people into categories. She was coediting *Feminist Theory: Critique of Ideology,* and, although she did not live to contribute an essay to the volume, those by Catherine MacKinnon, Mary O'Brien, and Jean Elshtain were overtly informed by Marxist theory (Keohane, Rosaldo, and Gelpi 1982). With a Marxist approach the focus shifts to the processes of production and reproduction that shape household and other social relationships. As early as 1960, well before publication of *Woman, Culture and Society* in 1974, Claude Meillassoux had been exploring the dynamic process of people's work upon the land in largely subsistence societies similar to the Ilongot. By 1964 he had published his monograph on the economy of the Gouro on the Ivory Coast, and in 1972 his classic essay, "From Reproduction to Production," had appeared. His ideas have been taken up by many, including Jack Goody (1976) and recently A. F. Robertson (1991).

In this essay I shall slip into a stream of discourse I might have had with Rosaldo when she was still alive, a discourse to which she may have contributed keen analysis had she remained alive.

Land, Labor, and Gender

The French and British Marxists have done a great deal to help us think more analytically about the kinds of rural societies much anthropological theory revolves around, but some intellectually exciting French anthropologists have been rather neglectful of placing their analyses within a feminist perspective. Considerable energy has been expended in extending Marx's concept of mode of production into precapitalist societies (see, e.g., Hindess and Hirst 1975). Put very briefly, a mode of production is the combination of complex social relations that limit access to land and other resources, and the labor process by which a swamp and rice seeds, for example, become food for consumption or exchange. Natural resources are not the entire environment but the parts that, by cultural definition, are seen to have cultural utility. Those definitions change over time. West African swamp, for example, is increasingly redefined as rice paddy (Boserup 1970; Dey 1981; Moore and Vaughan 1994). Such shifting definitions are in a feedback relationship with changing forms of social relationships and the way in which some people take surplus value from others.

Emanuel Terray (1969) saved us from using the concept of mode of production as yet another box for butterfly collecting. Societies—all societies—are not made up of a single mode of production but of combinations. At any point in time, however, one is dominant. This, of course, has implications for women's work and women's status. What we want to know is the process by which those involved in one type—but not with farming, which is characterized as women's production, for instance—come to define and govern basic social relationships in the society at large.

Meillassoux also sensitized us to this interplay in modes. In noncapitalist "developing" societies the web of interdependencies characterizing social and cultural systems are not necessarily egalitarian but are commonly exploitative, as, for example, with clients and aristocrats in rural Sierra Leone, the *jajmani* system in India, or entrepreneurship in Zaire. One then needs to fit gender into the framework, as Pat Caplan (1985) and Janet MacGaffey (1986) have done. When class and caste solidarity are being played off against gender solidarity, as they are every day, which wins? Or, of even more interest, how are social relations negotiated around and through such competing solidarities? There is no doubt that women are embedded in caste, class, and other institutional social categories, and Rosaldo was imprudent in saying that "in general, however, women are not differentiated except in terms of age, relationship to men, or idiosyncratic (and institutionally irrelevant) characteristics" (1974:29).

By focusing particularly on the resource of land as a key element in modes of production, we might tease out some reasons why gender, age, and class exploitation may be greater in some social formations than others. Marx suggested that land had two functions. One was as a subject of labor, the other as an instrument of labor (or an instrument of production). Land as a subject of labor shows a pattern of instantaneous production. It is the Ilongot hunters, the Inuit fishers, or !Kung gatherers who go out on the land or sea, which is to a large extent a free good, who live in a world where land is a subject of labor. Meillassoux (1972) suggests that the product of labor is immediately available, to be shared, rather than contractually exchanged. Reciprocities are not long delayed, and there is little incentive for the formation of social hierarchies or even extended family or lineage organization. Those egalitarian small-scale kindreds and ephemeral encampment groups have relatively little preoccupation with either biological reproduction or social reproduction. For example, these are the kinds of societies in which women are seldom in the socially defined role of midwife, having authority roles in control of other women's fertility (MacCormack 1994). Nor do we find, for example, dominant men who are marriage guardians over young women. Marjorie Shostak's (1983) biography of Nisa illustrates this kind of social formation.

On the other hand, land as an instrument of labor undergirds very different social, political, and ideological structures. Land as an instrument of labor characterizes settled agriculture of Ilongot rice farmers or Mende and Sherbro hoe cultivators on the coast of Sierra Leone. In the latter case traditional midwives are embedded within powerful ritual, economic, knowledge, and political hierarchies. In production people clear the land as the rains come on. They plant, transplant rice seedlings, weed, harvest, thresh, winnow, and store crops. Producers are bound together in interdependence until the harvest. They remain together in interdependence around their nonportable granaries. They must adjudicate disputes so those who produce may stay around to eat. They must protect their stored security from raids. The producers in the rainy season are eating the last of the grain produced by themselves and others in the previous rainy season. Thus, people are linked in interdependence not only spatially but also temporally, from year to year and generation to generation. Time and concepts of continuity are essential in the economy and thus color cultural ideologies about social relationships and social reproduction.

Over time, as infants are born and the elderly die, the working community changes but within a framework of hierarchy. Children who have been dependents begin to produce. Producers in time become elders and retire. Elders as such are not a class because all, in time, become elders. In rural Mandinka villages in the Gambia, for example, one sees men in the elder age grade lounging on a low platform near the entrance to the village. Men in the youngest of the three age grades are not so immediately visible, and women of all ages are not lounging but are in the fields until the sun sets. Perhaps that explains why women's robust village-wide organizations, present in all thirty-three villages we surveyed, had been invisible to the ethnographic literature on the Gambia (Cham et al. 1987).

Lineage organization seems quite logical where land is an instrument of production. One thinks of a newborn infant who owes his or her existence to older people who produce, nurture, and protect. As infants age, they are dependent on fewer and fewer people (unless they are permanently infantilized by gender role definition, socialized to participate in their own subordination as females are in some societies). Thinking metaphorically, in very old age only the ancestors and ancestresses have fed them and continue to bless them. All others, of the living, are in their debt. Empirically speaking, juniors feed the frail elderly but out of a sense of debt. It is therefore no surprise that sedentary agricultural economies in which land is a vital instrument of production are characterized by lineage ideology, the political, judicial, and ritual sanctioning power of elderhood, ancestor religion, fecundity cults, and culturally elaborated concern for reproduction in a wide sense.

Where land is an instrument of production we tend to find social control of people by age, class, caste, and gender linked with control of subsistence. Social control of women may be linked with concerns about biological reproduction of people as laborers on the land and the reproduction of social and cultural structures that ensure the continuity of productive relationships. Elaborate cultural rules govern marriage and residence. Groups cannot rely on blood kin only and seek to enhance their continuity through adoption, fosterage, and the accumulation of bridewealth for more wives. But the interesting question, still seldom asked, is: who is controlling all these people? Who are the elders and the heads of groups? In some cases women elders and chiefs may be controlling others—the subject of my contribution to the *Woman, Culture and Society* volume (Hoffer 1974).

In his book *Maidens, Meal and Money* Meillassoux makes the same assumption that Rosaldo did, that women are not differentiated from one another. Indeed, he lumps women and agricultural resources together as the means of production and concentrates on the social rules that reproduce men's control over those resources (1981:33–49). He describes a society organized around patrilineal descent and patrilocal residence following marriage. Both young men and women are in situations of dependency. Meillassoux assumes that male elders have a monopoly on marital exchanges, which gives them control over the labor of young men and women as well as control over the biological fertility of women. Young men cannot become social adults without their agnatic kins' assistance in accumulating bridewealth. He explains that young men carry out productive work for their elders in order to get wives, but he does not explain why girls and young women also work diligently weeding, harvesting, and making edible oil and many other things in the years before marriage. He is correct in focusing on marriage exchanges as important events in social reproduction, but he ignores other life cycle exchanges such as puberty, childbirth, or death, and he also lacks the careful ethnography to say exactly who all the actors are in the social processes he describes.

After marriage men remain dependent on fathers and male elders for usufruct access to farmland, seed stores, and other basic resources. Women at marriage are split off from the solidarity of their kin groups and live as solitary individuals among their husbands' kin. Young husbands are dependent on agnatic elders, and young wives are dependent on husbands, indeed, doubly dependent. But this kind of model building is oversimplified. Not all West African farming societies have classic patrilineal systems. Some have an ideology of matrilineal descent; others have cognatic, or double descent, systems. Now that we are looking for them, we seem to find women's organizations everywhere. There is a great deal of fosterage, and even where the ideology is patrilineal there is much scope for strategic rule bending or evading (Bohannon 1957; Bledsoe 1980). Even within a potentially dynamic Marxian framework, models of precapitalist modes of production may become static, rather mechanistic, constructs. They lose the fine-grained historical and ethnographic detail that allows us to see social and cultural change constantly arising. Change arises both endogenously and under the various external pressures of capitalist penetration. Narrow Marxist systemic models stand in danger of "egregious reductionism" (Comaroff 1987:64).

In his 1981 book Meillassoux was building a logical model by relating classic anthropological kinship theory to Marxian theory in the kind of subsistence agricultural societies for which Marx had little ethnographic description. At one level, however, Meillassoux is as unsatisfactory to read as Marx on precapitalist societies, because his monograph does not give enough empirical detail to inspire confidence in the model's validity. This is especially so where gender is concerned. We do not know whether women retain strong lineage identity. Can they separate or divorce when it suits them, returning home to give their farming labor to their own kin? If marriages are alliances between kin groups and women are the liaisons between the two groups, what information do they send home, and will their kin put pressure on an abusive or neglectful husband and his kin? Do they join religious congregations or other women's organizations in their marriage village? Also, we need to know more about productive relationships on the ground. What agricultural work do women do, what products do they control, and are they active in market and ritual exchange? Are their consanguineous kin their primary security, and are "onions their husband," with market skills and capital further security in greater measure than a husband would be (Clark 1995)?

Meillassoux writes of women as a homogeneous category, quite like the objects that, in structuralist theory, are whizzed about from one kin group to another. But many of us who work in West Africa know that aristocratic women have quite different powers from, for example, former slave women—and elderly aristocratic women are formidable. In the paramount chief's town of Shenge in coastal Sierra Leone I found 52 percent of residential compounds headed by women, most of them aristocratic elderly women. Some were widows, the first wife in a polygynous household, who continued to manage the labor of junior wives, kin, and clients. Some were cousin marriages, and the women married in their home village; others were in-marrying wives who remained in their virilocal village. Still others were local "owners of the land" who had gone off as young wives to reside virilocally in their husband's village but had come back in late middle age as elders, managing usufruct access to land, enjoying the productive labor of their junior kin and clients. In the past some of those aristocratic women were formidable slave owners, and some had even been slave dealers (MacCormack 1983). In summary, women are not objects as plots of farmland are but producers of the social relations of production.

Reproduction

There has been too much oversimplification of the concept of reproduction, either in an attempt to build models or out of unfamiliarity with detailed ethnography. Biological reproduction is not the same as the reproduction of the labor force. In the latter the labor process must be reproduced. Women do, of course, bear children. But to conflate the two leads us to miss the very details Meillassoux missed: how is the labor force constituted? What do men and women do, what do elders and juniors do, what do aristocrats and client "strangers" do? To conflate the two concepts is biological reductionism. Women's labor in social reproduction is far more complex than giving birth to children. In coastal Sierra Leone they have their own pervasive religious organization that ritually converts girls into marriageable women at puberty and collects wealth from men in the process. Those women are midwives and healers. They farm, cook, and teach good manners to children. The list of their activities in social reproduction is very long. None of the work of reproducing a labor force is "natural." This work done by women constitutes a huge part of the social order. In it lies much of the cultural superstructure, in a Marxist sense, which in turn shapes, sustains, and reproduces a particular economic base.

Land and Ecology

A Marxist historical perspective helps us to understand the changing relationships between what one might call a domestic domain and its links with external institutions. This essay suggests, however, that the analysis needs an ecological dimension as well. Just as "woman" is not a homogeneous category, neither is "land." In the tropical agricultural economies that have influenced so much anthropological theory we will be able to predict or explain more about women's status if we make a distinction between different ecologies and labor use. In very wet tropical environments land is indeed an instrument of production, and the economy is very labor intensive. In the cultural ecologies of coastal West Africa, South India, and perhaps even among the Ilongot of the Philippines the labor of both men and women is essential in production. In very labor-intensive ecologies one finds families making considerable social investments in girls, compared with their brothers: in girls' educations, in immunizing them, in feeding them adequately. Child mortality rates for boys and girls are about the same, which we may take as an empirical measure of rather equal social investments in both genders. In these ecologies one finds bridewealth, signifying that kinship groups must be compensated for releasing a valuable resource. Ideologies of matrilineality or cognatic descent are more common. Women are not likely to be in domestic seclusion but, rather, are out in the arenas of production and distribution of goods and services. They are more likely to speak in public and to have political and ritual offices. In this type of ecology women are more likely to retain the product of their labor and use it to transact, putting other people in their social debt and growing in social power.

On the other hand are the drier grasslands of East Africa or North India. A man and his plow and the draft animals he owns do most of the instrumental work upon the land. Little female labor is needed, and women are seen as a burden to support and are often secluded in domestic space. Dowry is necessary to get young women off one's hands, and patrilineal ideologies dominate the cultures. Women have value as little more than the producers of sons, and little social investment is made in girl children. Mortality for girls—even female fetuses—may greatly exceed mortality rates for boys (MacCormack 1988). These are the dynamics of the domestic versus the public face of women.

Models in the Modern World

With the penetration of capitalism the privileges of elders, aristocratic lineages, or whole ethnic groups may transmute into social class solidarities. This is a very disruptive process, and, when fed by the international arms trade, it accounts for much of the "free style" warfare going on in developing countries today. Social elites, or would-be elites, seek to gain more control over land and natural resources, converting them into cash. It is they who sign the strip-mining, toxic-dumping, and timber-leasing contracts with multinational firms and thus accumulate money capital. Inheritance of wealth becomes a major concern, and so too does the legitimation of heirs through marriage. Who is doing the controlling of resources and wealth in these transforming societies? We err in assuming it is always and everywhere men. There are some very wealthy and powerful urban elite women about in the Third World, merchant princesses who are working the parallel economies very well, as Janet MacGaffey has described in her books on the hidden economy of Zaire (MacGaffey 1987, 1991). Yet, as Gracia Clark (1994) shows in her study of women in Ghana, women are rarely at the top of the political corruption tree and have difficulty getting import licenses and the other perks that go with being a military officer or a high government official—positions still limited to men.

Terray and Meillassoux have helped us think more clearly about "developing" countries being clients of capitalist systems. The resultant societies often have parallel but interlinked modes of production. Multinational firms have a vested interest in preserving (or even encouraging the new development of) "indigenous" social structures, for those indigenous structures play a vital role in social reproduction. At a biological level they produce people for the labor supply, an abundant "reserve army" whose members might be invited in from the wings to industries on the Mexican border, for instance, to electronics factories in Thailand, or to German companies hiring Turkish guest workers. When capitalist cycles heat up, they are wanted but then are sent back to their villages when the cycle is in a slump. Indigenous social structures are vital to the reproduction of capitalist relationships over time (see, e.g., Roberts 1979; Young 1981; Murray 1981; Moore 1988).

Multinational firms and indigenous urban elites indeed find advantage in parallel economies, leaving many rural communities undisturbed. They maximize profits by not providing social services. The cheap cost of labor comes especially from the exploitation of poorly paid women. And the burden of this kind of development falls unequally on women who remain in domestic spaces to "grow" a labor force and care for men who are sent home, from the mines, for example, cold and ill (see Murray 1981). As Colin Murray shows in his work on Lesotho, the value of wives' unpaid labor cannot be measured directly in dollars, but it can be documented functionally, in careful ethnographic detail of how women maintain and reproduce labor power for the mines over generations. Their work is an undeniable part of the surplus value appropriated by mine owners and stockholders.

Mine owners maximize profits by paying a very low wage to migrant men, knowing that families provide food and other social services. They further maximize profits by not paying the kind of corporate taxes that would provide an urban physical and social infrastructure for the workforce. But the work of women is seldom measured or even conceptualized in these kinds of situations. Murray gives the case of a migrant miner whose wife died from cervical cancer (from untreated sexually transmitted diseases her husband brought home?). Having no one to look after the four children, he therefore could not return to the mines. Only after he remarried and had someone to rear his family and tend his farm could he return to mine labor.

What the dead wife and her successor provided were what Rosaldo would have placed in the domestic domain, but one cannot stop the analysis there. The labor they provided in both biological and social reproduction was an integral part of a transnational economic picture that must be scrutinized carefully with anthropological methods. We must look at the whole system of social relations of production, including the articulation of different modes of production within one system. If we looked only in the domestic domain, we would not know in any objective way the relative value of women's labor. It is not monetized for easy accounting, and, more important, it is seen to be "naturally" different from the work of men and thus noncomparable (Edholm, Harris, and Young 1977). There is much more in the domestic domain than met the eye in the very early days of the feminist critique in anthropology.

Editors' Note

Carol MacCormack opens her essay with an acknowledgment of the debates and disagreements that many of the contributors to the *Woman, Culture and Society* volume had in the early 1970s. Her essay stands as a continuation of those debates. Sadly, her death prevented her, and us, from more fully engaging them. We hope here, however, to provide a sketch of where we see both common ground and dissent between MacCormack's theorizing and that of Rosaldo and those who followed her. In a sense, then, just as MacCormack situates her essay as a piece of an ongoing conversation she would have liked to have had with Rosaldo had she lived, we situate these comments as a piece of a discussion we wish we had had the chance to pursue with MacCormack.

MacCormack's reinterpretation and critique of Meillassoux brings analysis of modes of production together with gender analysis in a way that seeks to transcend the public/domestic analytical dichotomy proposed by Rosaldo. MacCormack points out a contradiction in the analytical dichotomy and its translations (culture/nature, social good / self-interest, etc.) suggested by Rosaldo's own data from the Ilongot. Although Rosaldo's (and Ortner's) analytical dichotomies rank nature below culture, Ilongot men, "hunting in nature's wild," are accorded greater status than women, "working with planted crops in ordered fields." This apparent contradiction leads MacCormack to ask how the articulation of different modes of production—here hunting and farming—and not how supposed conceptual dichotomies between public and domestic, culture and nature, defines some people as more important than others and some people's products as more valued than others' products. The articulationist perspective also enables MacCormack to move beyond the traditional model of relatively autonomous "simple" societies carrying on their affairs in isolation from other "cultures" and toward an analysis that places such societies within the broader capitalist world system. This is an important and welcome move and forms the conclusion to her essay.

We think Rosaldo would have enjoyed this conclusion. But where Rosaldo might have disagreed with MacCormack is in the latter's emphasis on land as a key resource in different modes of production. Although MacCormack, like Marx, stresses that resources are not given elements of an environment but are the parts that are culturally defined as having utility, she nevertheless seems to hold land as a privileged and naturally given constraint on social systems. She does not inquire into the process of cultural definition that empowers certain understandings of "land" (or "utility," for that matter). Rather, she models two "functions" of land and postulates that one or the other comes to the fore based on certain natural features of an environment. This leads her to two broad types of societies. In those where land is the subject of labor—where land is essentially an unlimited, "free good"—we find widespread sharing, small-scale kindreds, ephemeral encampments, and little emphasis on biological or social reproduction or women's role in them. In those where land is an instrument of labor—and a relatively scarce good—we find concerns with proprietary rights, lineage ideologies, and an emphasis on the temporal depth of communities and an emphasis on women's roles in biological and social reproduction.

Such lineage-based societies were at the center of Meillassoux's theoretical intervention. He described social systems in which junior men are dependent on their seniors for access to farmland and seed stores and, by extension, the goods necessary to secure a wife. Men need wives to produce new laborers. Wives are dependent on their husbands for support since, at marriage, they are separated from their own kin. Yet, MacCormack points out, women in those systems never seem all that dependent on their men: there are many women's organizations, a great deal of fosterage in spite of lineage ideologies, and so forth. The model building of Meillassoux tended to cast women as just another resource, like land, caught up in transactions among men and not as "producers of the social relations of production" themselves. Once this productive role of women is acknowledged, MacCormack asserts, we begin to see the differences in the category "woman" within lineage-based societies— differences between aristocratic and slave women, for instance—that are themselves important bases for social and biological reproduction.

Here MacCormack addresses the question of the resource status of land but, again, not in a way we think Rosaldo would have found satisfactory. Mac-Cormack adds to her distinction between land as a subject of labor and land as an object of labor a dichotomy between more and less labor-intensive forms of production, based on climate and ecology. In wet tropical ecologies farming is very labor intensive and both men and women are needed to cultivate plots.

Women's labor is thus highly valued, and men wishing to marry must pay bridewealth in exchange for this valuable resource. In dry grasslands, where all a man needs is a plow and some draft animals, women's labor is not so highly valued, and "dowry is necessary to get young women off one's hands."

Rosaldo's quarrel with MacCormack would have been over the latter's adaptationist framework for understanding the relationships among land, labor, gender, and environment. In "Politics and Gender in Simple Societies" Collier and Rosaldo (1981) noted the tendency of anthropologists to attempt to describe "simple" societies in terms of their environmental and technological "adaptations" because of the widespread assumption that modern simple peoples represent the "elementary social forms and/or basic human nature," "before" culture, as it were. For Collier and Rosaldo the distinction between bridewealth societies and bride service societies (MacCormack's societies in which land is a subject of labor) lies in differences between "experiences of limitation and opportunities for exercising power" that go into the reproduction of "complex social wholes" (1981:277). Rather than beginning from land and working upward, Collier and Rosaldo begin with marriage and work outward, to paint a picture of production, marriage, gender, and politics as "mutually determining aspects" of a social system (279). The difference in approach is similar to the difference between historical materialism and practice theory, Marx and Bourdieu.

In her continuation of the "politics and gender" project begun with Rosaldo, Collier emphasizes that differences in men's and women's obligations, and not environmental determinants, structure marriage and inequality (see, e.g., Collier 1988:8, 16–17). In her analysis of bridewealth societies Collier makes the same criticism of Meillassoux as MacCormack—that women are missing from his discussion—but comes to a different conclusion. Collier notes that respect is a central value in bridewealth societies because of the structure of social obligations obtaining in these lineage-based societies. Juniors owe their existence to seniors; parents control the labor of their children, and children's products are not their own but their parents'. Collier's analysis suggests that gender and power are not so much the products of whether land is an object or subject of labor but whether people "have" the products of their labor (1988:86). Whether or not people have their products is a function of the system of social obligation. By looking at the structure of obligations entailed in affinal bonds, Collier suggests that grooms do not compensate senior men when they pay bridewealth for their wives but, rather, enact and constitute the cultural value of respect central to full adulthood. Grooms are not buying wives, or replacing a valuable resource; they are demonstrating respect and constituting themselves as entitled to the respect of others (1988:76–77, 81–85, 86–88).

In spite of MacCormack's and Rosaldo's different understandings of what constitutes "social relations," based on their emphasis on land as a subject or instrument of labor or on cultural values such as domestic and public ideologies, respectively, both were ultimately interested in trying to make sense of the production and reproduction of gendered social relations themselves, in both precapitalist and capitalist social formations. Both were interested in transcending "the static process of putting people into categories," as MacCormack puts it, and both, perhaps, failed (one not so much in identifying as privileging ecological categories, the other not so much in identifying as privileging public and domestic entities). In the final analysis, however, and at the end of their productive lives, both left similar anthropological legacies for feminist theory. If, in 1980, Michelle Rosaldo emphasized that, more than "documenting sexism as a social fact," feminist scholars should be "challenged to provide new ways of linking the particulars of women's lives, activities, and goals to inequalities wherever they exist" (1980:417), Carol MacCormack in this essay concludes, "we must look at the whole system of social relations of production" and argues that cultural ideologies about the gendered division of labor make the different tasks men and women do seem naturally different and noncomparable. Both were passionately devoted to tracing and identifying what Michelle Rosaldo called the "sources of power" that produce and reproduce gendered social relationships in society.

REFERENCES

Bledsoe, Caroline
1980   *Women and Marriage in Kpelle Society.* Stanford: Stanford University Press.
Bohannon, Laura
1952   "A Genealogical Charter." *Africa* 22:301–15.
Boserup, Esther
1970   *Women's Role in Economic Development.* London: George Allen and Unwin.
Caplan, Patricia
1985   *Class and Gender in India: Women and Their Organizations in a South Indian City.* London: Tavistock.
Cham, Kabbir, Carol MacCormack, Abdoulai Touray, and Susan Baldeh
1987   "Social Organization and Political Factionalism: Primary Health Care in the Gambia." *Health Policy and Planning* 2:214–26.
Clark, Gracia
1994   *Onions Are My Husband: Survival and Accumulation by West African Market Women.* Chicago: University of Chicago Press.
Collier, Jane
1988   *Marriage and Inequality in Classless Societies.* Stanford: Stanford University Press.
Collier, Jane, and Michelle Rosaldo
1981   "Politics and Gender in Simple Societies." In *Sexual Meanings,* ed. Sherry Ortner and Harriet Whitehead, 275–329. Cambridge: Cambridge University Press.
Comaroff, John
1987   "*Sui Genderis:* Feminism, Kinship Theory and Structural Domains." In *Gender and Kinship: Essays toward a Unified Analysis,* ed. Jane Collier and Sylvia Yanagisako, 53–85. Stanford: Stanford University Press.
Day, Jennie
1981   "Gambian Women: Unequal Partners in Rice Development Projects?" In *African Women in the Development Process,* ed. Nici Nelson, 109–22. London: Frank Cass.
Edholm, E., Olivia Harris, and Kate Young
1977   "Conceptualizing Women." *Critique of Anthropology* 3:101–30.
Goody, Jack
1976   *Production and Reproduction.* Cambridge: Cambridge University Press.
Hindess, Barry, and Paul Hirst
1975   *Pre-Capitalist Modes of Production.* London: Routledge and Kegan Paul.
Hoffer, Carol
1974   "Madam Yoko: Ruler of the Kpa Mende Confederacy." In *Woman, Culture and Society,* ed. Michelle Rosaldo and Louise Lamphere, 173–88. Stanford: Stanford University Press.

Keohane, Nannerl, Michelle Rosaldo, and Barbara Gelpi, eds.
1982 *Feminist Theory: A Critique of Ideology.* Chicago: University of Chicago Press.
MacCormack, Carol
1982 "Control of Land, Labor and Capital in Rural Southern Sierra Leone." In *Women and Work in Africa,* ed. Edna Ray, 19–33. Boulder: Westview.
1983 "Slaves, Slave Owners and Slave Dealers: Sherbro Coast and Hinterland." In *Women and Slavery in Africa,* ed. Claire Robertson and Martin Klein, 271–94. Madison: University of Wisconsin Press.
1988 "Health and the Social Power of Women." *Social Science and Medicine* 26:677–83.
1994 *Ethnography of Fertility and Birth,* 2d ed. Prospect Heights, Ill.: Waveland Press.
MacCormack, Carol, and Marilyn Strathern, eds.
1980 *Nature, Culture and Gender.* Cambridge: Cambridge University Press.
MacGaffey, Janet
1986 "Women and Class Formation in a Dependent Economy: Kisangani Entrepreneurs." In *Women and Class in Africa,* ed. Claire Robertson and Iris Berger, 161–77. New York: Holmes and Meier.
1987 *Entrepreneurs and Parasites: The Struggle for Indigenous Capitalism in Zaire.* Cambridge: Cambridge University Press.
1991 *The Real Economy of Zaire: An Anthropological Study.* Philadelphia: University of Pennsylvania Press.
Marx, Karl
1967 *Capital,* vol. 1. London: Lawrence and Wishart.
Meillassoux, Claude
1960 "Essai d'interpretation du phenomene économique dans las sociétés traditionelles d'autosubsistance." *Cahiers d'Etudes Africaines* 4:38–67.
1964 *Anthropologie économique des Gouro de Côte d'Ivoire.* Paris: Mouton.
1972 "From Reproduction to Production: A Marxist Approach to Economic Anthropology." *Economy and Society* 1:93–104.
1981 *Maidens, Meal and Money: Capitalism and the Domestic Community.* Cambridge: Cambridge University Press.
Moore, Henrietta
1988 *Feminism and Anthropology.* Cambridge: Polity Press.
Moore, Henrietta, and Megan Vaughan
1994 *Cutting Down Trees: Gender, Nutrition and Agricultural Change in Northern Province of Zambia, 1890–1990.* Portsmouth, N.H.: Heinemann.
Murray, Colin
1981 *Families Divided: The Impact of Migrant Labour in Lesotho.* Cambridge: Cambridge University Press.
Ortner, Sherry
1974 "Is Female to Male as Nature Is to Culture?" In *Woman, Culture and Society,* ed. Michelle Rosaldo and Louise Lamphere, 67–88. Stanford: Stanford University Press.

Roberts, Pepe
  1979 *The Integration of Women into the Development Process: Some Conceptual Problems.* Institute of Development Studies Bulletin, University of Sussex, vol.10.
Robertson, A. F.
  1991 *Beyond the Family: The Social Organization of Human Reproduction.* Berkeley: University of California Press.
Rosaldo, Michelle
  1974 "Woman, Culture and Society: A Theoretical Overview." In *Woman, Culture and Society,* ed. Michelle Rosaldo and Louise Lamphere, 17–42. Stanford: Stanford University Press.
  1980 "The Use and Abuse of Anthropology: Reflections on Feminism and Cross-Cultural Understanding." *Signs* 5:389–417.
Shostak, Marjorie
  1983 *Nisa: The Life and Work of a !Kung Woman.* New York: Random House.
Terray, Emanuel
  1972 [1969] *Marxism and "Primitive" Societies.* Trans. Mary Klopper. New York: Monthly Review Press.

Destabilizing the Masculine, Refocusing "Gender": Men and the Aura of Authority in Michelle Z. Rosaldo's Work

Alejandro Lugo

Societies . . . that place positive value on . . . the involvement of both men and women in the home seem to be most egalitarian in terms of sex roles. When a man is involved in domestic labor, in child care and cooking, he cannot establish an aura of authority and distance.
—Michelle Z. Rosaldo, "Woman, Culture, and Society"

I started working. I wasn't going as fast, but I was sewing kind of con-stantly. When I went to breakfast (3 hours later), I had 8 gowns assembled (last Friday, by this time, I had 3 or 4). At breakfast, "Arturo," a guy I briefly met while in training, sat with me. He is 19. He told me that a guy last Friday did sew his finger accidentally—five strikes . . . Arturo was telling me that even after the accident occurred, he kept on working. According to Arturo, the guy claimed it did not hurt; so he kept on work-ing for about two hours. He went to the nurse and she gave him a Band-Aid. Apparently, the nurse did not send him home because he had agreed to stay . . . After two hours, the guy's lower arm went numb. The guy could not work anymore, so he had to leave. According to Arturo, he did not show up today.
—Alejandro Lugo, in "Fragmented Lives, Assembled Goods"

The first epigraph—taken from Michelle Rosaldo's 1974 "Theoretical Overview"—manifests two areas of social analysis still not being addressed by the feminist anthropological literature: (1) Rosaldo's con-crete recommendation for social change in the West—to bring men into household obligations; and (2) her theoretical and practical strategy for the systematic study of men as gendered subjects in feminist anthropology as early as 1974. Together, the two epigraphs bring to light, first, Ros-aldo's insightful observation regarding the aura of authority and how it might be challenged and, second, a brief ethnographic attempt on my part to explore her intriguing suggestion: whether or not men who work in a "domestic" site (a garment factory) can establish an aura of authority vis-à-vis women.[1]

My main theoretical, methodological, and practical proposition in this essay is that feminist studies of women (usually done by women) and feminist studies of men or masculinity (usually done by men) do not necessarily add up, either together or separately, to studies of gender—that is, to studies of both men and women. In fact, when a sole feminist analyst examines, comprehensively, both men and women, new and productive categories of theoretical analysis and politics can emerge. In order to accomplish these objectives I will reflect on two broadly conceived interrelated projects for feminist anthropology, both of which constitute the main body of the essay. Part 1, "Rereading Michelle Z. Rosaldo's Domestic and Public," reexamines how Rosaldo's recommendations for social change were incorporated into her theoretical conceptualization of "domestic" and "public" and how her critics (including herself in 1980), while ignoring her practical suggestions for social transformation, disapproved of her early theorizing. Part 2, "Refocusing 'Gender': Destabilizing the Aura of Authority," explores several theoretical issues regarding the production of gender identity in specific social sites (i.e., late-capitalist shop floors) in which both men and women are involved in the same activity (either assembling microcircuits for computers, electric harnesses for automobiles, or hospital supplies). The ethnographic material presented in this part of the essay is based on field research conducted in Ciudad Juárez, Mexico, during the summers of 1987 and 1989 and in 1990–91.

More concretely, part 2 attempts to show that when both men and women are taken into consideration by the social analyst, the following theoretical and empirical problems seem to develop: (1) gender differentiation based on either biology or social tradition often loses significance for the actors involved, particularly if we examine "moments" of negotiation (Collier and Rosaldo 1981; Yanagisako and Collier 1987, 1994) that do not necessarily privilege either men or women (in Rosaldo's hypothetical cases of egalitarianism, when both men and women are involved in domestic chores; in my ethnographic cases, when both men and women are on the assembly line); (2) the narrow (though often useful) vision of studies of men becomes evident in either a prefeminist, masculinist text (in this case I revisit Napoleon Chagnon's ethnography of the Yanomamo) or in more recent feminist attempts (in this particular instance I present my own ethnography of maquiladora workers); and, finally, (3) our understanding of gendered subjectivities gets broadened by opening other avenues for feminist practice: for instance, domestic/public is transcended along with *simplistic* masculine/feminine distinctions.

Thus, I argue here that when both men and women are treated as gendered subjects in feminist projects, our usual analytical conceptions about gender, identity and power are redefined and, consequently, new political repercussions come to the fore. Attaining these goals, however—that is, getting more accurate descriptions of the human complexity in men and women—requires a specific ethnographic sensibility: skills that perhaps can only be acquired through a feminist consciousness and feminist anthropological training, as the one provided by the social lens of the late Michelle Zimbalist Rosaldo.

Part I: Rereading Michelle Z. Rosaldo's Domestic and Public

1 *domestic* adj 1: of or relating to the household or the family . . . TAME, DOMESTICATED; 5: devoted to home duties and pleasures
2 *domestic* n 1: a household servant
domestic animal n: any of various animals (as the horse and the sheep) domesticated by man so as to live and breed in a tame condition.
domesticate vt *-cated, -cating* 1: to bring into domestic use; ADOPT; 2: to fit for domestic life 3: to adapt (an animal or plant) to life in intimate association with and to the advantage of man
domesticity n 1: the quality or state of being domestic or domesticated; 2: domestic activities or life.

> Sexual asymmetries and visions convey what is "really" going on else-
> where, at another political epicenter.
> —Ann Laura Stoler, "Carnal Knowledge and Imperial Power"

In 1974 Michelle Rosaldo had a clear and definite political agenda: "to understand the nature of female subordination and the ways it may be overcome" (24). To this extent and in conjunction with most contributors to the Rosaldo and Lamphere volume (*Woman, Culture and Society*), her interest was, as Ortner stated, "of course more than academic" (1974:67).

Following the major anthropological tenet of the time—the search for universals, what was "broadly human"—she believed that the subordination of women was a cross-cultural phenomenon (Rosaldo 1974:19; Lamphere 1987:16). What constituted women's subordination for Rosaldo was in essence a "sexual asymmetry" embodied in "the fact that male, as opposed to female, activities are always recognized as predominantly important, and cultural systems give authority and value to the roles and activities of men" (1974:19). Although she was quite cautious in differentiating the theoretical implications of valued and devalued activities from the philosophical and political question of the subordinate status of women, Rosaldo tried to justify her stance regarding universal subordination by presenting specific ethnographic material (see 12–21, 28–41). More generally, she perhaps followed Ortner's position: "I think the onus is no longer upon us to demonstrate that female subordination is a cultural universal; it is up to those who would argue against the point to bring forth counter examples" (1974:71).

To what extent have Rosaldo's critics of the 1974 position brought counterexamples? Since then, for instance, Sacks (1979) argued for the complementarity of gender relations, Leacock (1981) analyzed so-called egalitarian societies, and Sanday and Goodenough (1991) have invited feminist anthropologists to go beyond the "second sex" syndrome. Alternatives such as these, however, which emphasize a move away from assuming too much about gender inequalities, were heavily questioned by Yanagisako and Collier (1987) and by Lamphere (1987). As Lamphere stated:

women . . . are rarely the "articulators" of decisions that involve the entire band or community . . . Usually this role falls to a male, though older women are not entirely excluded. The lack of recognition of this "male bias" in the way decisions are made . . . is, in my opinion, one of the critical deficiencies in the egalitarian hypothesis. (24)

Paradoxically, however, and perhaps optimistically, Rosaldo still hoped that we could achieve a certain form of egalitarianism.

Power and Gender, Biology and Practice

Although Rosaldo's preoccupation was more with finding ways to overcome the apparent universal oppression than with explaining universalism itself, she tried to understand why the activities of women were devalued cross-culturally, especially in comparison to men's practices. Her aim in this attempt was the search for the identification (in ethnography and in society) of the "sources of power" that kept women subordinated *as well as those that would help them escape the subordination* (1974:18)—or the devalued status. Thus, she proposed a "structural model" constituted of two dichotomous categories (public and domestic) that "underlay" the local "evaluations of the sexes" (23)—that is, the culturally specific values attached to male and female activities. The cultural values given to the sexual asymmetry were in themselves sources of power. They could work either against women as sources of domination and oppression or, as Rosaldo would prefer, for women as sources of empowerment and transformation.[2]

In 1987 Yanagisako and Collier, though critical of Rosaldo's use of domestic and public as "merely elaborations and extensions of the same natural fact: the biological difference between men and women" (15), still depend quite significantly on the notion of values applied to cultural practices carried out by men and women. They wrote regarding their concept of "systemic inequality":

> We begin with the premise that social systems are, by definition, systems of inequality. This premise . . . conforms to common usage. By most definitions, *a society is a system of social relationships and values. Values entail evaluation. Consequently, a society is a system of social relationships in which all things and actions are not equal.* (39; emph. added)

This focus on unequal values, as we have seen, was one of Rosaldo's main theoretical and practical preoccupations, as early as 1974. Yanagisako and Collier were extending "evaluation," in fact, to general studies of society, culture, and history—a direction, I believe, she would have taken.

The explanatory element that Yanagisako and Collier gave to Rosaldo's uses of domestic and public, however, is interpreted differently by Louise Lamphere. She noted, "Rosaldo did not attempt to *explain* women's subordination through the dichotomy, but saw it as an underlying structural framework in any society that supported subordination and that would have to be reorganized to change women's position" (1993:75). Rosaldo herself stated it quite explicitly:

> The opposition does not determine cultural stereotypes or asymmetries in the evaluation of the sexes, but rather underlies them, to support a very general (and, for women, often demeaning) identification of

women with domestic life and of men with public life. These identifications, themselves neither necessary nor desirable, can all be tied to the role of women in child rearing. (1974:23–24)

More than two decades later it should be evident that in 1974 Michelle Rosaldo was trying to come to grips with the ways men and women were given a social "identification," or, in more recent terminology, how they (or their identities) were produced socially—more concretely, how the asymmetry supported "a very general (and *for women, often demeaning*) identification of women with domestic life and of men with public life." Because of their socially produced nature, according to Rosaldo, these particular characterizations of men and women are "neither necessary nor desirable." Nonetheless, they provided a "framework for conceptualizing the activities of the sexes" (33). By *activities,* Rosaldo means human action, behavior happening on the ground—actual experience. With regard to the question of biology, she wrote, "I would suggest that anything so general as the universal asymmetry of sex roles is likely to be the result of a constellation of different factors . . . Biology may be one of these, but biology becomes significant only as it is interpreted by human actors and associated with characteristic modes of action" (23).

Plan of Action

The major arguments made so far must be well understood: (1) that Rosaldo formulated her theoretical model in order to identify the "sources" of power that subordinate women (here I stress, as I think she did, the sources of power and not "subordination"); (2) that she was theoretically, and politically, concerned with how women and men were given social identities (my phrase; her term, *identifications*); and (3) that she saw the problem of women as emerging mainly from their culturally perceived role as child rearers, and not so much as birth givers. As she held, "These identifications [of public and domestic] . . . can all be tied to the role of women in child rearing" (24). In order to subvert or transform the latter state of affairs—even though she stated that the "model has no necessary implications for the future"—Rosaldo delineated two possible sources of empowerment:

by using the structural model as a framework, we can identify the implications for female power, value, and status in various cross-cultural articulations of domestic and public roles . . . the model . . . permits us to identify two sorts of structural arrangements that elevate women's status: women may enter the public world, or *men may enter the home.* (35–36; emph. added)

Having handy Sacks's (1974) critique of Engels, it would not have been terribly illuminating to accentuate that women must enter the "public sphere." Instead, without denying such a strategy, it was the possibility that men could be brought into the "home" that stimulated Rosaldo to suggest that equality of the sexes could be attained. That is, only through such an alternative, cultural evaluations of the activities of men and women could be given equitable value. After all, she had found in the ethnographic literature of the time that societies

that place positive value on . . . the involvement of both men and women in the home seem to be most egalitarian in terms of sex roles. When a man is involved in domestic labor [i.e., as among the Ilongot, the Arapesh, and Mbuti; see 40–41] in child care and cooking, he cannot establish an aura of authority and distance. (39)

As I noted earlier, the latter statement about men involved in home activities and not establishing "an aura of authority" has not, as yet, been questioned (not even addressed) in the feminist anthropological literature. I will try to address it in part 2 of this essay. For the most part the main focus in feminist anthropology has been on women. As Judith Shapiro noted about the gender literature in anthropology: "much of the recent cross-cultural research is not only about women, but by women, and in some sense, for women" (1979:269). In this selective process of trying to "permit a grasp of women's lives," many feminist scholars forgot, as Michelle Rosaldo noted in 1980, that "men and women ultimately live together in the world." Yet, she argued, "we will never understand the lives that women lead without relating them to men" (396). This specific suggestion leads me, in turn, to argue categorically that this anthropological body of knowledge in the 1990s cries out for the systematic incorporation of men as gendered subjects (see, e.g., Brandes 1980; Herzfeld 1985; Shapiro 1987; Gilmore 1990; Lancaster 1992; Limon 1994; Behar 1995; Ong 1995; Tsing and Ebron 1995).[3]

Not surprisingly, then, as early as 1974, Michelle Rosaldo concluded her widely misunderstood feminist piece with the following suggestion for our society:

we must, like the Ilongots, bring men into the sphere of domestic concerns and responsibilities . . . the Ilongot example . . . suggests that men who in the past have committed their lives to public achievement will recognize women as true equals only when men themselves help raise new generations by taking on the responsibilities of the home. (42)

Some Repercussions, No Feminist Reaction

In the case of the United States, specifically in middle-class circles, bringing men into the home or into such activities as cooking their own meals, driving their kids to daycare centers, and helping to redefine their wives' reproductive lives, has perhaps been more influential in whatever autonomy women have achieved today than is commonly thought. Yet this does not mean that these new men and new women escape the hegemony of domestic/public discourses. For instance, in her study of new reproductive technologies (particularly amniocentesis and prenatal diagnoses) Rayna Rapp argues that, while recent medical technology allows women "like their male partners, to imagine voluntary limits to their commitments to children," it "does not transform the world of work, social services, media, and the like on which a different sense of maternity and the 'private' sphere would depend." Interestingly, Rapp does not reflect on Michelle Rosaldo's early work but makes the following apt claim: "Moreover, that 'private' sphere and its commitment to child bearing is now being enlarged to include men. Fathers, too, can now be socially created during the pregnancy, through birth-coaching and early bonding. These new fathers may also claim the right to comment on women's motives for pregnancy and abortion in powerful ways" (1997:138).

Thus, Michelle Rosaldo's framework of the domestic and public can still explain the gendered politics of everyday practices (although *private* is not synonymous with *domestic,* Rapp's specific usage is part of the hegemonic dichotomy Rosaldo was challenging). We, as scholars writing in the late twentieth century, must recognize that the identification of cultural and spatial male and female schematic worlds, or their inversions, is not necessarily futile; on the contrary, we must continue the disclosure of what Bourdieu calls "the schemes of the sexual division of labor and the division of sexual labor," since they manifest symptoms of broader hegemonic relations. As he convincingly argued with regard to Kabylian society in Algeria,

the opposition between . . . man, invested with protective, fecundating virtues, and woman, at once sacred and charged with maleficent forces

. . . is reproduced in the spatial division between male space, with the place of assembly, the market, or the fields, and female space, the house and its garden, the retreats of *haram.* (1978 [1972]:89)

Unfortunately, Bourdieu provided no critical commentary on the cultural positions of women. Nonetheless, he elaborated on how the correlation of space and gendered activities permeates other realms of everyday life by noting that

> this spatial organization (matched by a temporal organization obeying the same logic) governs practices and representations—far beyond the frequently described rough divisions between the male world and female world, the assembly and the fountain, public life and intimacy— and thereby contributes to the durable imposition of the schemes of perception, thought, and action. (89–90)

Perhaps much more intriguing and theoretically provoking than Bourdieu is Ann Stoler's critical observation regarding "sexual asymmetries" in colonial cultures: "Sexual asymmetries and visions convey what is 'really' going on elsewhere, at another political epicenter. They are tropes to depict other centers of power" (1991:54).

Interestingly, however, both the feminist movement and the gender literature have generally responded to Rosaldo's agenda very much as the Kibbutz social movement in Israel responded to gender issues. Judith Shapiro wrote about the Kibbutz:

> the attempt to achieve [sexual] equality is generally a matter of trying to turn women into social equivalents of men . . . Women had to be given the opportunity to work in agricultural production, in developing industries, and in the army. There was, however, no comparable effort to get men into the kitchens and laundries. (1991: n. 40)

Indeed, Rayna Rapp discusses how "white middle-class women," in their individualist fight for choice, "may be 'becoming more like men,' freer than ever before to enter hegemonic realms of the culture from which they were formerly barred, but at the price of questioning and altering their traditional gender identity" (1997:138). In Rapp's otherwise lucid analysis of amniocentesis there is no comment on the possibility, essentialist notwithstanding, of the "new fathers" becoming social equivalents of women:

unlike their female counterparts who get transformed into social males, they remain men but shift from biological into socially created fathers (through birth coaching, e.g.).

Lest there might be misunderstanding, the point of this discussion is twofold: that domestic/public narratives affecting both men and women continue to reproduce themselves and that their identification on the part of the analyst might help demonstrate some of the social victories, and the lost battles as well, of the feminist movement itself (at least in Western society—the dominant context in which most anthropologists still write).

We the Victorians: Historical Realizations, Static Applications

In her 1980 article "The Use and Abuse of Anthropology" Rosaldo reconsiders her 1974 position by reanalyzing her use of human universals, her use of dichotomies, and her abuse of Western concepts. Undoubtedly, after Reiter's (Rapp's) 1975 historical contextualization of our folk concepts of the domestic and the public, and their respective association with women and men, she suggested, and clarified, that her model was dichotomous because such dualities had constituted in our culture a heritage from Victorian England. This ideological legacy, she agreed, we have not escaped (Rosaldo 1980; also see Collier, this vol.).

This valid recognition on her part, however, which mainly traces her theoretical position historically and culturally, does not necessarily make invalid the ethnographic cases she used in 1974. In the examination of the secondary texts presented, the reader is not so naive as to fail to distinguish between Rosaldo's imposition of the dichotomy and the data that those ethnographies provided. In fact, the latter were simply illuminated by Rosaldo's interpretation. After all, we must remember that ideology in different contexts can be put to different uses. As we have seen, her specific political purpose of the application of the dichotomy was opposed to that of Victorian thinking—bringing men into the household.

Moreover, Rosaldo was interested in power relations and, being a cultural relativist, in cultural variation. When she thought of sexual asymmetry in 1974, she was not thinking of how "gender works" (1980:399), as she believed in 1980. Instead, her preoccupation concerned the ideological sources of power that tend to produce or give rise to the asymmetry. Indeed, it was the purpose of her essay to present an agenda about how to subvert the nature of the Western asymmetry. Perhaps without fully knowing it, she was already making a critique of Victorian ideology. Thus, her belief in 1980 that she was "assuming too much" with her use of the two spheres is, more than anything and for the most part, the influence of her critics. Realizing that her theoretical framework was based on a hegemonic Victorian tenet does not necessarily make the ethnographic material Victorian. As she noted in 1980 about the empirical element in the dichotomy debates:

> My earlier account of sexual asymmetry in terms of the inevitable ranking of opposed domestic and public spheres is *not . . . one that I am willing to reject for being wrong.* Rather, I have suggested that the reasons that account made sense are to be found not in empirical detail, but in the categories, biases, and limitations of a traditionally individualistic and male-oriented sociology. (Rosaldo 1980:415)

Rosaldo was a product and an example of a social transformation (the feminist movement): by bringing men into the home, she was turning the Victorian dichotomy on its head. As she argued about the public *in* the domestic: "when *public decisions are made in the household,* women may have a legitimate public role" (1974:39; emph. added). And so, I argue, there must be domesticity—"the quality or state of being domestic or domesticated"—in (so-called) public terrains of struggle.

Michelle Rosaldo's Articulation of Theory and Practice

Rosaldo's practical political agenda and her theoretical formulations went hand in hand. They could not be, and should not have been, separated. The alternative itself was not taken into consideration by her peers in the 1974 book. She wrote, "none of the other papers in this volume consider this alternative"—that is, bringing men into the household. Her critics have ignored her most specific political strategy. Yet, by separating the dichotomous framework (domestic and public) from the concrete recommendation for change in our society, they managed conveniently to discard her theoretical proposition (see, e.g., Reiter 1975; Sacks 1979; MacCormack and Strathern 1980; Leacock 1981; J. Comaroff 1987; Yanagisako and Collier 1987; Strathern 1988). Perhaps having considered "the Michelle Rosaldo case" closed, the following feminists did not challenge her critics: Tsing and Ginsburg (1990), di Leonardo (1991), Behar and Gordon (1995). (In fact, in one of the most recent collections addressing gender issues—*Situated Lives: Gender and Culture in Everyday Life,* edited by Louise Lamphere, Helena Ragone, and Patricia Zavella [1997]— Michelle Rosaldo is completely absent from the discussion about what constitutes feminist anthropology in the late 1990s.)

We must realize that gender relations can only be better understood by analyzing the complex sociopolitical processes affecting both women and men in their culturally and historically ordered worlds (Rosaldo 1980; Yanagisako and Collier 1987; Lugo and Maurer, this vol.). One of the initial attempts to deal with men as gendered (i.e., domesticated) subjects was already theoretically and politically inherent in Rosaldo's pioneering formulation. By 1980 Michelle Rosaldo invited feminist scholars "to ask just how it comes about—in a world where people of both sexes make choices that count—that men come to be seen as the creators of collective good and the preeminent force in local politics" (414–15). Thus, without leaving behind the feminist project for social justice, we must systematically study men as culturohistorical products themselves and with the same care and rigor undertaken when studying women.

Part 2: Refocusing "Gender":
Destabilizing the Aura of Authority

1 *domestic* / of or relating to the household or the family . . . TAME, DOMES-
TICATED.

1 *private* / adj 1 a: intended for or restricted to the use of a particular person, group, or class; b: belonging to or concerning an individual person, company, or interest; c (1) restricted to the individual; 2: carried on by the individual independently of the institutions; 2 a (1): not holding public office or employment; (2): not related to one's official position: PERSONAL; 3 a: withdrawn from company or observation : not known or intended to be known publicly: SECRET; c: unsuitable for public use or display.

1 *tame* adj 1: reduced from a state of native wildness especially so as to be tractable and useful to man: DOMESTICATED; 2; made docile and submissive: SUBDUED; 3: lacking spirit, zest, or interest
syn TAME, SUBDUED, SUBMISSIVE shared meaning element: docilely tractable
ant FIERCE.

2 *tame* vb, *tamed; taming* vt 1 a: to reduce from a wild to a domestic state; b: to subject to cultivation; 2: to deprive of spirit: HUMBLE, SUBDUE; 3: tone down: SOFTEN vt: to become tame-tamable.

tameless adj not tamed or not capable of being tamed.

A few of the younger men retired after a single blow, privately admitting to me later that they pretended to be injured to avoid being forced to fight more.
      —Napoleon Chagnon, *Yanomamo*

The whistling of the people is important. When someone drops something noisy, or forgets to wear his or her hair cover, everybody whistles. In Juárez, you are expected to be perfect in your behavior. You cannot be weak, forgetful, or careless. To present yourself as such, it would only show that you are not capable of doing what you are expected to do. Thus, if you drop something, or forget to cover your head after the break or after lunch, they will whistle, mainly the men. One time, the whistling was so constant (apparently, the target had not noticed it was he who had been whistled at; most of the time you think it is someone else) until one guy finally yelled, "Tu gorro pendejo" (Your cap, stupid!).
      —Alejandro Lugo, *Fragmented Lives, Assembled Goods*

Men began to get employed in *maquiladoras* (global assembly plants) in the early 1980s—on electronic, garment, and automobile assembly lines. At the time Fernández-Kelly published her pioneering work in 1983 (Fernández-Kelly 1983) hundreds of new maquiladoras were arriving to Ciudad Juárez due to the so-called Mexican Crisis and its subsequent devaluation of the peso. Throughout the 1980s anyone could be hired throughout the industrial parks of the city (though not in all factories): young and older women, young and older men, educated and uneducated. Since the early 1980s the male maquiladora labor force in Ciudad Juárez has fluctuated between 35 and 45 percent (Lugo 1995). Throughout the 1970s, however, women constituted the majority of the maquiladora labor force, fluctuating between 80 and 90 percent (Fernández-Kelly 1983).

  Strongly believing in "participant observation," I worked as an assembly line operator in three maquiladoras: one electronic (1987), one garment (1989), and one of the automobile type (1991). I was interested in studying both men and women, especially the interactions between them, inside and outside the factory. It never occurred to me to study either exclusively men or the issue of masculinity per se. While I asked both men and women about their conceptions of machismo, I never asked about their own local conceptions of "masculinity" or how they defined "the masculine," "manliness," or "manly" virtues (see Gutmann, this vol.). After all (I now ask myself), did feminist scholars approach the "woman question" in terms of the "feminine"? How far would they have gone if they had continued along those lines? In trying to understand men, how truly critical is the issue of the masculine? Regarding these kinds of questions, though related to women, Michelle Rosaldo knew better. As early as 1974, she examined or asked questions about the *activities of women,* not about their femininity; even more important for our purposes here, in 1980 she argued that women's place in society was a product of "the meaning [their] activities acquire through concrete social interactions" (1980:400).

In the last fifteen years most ethnographic studies about men by male anthropologists (e.g., Herdt 1981; Herzfeld 1985; Lancaster 1986, 1988, 1992; Limon 1989, 1994; Lugo 1990) have focused on the cultural construction of masculinity, or manliness (machismo) vis-à-vis men, and not necessarily vis-à-vis "gender." To this extent most of these works do not engage directly with feminist theorists nor with feminist theorizing about gender (for an unfortunate attempt by a male anthropologist who caricatures feminist anthropology, see Gilmore 1990:23–24). And in the cases where more serious and sophisticated theorizing occurs (e.g., John Comaroff 1987; Valeri 1990; Scheffler 1991; Lancaster 1992) it has not been applied to concrete innovative ethnographic projects that would enrich our representations of *both* men and women—gender relations—in feminist anthropology. One recent exception, however, is Matthew Gutmann's extraordinary work among working-class Mexican men in Mexico City (1996).[4]

Yet, perhaps ironically, we cannot claim that before the feminist movement men were not being studied. After all, was not this privileging of men in previous prefeminist ethnographies what triggered feminist anthropology in the 1970s? To what analytical degree is it possible to claim that those studies were "in fact" studies of masculinity?

With these questions in mind, in what follows I will examine certain social occurrences that Yanagisako and Collier call "moments when practice and meaning are negotiated together" (1994:198). My analysis of such moments of negotiation will consist of a juxtaposition between my own ethnographic narratives of maquiladora men and women conducting their working journey and Napoleon Chagnon's ethnographic descriptions of Yanomamo men as aggressive/violent masculine subjects. This juxtaposition serves several purposes: (1) it shows one treatment of masculinities in what Renato Rosaldo calls "a classic ethnography"; (2) it shows the critical difference between Chagnon's masculinist, prefeminist vision and my own feminist consciousness—a product of my specific graduate training in the 1980s; (3) it shows the limitations in exclusively examining men's lives in so-called masculine terms; (4) it tries to show how *maquila* men's lives as well as Yanomamo men's experiences cannot be described by excluding from our analyses men's vulnerabilities as part of their gendered subjectivities (i.e., feeling frightened, intimidated, and ineffective); and, finally, (5) by focusing on these feelings of vulnerability, the following also sheds light on Michelle Rosaldo's analytical insight, though inverted, that "*when public decisions are made in the household, women may have a legitimate public role*" (Rosaldo 1974:39; emph. added); in other words, when this same insight is applied to men in public settings—that is, when "domestic" decisions are made by men in public settings, the domestic is inevitably turned into the "private/personal/intimate," allowing or leading men to play a legitimate and necessary, though not always desired, domestic (if not tamed/domesticated) role.

Yanomamo Men: The Fierce, the Frightened,
and Chagnon's Masculine Heroics

> We would raise the question, nonetheless, of whether a postmodern feminism can afford, any more than modernist feminism, to be a project for women only.
>
> —Judith Newton and Judith Stacey,
> "Reflections on Studying Academic Men"

Whereas feminist anthropological projects of gender, after 1970, were consciously, decidedly, and politically explicit about, by, and for women, during the classic period of anthropology (more or less between 1920 and 1970) most studies of culture and society were, for the most part, unconsciously and "apolitically," about men, by men, and probably for men, who dominated the academy. This confusion of masculinity with culture and society is quite evident in *Yanomamo,* by Napoleon Chagnon (there have been several editions: 1968, 1977, 1983, and 1992). Chagnon's ethnography can be read in many different ways: as a study of marriage, kinship, and descent; as a study of warfare; or as a study of cultural ecology and social structure—or, perhaps more simply, but more exact, as a study of sedentary gardeners and hunters who live in dispersed villages in the Venezuela-Brazil Amazonian border and who speak the Yanomamo language. Perhaps for historical reasons related to the birth and development of the classic ethnography (see R. Rosaldo 1989), the text is believed to be, and is presented by Chagnon as, a study of a *whole* people and their culture. After all, the first three editions of Chagnon's case study were subtitled "The Fierce People." After he consulted with some Apache friends of his, Chagnon dropped the subtitle because *they* (not he) felt "some white people might read the wrong thing into a word that attempted to represent valor, honor, and independence" (1992:xvi). In spite of this change in the new title to his book, Chagnon confuses not only the notion of "fierce" with violence (he explains to the readers the different "Levels of Violence"—chest pounding, side slapping, club fighting, and raiding), but he also confuses what he thinks is a study of *the* "Yanomamo culture" with, at best, a study of masculinities and, at worst, a study of a few men who acted "violently."

Allow me to present three moments in which feeling fear and feeling intimidated by others were probably more common in his ethnography than the acts of fierceness Chagnon believes to be describing. Chagnon identifies two men (Rerebawa and Kaobawa) as his key informants: Rerebawa is in his early twenties, and Kaobawa, the head of the village, is in his early forties. According to Chagnon, "Of all the Yanomamo I know, [Rerebawa] is the most genuine and the most devoted to his culture's ways and values." Whereas "Kaobawa is older and wiser, a polished diplomat," Rerebawa "is fierce and capable of considerable nastiness" (1992:31). Chagnon presents at least two examples of Rerebawa's "ferocity," one being when he challenged Bakotawa, who had an affair with one of Rerebawa's potential wives:

Rerebawa challenged Bakotawa to a club fight . . . He hurled insult after insult at both Bakotawa and his father, trying to goad them into a fight. His insults were bitter and nasty. They tolerated them for a few moments, but Rerebawa's biting insults provoked them to rage. Finally, they stormed angrily out of their hammocks and ripped out roof-poles, now returning the insults verbally, and rushed to the village clearing. Rerebawa continued to insult them, goading them into striking him on the head with their equally long clubs. Had either of them struck his head . . . he would then have the right to take his turn on their heads with his club. His opponents were intimidated by his fury, and

simply backed down, refusing to strike him, and the argument ended.
He had intimidated them into submission . . . Rerebawa had won the
showdown and thereafter swaggered around the village, insulting the
two men behind their backs at every opportunity. (22)

While I would like to emphasize rage, the process of intimidating and
the submission (taming/domestication) of two men (father and son),
Chagnon wants to emphasize the fury and anger of Rerebawa but with a
strategic purpose in mind—to get at people's genealogies: "He was genuinely angry with them, to the point of calling the older man by the name
of his long-deceased father. I quickly seized the opportunity to collect an
accurate genealogy and confidentially asked Rerebawa about his adver-
sary's ancestors" (1992: 22). Evidently, Chagnon's seizing of violent occasions in order to trace genealogical relationships constitutes an extreme
methodological strategy of classic anthropology's privileging of social
structure over structures of feeling. This theoretical preference omitted
what Michelle Rosaldo would have emphasized: that when individuals
make private/personal decisions (tolerating insults, experiencing rage, and
feeling intimidated into submission) in public places, they tend to play a
culturally legitimate domestic (if not domesticated) role. Thus, while masculinist decisions or feelings of fury do not escape Chagnon's ethnographic
sensibility (particularly in figuring out social networks), other public forms
of intimate "identifications" become blurred if not erased in front of his
analytical gaze. In leaving out of his analysis what he would probably consider *nonmasculine* vulnerabilities of men (feeling fear and intimidated),
Chagnon reduces, or rather elevates, "the Yanomamo," particularly
Yanomamo men, to masculine—in this case, fierce—proportions.
　In yet another example of what it means to be fierce Chagnon tells us
that:

Rerebawa has displaced his ferocity in many ways, one incident in particular illustrates what his character can be like. Before he left his own
village to take his new wife . . . he had an affair with the wife of an older
brother. When it was discovered, his brother attacked him with a club.
Rerebawa responded furiously: He grabbed an ax and drove his brother
out of the village after soundly beating him with the blunt side of the
single-bit ax. His brother was so intimidated by the thrashing and
promise of more to come that he did not return to the village for several
days. I visited the village . . . shortly after this event had taken place;

Rerebawa was my guide. He made it a point to introduce me to this man. He approached his hammock, grabbed him by the wrist, and dragged him out on the ground: "This is the brother whose wife I screwed when he wasn't around!" A deadly insult, one that would usually provoke a bloody club fight among more valiant Yanomamo. The man did nothing. He slunk sheepishly back into his hammock, shamed, but relieved to have Rerebawa release his grip. (1992:30)

While I would like to call attention, once again, to the shame, the fear, and the intimidation felt by Rerebawa's brother (we do not get his name), Chagnon repeatedly ignores these public demonstrations of domesticated feelings among the Yanomamo and instead makes the observation that Rerebawa "has a charming, witty side as well." Yet, just as he provided Chagnon with genealogies, Rerebawa also seemed to give the most charming treatment to the anthropologist (unlike the blows given to his cultural peers). For instance, Chagnon wrote: "he is one of few Yanomamo that I feel I can trust. I recall indelibly my return to [the village] after being away a year . . . He greeted me with an immense bear hug and exclaimed, with tears welling up in his eyes, 'Shaki! Why did you stay away so long? . . . I could not at times eat for want of seeing you again?' I, too [Chagnon continues], felt the same way about him—then and now . . . Of all the Yanomamo I know, he is the most genuine and most devoted to his culture's ways and values" (1992:30–31). Thus, even though Rerebawa intimidated everyone else in the village, Chagnon considered him a typical Yanomamo, with all kinds of evidence to the contrary.

One last example of the terror felt by the young men (and the avoidance practiced by older men) should suffice to demonstrate that Chagnon's ideal spectacle about "fierceness" was mostly in his own masculinist imagination. He wrote:

Some of the younger men in Kaobawa's group were reluctant to participate in the fighting because *they were afraid of being injured, remaining on the periphery so as to not be easily seen.* This put more strain on the others, who were forced to take extra turns in order to preserve the group's reputation. At one point Kaobawa's men, sore from the punishment they had taken and worried that they would ultimately lose the fight, wanted to escalate the contest to an ax duel . . . Kaobawa was adamantly opposed to this, as he knew it would bring bloodshed. He therefore recruited the younger men into the fighting, as well as a few of the older ones who had nothing but demand the *others* step into the arena . . . *A few of the younger men retired after a single blow, privately admitting to me later that they pretended to be injured to avoid being forced to fight more.* The fighting continued in this fashion for nearly three hours . . . Kaobawa and the headman from the other group stood by with their weapons, attempting to keep the fighting under control but not participating in it. (1992:180; emph. added)

This chest-pounding duel, which eventually led to "women and children from both groups . . . fleeing from the village, screaming and crying," was a product of a feast. Even though the relationship between the two groups remained "somewhat strained and potentially hostile," Chagnon ends his analysis with a sort of happy, structural-functional note: "In general, feasts are exciting for both the hosts and the guests and contribute to their solidarity . . . Of the six feasts I witnessed during the first 18 months I spent with the Yanomamo, two of them ended in fighting" (183).

In spite of the complex life lived by the people Chagnon studied and in spite of his (almost exclusive) interaction with men—and not all of them "violent"—Chagnon reached explicit conclusions not only about culture, society, social structure, and the nature of violence in human beings (of course, a feminist anthropological nightmare). He also reached *implicit* conclusions about Yanomamo men as if they all were exclusively masculine and, thus, fierce beings.

From Masculinity to Gender Studies

In Chagnon's ethnography, and most visibly in the ethnographic films he made, women (as gendered subjects) are present but hardly ever discussed. For that to occur in anthropology it took a feminist turn in the discipline, a shift driven quite effectively by the female generation of Michelle Rosaldo. This feminist turn constituted not only a feminist critique of gender roles; it also implied (though informally) some kind of anthropological training in the development of a feminist sensibility and consciousness on the part of the ethnographer—something that Chagnon and most anthropologists of his generation either rejected or simply did not get. By the mid- and late 1980s, the period in which I was a graduate student at the University of Wisconsin–Madison and Stanford, several of my feminist professors (who were themselves trained in a critical feminist and/or Marxist anthropology in the late 1960s and 1970s) were reshaping a theoretically pervasive and ethnographically convincing kind of feminist anthropological tradition that their students, female or male, could easily incorporate into their general training of the discipline (if they so desired) and into their general vision of the social and academic worlds they inhabited. Yet in the 1990s, perhaps ironically, the move from women's studies and masculinist studies to gender studies has been characteristic of gaps and contradictions, particularly concerning the production of a scholarly field that would genuinely take the feminist study of gender—of *both* men and women—to rigorous task.

With the intention of exploring possibilities, in what follows I will displace or change the focus on masculinity to refocus on gender in order to: (1) challenge more effectively the aura of authority (as Michelle Rosaldo suggested); and (2) argue that neither men nor women can be properly understood separately, especially in the cultural contexts of maquiladora production in the late 1980s and early 1990s. Following Rosaldo's inquisitive logic, I would like to address in this section two interrelated questions: (1) are gender subjectivities and identities transformed when men are incorporated into social spaces, such as maquiladoras, which are culturally conceptualized as domestic or for females? and (2) is the aura of authority effectively challenged in this process?

In 1990, based on my 1987 fieldwork experience in a maquiladora (in which the workers and myself assembled microcircuits), I made several arguments about gender, culture, and late-capitalist production (Lugo 1990). I examined how sociohistorical notions of laziness constitute in themselves cultural enactments or performances that enrich, in the eyes of the capitalist, the global assembling process. More specifically, I tried to show how new notions of machismo (manliness and masculinity) were produced and reproduced through the production and reproduction of microcircuits on the assembly line. This production and reproduction of culture and gender identity occurred (1) through the public enactment of *huevón(a)* and *barra*—two different linguistic terms that mean the same thing: lazy—and (2) through the cultural expectation, on the part of Mexican men, to have *huevos,* or courage/strength, in everyday life (here the metaphor *huevos,* translated as "eggs," implies testicles, or "balls"). The most important tool necessary to assemble the microcircuits was a *barra,* a piece of iron (a beam), one foot long, one and a half inches wide. In Ciudad Juárez, however, the term *barra,* as noted, also means "lazy"—as in "Como eres barra" (You are so lazy). In this particular transnational corporation both men and women worked together on the same table of production or assembly line. The multiple uses and multiple meanings of the term *barra* led me to give the following ethnographic description about gender and capitalist production:

In the attempt to produce enough microcircuits to fulfill the quota, the workers are pressed by other workers (either male or female) to work harder and faster by yelling *barra!* to each other. Even though women are not associated with machismo, that is, they do not enact macho behavior, per se, they also work faster when pressed with the term *barra.* They are being called "lazy" women: *huevonas*. . . [the masculine *huevón* is used to call a man lazy]. If a man gets behind, however, he might not be considered to be macho [or masculine]; he might be thought of as not having *huevos* (testicles/courage/strength). Consequently, he loses status as a male, not only in terms of the "border culture," but also in the Mexican national culture. The image that he might reflect is that of an unmasculine male, especially in front of the women and the other "machista" men. Thus, part of being able to keep up with the quota [part of being able to show physical strength] is, to a large extent, part of maintaining the macho image. This machismo is in turn transformed from cultural behavior (or practice) to a system of labor control, or [rather], of capitalist discipline . . . Consequently, in making themselves work faster at the command of *barras!* the men are actually reproducing themselves as machos, and thus, are reproducing their own macho culture. (Lugo 1990:187–88)

It is obvious that my narrative was implicitly dominated by the machismo/marianismo distinction, stereotypically associated with gender differences in Latin America (see Twinam 1989:120). Yet it is more true that part of the psychological pressure the men felt when getting behind was a product of the negotiation taking place not only with other men but also with the women who were assembling in the same table of production. In other words, the reproduction of masculinity was not only a male thing (see also Gutmann 1996); it acquired deeper meaning precisely because of the power behind the women's gazes. Interestingly, however, in spite of this masculinist cultural process, as Michelle Rosaldo argued, men cannot easily establish an aura of authority—precisely because of the similarly valued involvement of both men and women in the same kind of activity.

This transfiguration in the dynamic of the workings of authority has unintended and unexpected consequences for the transformation of gender identity and subjectivity. If in this particular global factory being masculine meant keeping up with the quota in an efficient manner, then the women at the table of production also engaged in a "masculine" praxis of their own. Thus, biological notions of femininity and masculinity collapse when, for example, social and productive effectiveness is the dominant discourse challenging and shaping/domesticating, or taming, all workers (both men and women) as gendered (and class) subjects.

Without this specific analysis of gender subjectivity, it is possible, though a serious theoretical problem, to reduce complex social processes to either men or women. For example, Salvador Reyes Nevares limits the notion of effectiveness to issues of masculinity and manliness exclusively, leaving women out of his analysis; he argued that manliness "involves the notion of effectiveness. The man must be self-sufficient and able to solve the problem in life without hesitation or confusion" (qtd. in Arnold 1977:179–80); under these specific circumstances of production (with both men and women producing), in which it is uncertain whether the worker will be effective or not, gender identities are improvised and negotiated, specifically at the table of production. In fact, one day we ran out of material to assemble; they still had to bring it from El Paso. It looked like a late arrival. During this time the workers automatically separated themselves into small groups to talk about incidents at work, dances they had attended, or incidents at home. While we were talking, a young man (teenager) seriously commented that he had a headache. In the border city of Ciudad Juárez working-class men often joke with the linguistic expression *dolor de cabeza,* or having a "headache." Metonymically, *cabeza,* or "head," can be jokingly taken to mean the head of the penis (just as *head* is used in the American expression "giving head"). Consequently, when the young man seriously said, "Me duele la cabeza," a young woman immediately responded by yelling, "Sumo!" an expression meaning "Fuck You! [with the head of my penis]," which is commonly used by males to express real and ideal sexual domination over others, but here it was appropriated by a woman. Feeling challenged in their own subculture, the men nodded with a smile, whereas other women simultaneously showed, with a different kind of smile, both a sign of approval of the cultural inversion, or rather cultural shift, taking place and a sign of momentary disassociation from that type of women—*ese tipo de mujeres.* Thus, as we can see, the appropriation of male discourse on the part of women evidently dissolves facile masculine/feminine distinctions, yet it does not necessarily transcend or transform the male ideology that often marks as *locas,* or "loose," the women who cross conventional gendered boundaries.

Nonetheless, we must still ask the following question about the workers: what strategies do they (men or women) have for coping with group pressure (which, when actively assembling a product, is not fully dissimilar to the group pressure felt by the young Yanomamo men in chest-pounding duels)? Just as Yanomomo men "remain on the periphery so as to not be easily seen" and "pretend to be injured," maquiladora workers sometimes opt for simply leaving the job, especially if the pressure gets too high. This is part of the problem of turnover, or rotation, which has characterized maquiladora production in the last fifteen years. The following description by "Carlos" about what it means to work under pressure in an automobile *maquila,* where he assembled electric harnesses, vividly explains what experiences lead a worker (male or female) simply to quit:

Since it is very hard work, people leave constantly. They cannot take it any longer. Most electric harness factories are always hiring. Some workers only last two months, some last three months, some last longer! At the [assembly] lines, our fingers get tired of grabbing the terminals. We have to press our fingers onto the terminals; often they go numb. They give you masking tape so that our fingers will not get damaged, since the terminal is pure metal. We had to work fast, very fast. For example, I used to work assembling three cables. I knew it was a lot of work: the first cable had eight or nine terminals to insert, the second cable had one terminal, and the third one had two or three terminals. Then, in one fraction of a minute, as the machine rotates, we only had six or seven seconds to assemble all the cables. There was a quota. The line where I was working had to produce between 150 and 200 harnesses . . . it was a lot. If we ran out of material, then you rest. If a person got behind, as one of my [male] friends used to do . . . [*pause*] . . . he would always get behind, always. He was five persons behind me. I was the last one. He had very long cables . . . do you understand? . . . Very long cables. Where they were hung, the cables would make three big circles. When my friend would pull the cables, he would get desperate because he would not pull them right. With the preoccupation that the machine was rotating, he would get behind. Then everybody would fall behind . . . everybody: the five persons behind him and five guys between us. So the machine would have to be stopped. Since no one wanted to get behind, all the workers [women and men] would get on top of each other, trying to assemble their own cables. See, the machine could not be stopped. The most it would stop was two or three minutes, and that was a lot. They would tell us, "You have to keep up with it. That's why you are here, because you are good at what you do" . . . They would brainwash us. "Otherwise, we wouldn't have placed you here," they would say. We know that it is hard work. But because it is a job, because you want them to like you, you try your best. (Qtd. in Lugo 1995:142–43)

After a long journey Carlos and his friend (they lived in the same neighborhood) would go home and dream about work. He told me that they used to joke with the supervisor by asking him who would pay the extra hours labored. The supervisor would ask, what extra hours? Carlos would answer: "The evening hours. We go home and dream that we are inserting terminals. Who is gonna pay for those hours?" When I worked in the electronic *maquila* assembling microcircuits and distributing *barras* through the conveyor belt, I used to dream that I was passing *barras* to the other workers. My wife used to tell me that I kept on giving my pillow to her while I sat (asleep) on our bed. Carlos then told me that he and his friend resigned, both on the same day.

In the garment maquiladora where I conducted fieldwork in 1989 notions of aggressiveness, which tend to be associated with the masculine *in men,* were more characteristic of *the workplace* than of either men or women; this is the case even if it is through gendered subjects that these cultural practices are manifested. In this particular garment factory there were not enough decent chairs on which to sit in order to sew the hospital gowns we were supposed to assemble. Cultural notions of respect toward *lo ajeno* (what does not belong to you) or toward Latin American *caballerismo* (expected gentleness toward women) on the part of men, as when giving the chair or the seat to a woman, had to be discarded if the workers wanted to carry out their jobs. It is impossible to sew without a chair in garment factories. Yet every morning at 6 A.M. workers had to confront others in their daily struggles for chairs. The chair had to be negotiated every morning, along with their dignity and, of course, their gender subjectivity.

The following journal entries from my field notes attempt to portray how the workers and myself negotiated chairs in the garment maquiladora:

August 21, 1989, Monday—"Victor" was looking for his chair. Finally, he went to me; he said mine was his. "Juan," another worker said, "*No te creas*" (Don't believe him). Victor insisted. I said, "Go tell Pablo (the foreman). He assigned it to me." Victor did not say anything. He just wanted a chair. I don't know why no one is assigned one. It's not even good for productivity. I liked that chair. At the end of the day, I marked it with "Lugo" on it. I went to tell Pablo that because so many people were absent, if the owner shows up tomorrow, I would give it back to him or her. Then Pablo, the foreman, said, "No, Defend it! Defend that one!"

On the next day, August 22, 1989, I wrote the following:

Remember, I was to defend my chair, the chair I had labeled "Lugo." I was hoping that a *cholo* (a gang member) would not have it. But then, to my surprise, a young, quiet (sixteen- or seventeen-year-old) woman had it. I went to her and said, "*Oiga, esta es mi silla*" (Excuse me, this is my chair). She said, "I always use this one." Then I asked, "Were you here yesterday? Why didn't you have it?" She answered, "Yesterday, everything was very confusing, so I ended up with another one." I said to her, "Pablo told me to label this one. Tell Pablo to assign you one" (By this time, I do not know why I insisted on assigning chairs). While talking to her, I couldn't help but realize that she was so young (I was twenty-seven years old at that time). Yet, I was told to "defend" that chair. I remembered my feminist intructors from graduate school (Ann Stoler, Florencia Mallon, Maria Lepowsky, Jane Collier). I thought about Fernández-Kelly (through her book). I could see their faces inside my mind. Believe me, you gals, I didn't mistreat her. I've learned from your teachings. We didn't have a discussion or argument about the chair; we had a dialogue. I was aware of gender relations (power) there, at that moment. I was gentle to her. I even felt bad when she was giving the chair back to me. She said, "I'll talk to Pablo. I'll tell him to find me one" . . . When I went to my place, I saw her grabbing another chair (from another machine). I went to her and said, "Make sure you label that one" . . . She said, "I always use this one or the one you have. So I'll stay with this one." "Label it," I said again. She answered, "I'll recognize the chair." Of course, I felt ridiculously patronizing and stupid. Both of us had different ways of approaching the chairs . . . When I came back, "María" thought the young woman was taking away my chair. She said to me, "If that chair is yours, make sure you claim it . . . *Que a usted le valga.*" María had described the attitude that one has to have under these working conditions. Whether the person is a woman, a man, a young woman, an older woman, an older man, or a younger man: you must defend your chair. It was survival of the fittest in the late twentieth century inside a multinational assembly plant. Yet the young women are and can still be at a disadvantage. This is why the feminist arguments of Fernández-Kelly, Stoler, Mallon, Lepowsky, and Collier came to my mind at that particular moment. I saw and experienced the situations they claim injure particular women, especially the young ones. I saw Rosa, however, an older woman (with seniority) defending her positions, regarding chairs, fans, gums, etc. not only from older men with experience, but also from inexperienced, male newcomers.

Thus, it is evident that many times, and depending on their circumstances, gender identities and notions of "aggressiveness" cannot be defined either as masculine or as feminine: these meanings can be uncertain and tend to get negotiated; in this case, as Michelle Rosaldo would have suggested, precisely because both men and women are involved in work activities that are given the same value—either by the capitalist or by the coworker. In this regard notions of Latin American *caballerismo* on the part of men, "giving your chair to a woman," had to be discarded. (In fact, it is common nowadays, when the workers get on the bus hoping to find a seat where they can rest, to see men *not* giving their seat to women who might be standing on their way home at the end of a long working day.) Consequently, the question of "the masculine" or "the feminine" is not always the right question to ask, even if it seems that the question of gender is the issue. It is thus clear that the social context and the circumstances themselves (late capitalism) had a dominant role in producing aggressive practices and subjectivities. In Chagnon's masculinist ethnography it is the Yanomamo themselves who are fierce. The circumstances and social contexts are presented by Chagnon solely as arenas in which Yanomamo men express and manifest levels of violence.

Social reality, however, either in its negotiated or inverted version, does not necessarily transcend the power inequalities that still place subordinate/domesticated subjects at a disadvantage in the process of negotiation. Men and women in Ciudad Juárez, for example, are still victims of patriarchal ideologies: some physically stronger men still injure the weaker males in violent fights, which take place inside and outside the factories (in the buses, in the streets of their neighborhoods); some of these men batter their wives and girlfriends. Physical violence against women, children, and gay men is one of the most common problems the Juárez community still associates with the use and abuse of authority and physical strength, whether on the part of male police or on the part of other victimizers of violence, who tend to be males (I have noticed, however, that most male victimizers of violence are nonmaquiladora men: they tend to be street vendors, construction workers, drug dealers, and, more recently, bus drivers). Although these cases of conflict deserve to be examined, they are beyond the scope of this essay. I would argue, however, that the cultural meanings given to these occurrences relate more to discourses of power—which disembody gender from the body itself—manifested in particular contexts of late capitalism, than to essentializing notions of a masculinity and a femininity, sociobiologically inscribed exclusively on already naturalized male or female bodies (see Ginsburg 1997).

Conclusion

The particular displacements of gender identity examined in this essay—the unpredictability, uncertainty, and unexpected inversions and subversions of gender relations and gendered subjectivities—are products of the destabilization (at strategic moments) of the aura of male authority in gender relations; these social products and social transformations, however, were not imagined by Michelle Rosaldo when she proposed her hypothetical recommendations for social change in Western capitalist society: to bring men into household obligations. Thus, it seems that a more extensive and multilayered concept of gender is our best option for understanding and examining relations among men, among women (not explored here), and between men and women, in the multiple "fields" of feminist anthropology.

In this essay I have made several arguments. In part 1 I suggested that Rosaldo's articulation of theory and practice was reflected through complex (instead of simplistic) understandings of domestic and public spheres and through the political spaces her theorizing tried to create for the social transformation of gender relations, at least in capitalist societies. Bringing men into household obligations and responsibilities, she thought, would not allow men to establish an aura of authority and distance vis-à-vis women. I argued in part 1 that her critics misunderstood her political project and, as a consequence, her theoretical project as well. Part 2 examines the social repercussions and theoretical implications associated with "bringing men into the home," or with destabilizing the aura of authority in an ideologically and materially unfixed domestic space. Through ethnographic detail I tried to address the following question: are gender subjectivities and identities transformed when men are incorporated into the global assembly line (an economic sector historically associated with female labor in Ciudad Juárez, Mexico)?

Before attempting to answer this question, I analyzed certain limitations with studies of men vis-à-vis men (as opposed to gender) by using as an example Napoleon Chagnon's masculinized representations of the Yanomamo. In critically examining Chagnon's ethnographic representations of Yanomamo men, I made the following arguments: first, that if we are going to focus on men in ethnography and consider in turn only their strengths in our analysis (just as Chagnon focused exclusively on masculinist fury and on being fierce), we end up not only with poorly understood, reductionistic notions of the masculine in men but also with masculinist representations of what otherwise are complex human beings; second, a more accurate description of this human complexity in men and women requires particular ethnographic sensibility and training—skills that perhaps can only be acquired through a feminist consciousness and feminist anthropological training, as the one provided by the sophisticated lens of the late Michelle Zimbalist Rosaldo (and of several female anthropologists of her generation). Finally, I argued in this section, though implicitly, that in the 1990s the new generations of feminist anthropologists, especially those trained in the last decade, should have the capacity to carry out (if the analyst so desires) gender analysis that transcends either the masculinist studies of the classic tradition (which should not be reproduced in any form or content in the future) or the kind of studies of women that, according to Rosaldo, "by stressing female action" fail "to ask just how it comes about—in a world in which people of both sexes make choices that count—that men come to be seen as the creators of collective good and the preeminent force in local politics" (1980:414–15; emph. added).

In part 2 I also juxtaposed Chagnon's analysis of Yanomamo men with my own analysis of factory men and women at the U.S.-Mexico border. Through such juxtaposition I raised certain theoretical issues that, I believe, redefine our conception of gender in feminist anthropology. For example, I have demonstrated that, in destabilizing the aura of authority, there are no empirical grounds for reducing either masculinity to men or femininity to women. In this process I have also claimed that men, if they are to be studied, should be understood through both their strengths and vulnerabilities as human beings. Here I emphasized vulnerabilities: feeling fear, frightened, intimidated, getting hurt, being careless, feeling pressure (at work or in dreams), and, finally, feeling physically ineffective, whether among maquiladora men or among Yanomamo men. This discussion of the domestic and of private and personal feelings of men in so-called public places constituted as well my reflections on the theoretical insights Michelle Rosaldo had for inversions in gender relations: just as she claimed that "when public decisions are made in the household, women may have a legitimate public role" (1974:39), I also argued that, when undesired personal decisions are made in public settings, men often do play a domestic (if not domesticated/tamed) role.

In all the maquiladora cases examined here an aura of static, pervasive, or persistent authority on the part of men cannot be established precisely because both genders are actively involved in the same activities, and on more or less equal terms. This was Michelle Rosaldo's suggestive hypothesis, which I tried to put to the test.

Despite the undeniable self-presentation of men and women in terms of what they believe to be a culturally acceptable image along masculine and feminine lines, the complexity of everyday life should remind at least those of us who study human beings in their sociohistorical contexts that questions of "the masculine" and "the feminine" should be addressed not through our powerful (but probably false) assumptions of what biology and society should dictate but, rather, through our analyses of power, context, and gender—of how human beings (both men and women) interact and negotiate their cultural subjectivities in particular social contexts.

To conclude, just as Michelle Rosaldo tried to invert the domestic/public dichotomy, I tried to show that the masculine and feminine subjectivities of men and women, respectively, are also inverted in the shop floor, many times transcending what it means to be a man and what it means to be a woman. The identification of these problems of identity and politics is just the beginning of our understanding of the unintended consequences of the destabilization of the aura of authority in gender relations. These are the particular social contexts that constrain, transform, and, finally, give shape to what Michelle Rosaldo called our identifications. By the same token I hope that these observations make evident that our traditional conception of what constitutes gender studies or studies of gender must also be transformed into a notion that encompasses specific studies of both men and women and not only studies of women or studies of men.

NOTES

Earlier versions of this essay were presented at the AAA Meetings in San Francisco in 1992, at the Latin American Studies Association meetings in 1995 at Washington, D.C., at the University of Illinois in the fall of 1997, and at Knox College in the spring of 1998. For comments on some of those presentations I would like to thank June Nash, the late Carol MacCormack, Matthew Gutmann, Brenda Farnell, Bill Kelleher, Andy Orta, Helaine Silverman, Nancy Eberhart, Jon Wagner, Yvonne Lassalle-Lopez, Magali Roy-Feguiere, Ann Janette Rosga, and, especially, Alma Gottlieb, Claudio Lomnitz, Bill Maurer, Sonya Michel, and Anna Tsing. Ruth Behar, Ed Bruner, Richard King, Lynn Stephen, and Arlene Torres also read and commented on earlier drafts of this essay. I am deeply grateful to all of them. Needless to say, I am solely responsible for any error.

1. Transnational assembly plants, and especially garment factories, have been historically perceived as what I call "domesticated" public spaces, both metaphorically and literally, mainly because they have been associated with women. Elson and Pearson, for instance, describe what Pearson and others call "the changing forms of the subordination of women" (1984:xiii) in the development of capitalist social production, as follows: "Though one form of gender subordination, the subordination of daughters to their fathers, may visibly crumble [once they find work in global factories], another form of gender subordination, that of women employees to male factory bosses, just as visibly is built up . . . In study after study the same pattern is revealed: the young female employees are almost exclusively at the bottom of this hierarchy; the upper levels of the hierarchy are almost invariably male" (1984:33). Before men were hired in transnational factories in the early 1980s at the U.S.-Mexico border (see Lugo 1990), the following characterization of what I will call the "domestication" of women either at home or in the factory would have applied as well to female factory workers in Mexico: "But the problem is not simply that young women may, through factory work, escape the domination of fathers and brothers only to become subordinate to male managers and supervisors, or escape the domination of managers and supervisors only to become subordinate to husbands or lovers. There is also the problem that the domination of managers and supervisors may be withdrawn—the woman may be sacked from her job—while the woman is without the "protection" of subordination to father, brother, husband" (Elson and Pearson 1984:33). In what follows I will remap Elson and Pearson's discourse of domination/subordination in the current context of narratives about the domestic and the public both as they appear in Michelle Rosaldo's work and as they might relate to the Foucauldian notion of "the subject" as "always already subjected" (Grossberg 1996) and "suggesting forms of power which subject and make subject to" (Foucault in Alonso and Koreck

1988:119; also see Stuart Hall for "Foucault's discussion of the double-sided character of subjection/subjectification" [1996:10]). Thus, in this essay I will extend Michelle Rosaldo's use of "the domestic" into the "already domesticated"—as an element of particular "forms of power that subject [domesticate] and make subject to." For a different, though not totally unrelated, use of domestication—as a form of empowerment on the part of particular groups of women who have domesticated public places in England and in Argentina—see Schirmer 1994:203–16.

2. Jeniffer Schirmer has provided explicit examples of these sources of power as forms of empowerment. For example, she has shown how the Plaza de Mayo Madres of Argentina have used photographs of children and of the disappeared to subvert or domesticate the public plazas: "The Madres have used the conservative image of women without husbands to care for them, together with photographs of children, to appeal to a 'natural order' that the state does not respect . . . photographs also serve to reassert the presence of the disappeared in the mind of the public and to negate the 'chronicle of announced death.' Photographs exhibited publicly break the state's monopoly over memory and, together with the domestication of political space, serve, in turn to substantiate these women's political shape and purpose" (Schirmer 1994:204). Schirmer also gave a captivating example of domestication of public space from England. The Greenham Common women, who have protested nuclear weapons since the eary 1980s, domesticated with a sofa the "roadway on which camouflaged missile convoys exercised maneuvers": "in March 1987 a Cruise missile truck convoy, returning from driving missiles around on the Salisbury Plain to 'distract the enemy,' found the turning to the main gate at Greenham blocked by a dilapidated sofa upon which three women sat chatting. When the convoy arrived, one of the women said in a very matter-of-fact tone through a megaphone . . . 'As you will notice, this road is now occupied by women. The road is now closed. The road is now closed. Please turn back and go away'" (207). Schirmer's work in Latin America and in England is a reincarnation of Temma Kaplan's classic work on Barcelona (see preface, this vol.): both, it seems to me, show how Michelle Rosaldo's ideas about the mobilizing potential of the domestic were and have been ignored, while the wheel continues to be reinvented.

3. For a much needed examination of the gender and sexuality of academic anthropology, see Lutz 1995; Tedlock 1995; Newton and Stacey 1995; Dubois 1995; and Lewin 1995—all in Behar and Gordon 1995.

4. Ironically, in an otherwise illuminating discussion of feminist thought in anthropology, Gutmann sets aside Michelle Rosaldo's import regarding the study of both men and women not only by reducing it to an "awkward" formulation but also by erroneously conflating *private* with *domestic* (see the section "Part 2: Refocusing "Gender" in this essay as well as Maurer, this vol., for a much needed distinction between the latter two terms). Gutmann wrote:

To better understand the relation between domesticity, economics, and masculinity we should reexamine one of feminist anthropology's hoary debates: the association of public life with men and of private life with women. As an early proponent of this dichotomy came herself to conclude, such typologizing can tend to overlook the numerous situations in which such associations do not apply . . Yet if Rosaldo's original formulation remains awkward, perhaps, as Ortner points out, a public/private distinction should nonetheless not be jettisoned too hastily. (1996:147)

Following, instead, a combination of Nancy Fraser's and Jurgen Habermas's ideas, Gutmann concludes that "the problem lies not so much with the terms *public* and *private* as with the inappropriate application of these concepts, as though they everywhere coincided with rigidly delineated categories" (1996:148).

REFERENCES

Alonso, Ana María, and María Teresa Koreck
1988   "Silences: Hispanics, AIDS, and Sexual Practices." *Differences* 1:101–24.
Arnold, Katherine
1977   "The Introduction of Poses to a Peruvian Brothel and Changing Images of Male and Female." In *The Anthropology of Body,* ed. John Blacking, 179–97. London: Academic Press.
Behar, Ruth
1995   "Writing in my Father's Name: A Diary of *Translated Woman's* First Year." In *Women Writing Culture,* ed. Ruth Behar and Deborah A. Gordon, 65–82. Berkeley: University of California Press.
Behar, Ruth, and Deborah Gordon, eds.
1995   *Women Writing Culture.* Berkeley: University of California Press.
Bourdieu, Pierre
1978   *Outline of a Theory of Practice.* Cambridge: Cambridge University Press.
Brandes, Stanley
1981   "Like Wounded Stags: Male Sexual Ideology in an Andalusian Town." In *Sexual Meanings,* ed. Sherry Ortner and Harriet Whitehead, 216–39. Cambridge: Cambridge University Press.
1980   *Metaphors of Masculinity: Sex and Status in Andalusian Folklore.* Philadelphia: University of Pennsylvania Press.
Chagnon, Napoleon
1992   *Yanomamo.* 4th ed. Fort Worth, Tex.: Hartcourt Brace College Publishers.
Collier, Jane F., and Michelle Z. Rosaldo
1981   "Politics and Gender in Simple Societies." In *Sexual Meanings,* ed. Sherry Ortner and Harriet Whitehead, 275–329. New York: Cambridge University Press.
Comaroff, John L.
1987   "*Sui Generis:* Feminism, Kinship Theory, and Structural 'Domains.'" In *Gender and Kinship: Essays toward a Unified Analysis,* ed. Jane Fishburne Collier and Sylvia Junko Yanagisako, 53–85. Stanford: Stanford University Press.

di Leonardo, Micaela
1991 "Introduction: Gender, Culture, and Political Economy: Feminist Anthropology in Historical Perspective." In *Gender at the Crossroads of Knowledge: Feminist Anthropology in the Postmodern Era,* ed. Micaela di Leonardo, 1–48. Berkeley: University of California Press.

Dubois, Laurent
1995 "'Man's Darkest Hours': Maleness, Travel, and Anthropology." In *Women Writing Culture,* ed. Ruth Behar and Deborah A. Gordon, 306–21. Berkeley: University of California Press.

Ebron, Paulla, and Anna Lowenhaupt Tsing
1995 "In Dialogue? Reading across Minority Discourses." In *Women Writing Culture,* ed. Ruth Behar and Deborah A. Gordon, 373–89. Berkeley: University of California Press.

Elson, Diane, and Ruth Pearson
1984 "The Subordination of Women and the Internalization of Factory Production." In *Of Marriage and the Market,* ed. Kate Young, Carol Wolkowitz, and Roslyn McCullagh, 18–40. London: Routledge.

Fernández-Kelly, María Patricia
1983 *For We Are Sold, I and My People: Women and Industry in Mexico's Frontier.* Albany: State University of New York Press.

Gilmore, David D.
1990 *Manhood in the Making: Cultural Concepts of Masculinity.* New Haven: Yale University Press.

Ginsburg, Faye
1997 "The 'Word-Made' Flesh: The Disembodiment of Gender in the Abortion Debate." In *Situated Lives,* ed. Louise Lamphere, Helena Ragone, and Patricia Zavella, 142–56. New York: Routledge.

Ginsburg, Faye, and Anna Lowenhaut Tsing, eds.
1990 *Uncertain Terms: Negotiating Gender in American Culture.* Boston: Beacon Press.

Grossberg, Lawrence
1996 "Identity and Cultural Studies—Is That All There Is?" In *Questions of Cultural Identity,* ed. Stuart Hall and Paul du Gay, 87–107. London: Sage Publications.

Gutmann, Matthew C.
1996 *The Meanings of Macho: Being a Man in Mexico City.* Berkeley: University of California Press.

Hall, Stuart
1996 "Introduction: Who Needs 'Identity'?" In *Questions of Cultural Identity,* ed. Stuart Hall and Paul du Gay, 1–17. London: Sage Publications.

Herdt, Gilbert H.
1981 *Guardians of the Flutes: Idioms of Masculinity.* New York: McGraw-Hill.

Herzfeld, Michael
1985 *Poetics of Manhood: Contest and Identity in a Cretan Mountain Village.* Princeton: Princeton University Press.

Lamphere, Louise
1987 "Feminism and Anthropology: The Struggle to Reshape Our Thinking

about Gender." In *The Impact of Feminist Research in the Academy*, ed. Christie Farnham, 67–77. Bloomington: Indiana University Press.

1993 "The Domestic Sphere of Women and the Public World of Men: The Strengths and Limitations of an Anthropological Dichotomy." In *Gender in Cross-Cultural Perspective*, ed. Caroline B. Brettell and Carolyn F. Sargent, 67–77. Englewood, N.J.: Prentice-Hall.

Lancaster, Roger N.

1988 "Subject Honor and Object Shame: The Construction of Male Homosexuality and Stigma in Nicaragua." *Ethnology* 27 (2): 111–25.

1992 *Life Is Hard: Machismo, Danger, and the Intimacy of Power in Nicaragua.* Berkeley: University of California Press.

Leacock, Eleanor

1981 *Myths of Male Dominance.* New York: Monthly Review Press.

Lewin, Ellen

1995 "Writing Lesbian Ethnography." In *Women Writing Culture*, ed. Ruth Behar and Deborah A. Gordon, 322–35. Berkeley: University of California Press.

Limón, José E.

1989 "*Carne, Carnales,* and the Carnivalesque: Bakhtinian *Batos,* Disorder, and Narrative Discourses." *American Ethnologist* 16:471–86.

1994 *Dancing with the Devil: Society and Cultural Poetics in Mexican-American South Texas.* Madison: University of Wisconsin Press.

Lugo, Alejandro

1990 "Cultural Production and Reproduction in Ciudad Juárez, México: Tropes at Play among Maquiladora Workers." *Cultural Anthropology* 5 (2): 173–96.

1995 "Fragmented Lives, Assembled Goods: A Study in Maquilas, Culture, and History at the Mexican Borderlands." Ph.D. diss., Department of Anthropology, Stanford University.

Lutz, Catherine

1995 "The Gender of Theory." In *Women Writing Culture*, ed. Ruth Behar and Deborah A. Gordon, 249–66. Berkeley: University of California Press.

MacCormack, Carol, and Marilyn Strathern, eds.

1980 *Nature, Culture, and Gender.* Cambridge: Cambridge University Press.

Newton, Judith, and Judith Stacey

1995 "Reflections on Studying Academic Men." In *Women Writing Culture*, ed. Ruth Behar and Deborah A. Gordon, 287–305. Berkeley: University of California Press.

Ong, Aihwa

1995 "Women Out of China: Traveling Tales and Traveling Theories in Postcolonial Feminism." In *Women Writing Culture*, ed. Ruth Behar and Deborah A. Gordon, 350–72. Berkeley: University of California Press.

Ortner, Sherry B.

1974 "Is Female to Male as Nature Is to Culture?" In *Woman, Culture, and Society*, ed. Michelle Zimbalist Rosaldo and Louise Lamphere, 67–87. Stanford: Stanford University Press.

Rapp, Rayna
1997 "Constructing Amniocentesis: Maternal and Medical Discourses." In *Situated Lives,* ed. Louise Lamphere, Helena Ragone, and Patricia Zavella, 128–41. New York: Routledge.
Reiter, Rayna
1975 "Men and Women in the South of France: Public and Private Domains." *Toward an Anthropology of Women,* ed. Rayna Reiter. New York: Monthly Review Press.
Rosaldo, Michelle Zimbalist
1974 "Woman, Culture, and Society: A Theoretical Overview." In *Woman, Culture, and Society,* ed. Michelle Zimbalist Rosaldo and Louise Lamphere, 17–42. Stanford: Stanford University Press.
1980 "The Use and Abuse of Anthropology: Reflections on Feminism and Cross-Cultural Understanding." *Signs* 5 (3): 389–417.
Rosaldo, Michelle Zimbalist, and Louise Lamphere, eds.
1974 *Woman, Culture, and Society.* Stanford: Stanford University Press.
Rosaldo, Renato
1989 [1993] *Culture and Truth: The Remaking of Social Analysis.* Boston: Beacon Press.
Sacks, Karen
1974 "Engels Revisited: Women, the Organization of Production and Private Property." In *Woman, Culture, and Society,* ed. Michelle Zimbalist Rosaldo and Louise Lamphere, 207–22. Stanford: Stanford University Press.
1979 *Sisters and Wives: The Past and the Future of Sexual Equality.* Westport, Conn.: Greenwood Press.
Sanday, Peggy Reeves, and Ruth Gallagher Goodenough, eds.
1990 *Beyond the Second Sex: New Directions in the Anthropology of Gender.* Philadelphia: University of Pennsylvania Press.
Scheffler, Harold W.
1991 "Sexism and Naturalism in the Study of Kinship." In *Gender at the Crossroads of Knowledge: Feminist Anthropology in the Postmodern Era,* ed. Micaela di Leonardo, 361–82. Berkeley: University of California Press.
Schirmer, Jennifer
1994 "The Claiming of Space and the Body Politic within National-Security States: The Plaza de Mayo Madres and the Greenham Common Women." In *Remapping Memory: The Politics of TimeSpace,* ed. Jonathan Boyarin, 185–220. Minneapolis: University of Minnesota Press.
Shapiro, Judith
1979 "Cross-Cultural Perspectives on Sexual Differentiation." In *Human Sexuality: A Comparative and Developmental Perspective,* ed. Herant Katchadourian, 269–308. Berkeley: University of California Press.
1987 "Men in Groups: A Reexamination of Patriliny in Lowland South America." In *Gender and Kinship: Essays toward a Unified Analysis,* ed. Jane F.

Collier and Sylvia J. Yanagisako, 301–23. Stanford: Stanford University Press.

1991 "Transsexualism: Reflections on the Persistence of Gender and the Mutability of Sex." In *Body Guards: The Cultural Politics of Gender Ambiguity,* ed. Julia Epstein and Kristina Straubb, 248–79. New York: Routledge.

Stoler, Ann Laura

1991 "Carnal Knowledge and Imperial Power: Gender, Race, and Morality in Colonial Asia." In *Gender at the Crossroads of Knowledge: Feminist Anthropology in the Postmodern Era,* ed. Micaela di Leonardo, 51–101. Berkeley: University of California Press.

Strathern, Marilyn

1988 *The Gender of the Gift: Problems with Women and with Society in Melanesia.* Berkeley: University of California Press.

Tedlock, Barbara

1995 "Works and Wives: On the Sexual Division of Textual Labor." In *Women Writing Culture,* ed. Ruth Behar and Deborah A. Gordon, 267–86. Berkeley: University of California Press.

Twinam, Ann

1989 "Honor, Sexuality, and Illegitimacy in Colonial Spanish America." In *Sexuality and Marriage in Colonial Latin America,* ed. Asunción Lavrin, 118–55. Lincoln: University of Nebraska Press.

Valeri, Valerio

1990 "Both Nature and Culture: Reflections on Menstrual and Parturitional Taboos in Huaulu (Seram)." In *Power and Difference: Gender in Island Southeast Asia,* ed. Jane M. Atkinson and Shelly Errington, 235–72. Stanford: Stanford University Press.

Yanagisako, Sylvia, and Jane F. Collier

1987 "Toward a Unified Analysis of Gender and Kinship." In *Gender and Kinship: Essays toward a Unified Analysis,* ed. Jane Collier and Sylvia Yanagisako, 14–50. Stanford: Stanford University Press.

1994 "Gender and Kinship Reconsidered: Toward a Unified Analysis." In *Assessing Cultural Anthropology,* ed. Robert Borofsky, 190–201. New York: McGraw-Hill.

Sexualities and Separate Spheres: Gender, Sexual Identity, and Work in Dominica and Beyond

Bill Maurer

In 1988 I wrote an essay on the conceptual vocabularies of sexuality and work in Dominica, a small island in the eastern Caribbean. That essay began with a critique of the public/domestic dichotomy in the literature on women in Caribbean development. The crux of my argument was that the way some researchers had deployed the public/domestic analytic naturalized sexuality by locating it in the "private" domain of procreation and thus removed from view the relationship between the devaluation of women's sexuality and the devaluation of women's work (Maurer 1991). I was attempting to outline the shortcomings of feminist scholarship that had explored Michelle Rosaldo's (1974) proposal that the public/domestic dichotomy should prove a useful device for looking at gender inequality cross-culturally, and I was interested in bringing the dichotomy to bear on the issue of sexuality, a theme not explored in Rosaldo's work or in any feminist work following in her footsteps.

This essay represents an attempt to rethink the utility of the public/domestic dichotomy for the study of the production of sexualities. The public/domestic dichotomy structures Dominican people's understandings of both sexuality and work. But, since the dichotomy is hegemonic for both Caribbean peoples and the analysts who study them, it has tended to be used in Caribbeanist scholarship as a mirror of the "facts" of gender, sexuality, and work. Without really questioning these facts themselves, analysts ended up replicating the very essentialisms Rosaldo was trying to destabilize. Previous researchers who made use of the public/domestic dichotomy obscured the issue of sexuality, because they connected sex to reproduction as a matter of course. They also committed the error of overlooking the acts women performed in "public," since they presumed all women's work occurred in the "domestic" sphere, or, if performed in public, nevertheless contributed mainly to the domestic sphere. I argued in my original essay that women's public acts seem to be devalued because *women* did them and not because they were conceptually linked to the domestic sphere. And I argued that the devaluation of women had to do with linkages between conceptualizations of their sexuality and their work.

Here, however, I too was caught up in the taken-for-granted logic of the public/domestic dichotomy. In attempting to show that domesticity alone could not explain the devaluation of women's work and by suggesting instead that constructions of women's sexuality told us more about the devaluation of women as *women,* I ended up taking the category "women" for granted and grossly simplified the structures and processes contributing to this categorization in Dominican and other Western postcolonial societies. As I take another look at my material from Dominica, I find I ought to attend more carefully to the kinds of work and sexuality that men and women were telling me about.

Men were primarily wage workers; women grew and marketed subsistence crops but for the most part did not earn a wage. Subsequently, men, in discussing their work, listed the occupations they were engaged in. Women, meanwhile, saw themselves as doing "only housework." Similarly, people talked about men's sexuality using a multiplicity of identity and descriptive categories, while the words and phrases people used to describe women's sexuality implied that women did not "have" sexuality or sexual identity apart from their relations with men. Why were men's sexualities and men's work described as things that men "are" and "have," while sexuality and work, as cultural categories, were rarely applied to women and, when they were, only came up in connection with women's relationships to men?

"Queer theory" emerging in literary fields and theories of performance that cross disciplinary boundaries draw our attention to the always-enacted nature of identity, the performative reiterations of preexisting norms that temporarily stabilize or render apparently immutable such categories as gender, sex, and sexuality (de Lauretis 1987; Butler 1993; Morris 1995). While this literature on sexuality has done a nice job of destabilizing the taken-for-granted categories of, say, "gay" or "lesbian" identity, it has not fully explored the connection between the performance of identity and capitalist relations of production. It has also paid scant attention to the formerly colonized world and the performative twists and turns played out by postcolonial subjects setting sexuality norms to new practices and new identities (but see Boellstorff 1996; Lancaster 1992; and Stoler 1995, for suggestive analyses in this direction). My contention in this essay is that the Dominica case helps us to see that the norms of sexuality-as-identity are historically and culturally specific and are bound up with the emergence of capitalism, wage work, and the reification of the public/domestic dichotomy that wage work engenders.[1] I write, then, in the spirit of recuperating Rosaldo's project of understanding and not taking for granted the doctrine of "separate spheres" in societies influenced by Enlightenment and Victorian social worlds (see Collier, this vol.).

The Public/Domestic Dichotomy
in Caribbean Gender Studies

The study of gender and work in the Caribbean has employed the public/domestic dichotomy as a tool for understanding women's and men's work and social status. Rather than using the dichotomy critically, many researchers simply took it as a handy way to reflect the lived realities they observed. The dichotomy has been taken in a positivist spirit that Rosaldo herself did not intend (Lugo, this vol.). Thus, gendered activities and identities are seen to fall into two spheres of activity. Activities in the public sphere "link, rank, organize or subsume particular mother-child groups," while those in the domestic "are organized immediately around one or more mothers and their children" (Rosaldo 1974:23). In much of the literature on gender in the Caribbean women's and men's work are described in terms of interconnected networks through which people carry out economic and social exchanges (Anderson 1986; Ellis 1986; Berleant-Schiller 1977; Safa 1986). Analysts use the public/domestic dichotomy, implicitly or explicitly, to delineate these networks and the positions of women and men within them. They maintain that women's place in networks is within the sphere of the household and that women, in conducting household activities, obtain a limited degree of influence in the public sphere through their affiliations with men.

Several Caribbeanists have pointed out that the public/domestic dichotomy seems to soften when women's activities in "public" are taken into account (Barrow 1986; Sutton and Makiesky-Barrow 1977; Gussler 1980). Many women's activities, the purpose of which is to maintain the household, are performed in the public arena. This public performance often has far-reaching public effects, "and the social system itself depend[s] on the ability of the female to be mobile, flexible, and resourceful, rather than tied to a specific structure or role" (Gussler 1980:208). Women's economic activities, for instance, not only "affect" the public sphere but partially constitute it. And women's "household" work is about more than the household; we must examine the importance of so-called domestic activities to the political, economic, and social life of communities before jumping to the conclusion that such tasks enacted in public are domestic simply because the actors are female and the activities contribute to household maintenance (Berleant-Schiller and Maurer 1993:66).

Another problem with the Caribbeanist version of the public/domestic dichotomy is its neglect of sexuality. When taken as a positive reflection of social facts, and not a way to interrogate them, Rosaldo's initial formulation appears to rest on women's social role in bearing and, more important, raising children. This is rooted in Western logic, which links women and sex to babies and procreation "naturally" and which assumes women are mothers (Delaney 1991). When this logic is imported into feminist scholarship on women's work in "developing" societies, it gets rewritten in terms of a simplified version of the Marxist dichotomy between reproduction and production. Criticisms of the gender and sex assumptions of the reproduction/production dichotomy in Marxist theory are well rehearsed (Harris and Young 1981; Yanagisako and Collier 1987; Collier, this vol.; MacCormack, this vol.). The problem stems from the initial feminist conception of "sex" as the "natural" substrate on which "gender" is culturally constructed. The distinction intended between biology and culture has indeed been useful in establishing the arbitrary quality of gender and in combating essentialism (Mead 1935; Beauvoir 1953; Oakley 1972). The two terms, *sex* and *gender,* "serve a useful analytic purpose in contrasting a set of biological facts with a set of cultural facts" (Shapiro 1981:449). But they are limiting as well.

Donna Haraway and others have repeatedly made the case that, like gender, sex itself must be seen as "constructed and social" (Haraway 1986:85; Strathern 1992; Delaney 1991). The work of Michel Foucault has been extremely influential in redirecting studies of gender, sex, and sexuality away from the sex/gender distinction and toward the discursive regimes that empower this dichotomy. Judith Butler, drawing on Foucault, J. L. Austin's speech-act theory (Austin 1955), and a Derridean critique of it, has persuasively argued that, to explore the apparent "ground" of sex in Western conceptions of sex and gender, one must investigate the discursive relationships in which the category "sex" is embedded. When does sex as a natural category become important to people? How do people make sex a material fact of their existence? When do they see it as determinative of other domains of social identity or interaction? The Dominica case suggests that people "make sex" and sexuality as stable, given identities only in certain contexts and under regimes of wage work.

Women's and Men's Work in Dominica

Dominica is an island in the eastern Caribbean, located between the French islands of Martinique and Guadeloupe. Its inhabitants are English and French creole speaking, and the island gained independence from the United Kingdom in 1978. It is one of the wetter and more mountainous islands of the Caribbean, and, in part because of its climate and difficult terrain, Dominica has never experienced large-scale plantation development in quite the same way as the neighboring islands. Dominican agriculture is mainly carried out on small-plot family farms. Bananas are the chief export crop and, at present, the mainstay of the economy (McAfee 1991; Trouillot 1988; Yankey 1969).[2]

Most family farms occupy between one-half and two and a half acres of land. Inheritance of land is bilateral, and almost all farms are maintained by family labor. To prepare a plot for banana cultivation the men of a family will first clear the land using slash-and-burn techniques. Getting a plot ready for planting can take as long as a week. Men use pickaxs, plows, and heavy wooden tools called *louchettes* for digging and planting, and men work chemical and organic fertilizers into the soil. Once the banana plants are established their maintenance entails frequent applications of pesticides and fungicides. Both men and women do this, usually under men's supervision. Women are responsible for weeding under the plants. Both men and women harvest the fruits. Women also sometimes work in the boxing plants scattered across the island to prepare the bananas for transport. Groups of men and some women come together to transport the boxed bananas by motor vehicles once every two weeks. These are brought to the dock and loaded onto the boats of the Geest Company. Men earn a wage proportional to the weight of the bananas they deliver.

Women maintain small plots of vegetables independently of the banana farms. Some women also raise small stock such as goats, rabbits, and chickens. They provide food for their households and for sale at the local market. Women produce almost all of Dominica's vegetables and ground provisions, and women are completely responsible for the planting, care, harvesting, and marketing of their crops. Through their marketing activities women sustain the island's internal economy and maintain social networks that facilitate interisland communication. News frequently travels through the Saturday market. My landlady and I, for example, found out about a friend's nomination to town council at the market a good three or four hours before the nominations were made "public."

Women's agricultural activities are more labor intensive than men's, especially since women are also responsible for cooking, laundry, and other forms of housework. At the time of my research (1987) many rural women could not afford coal or cooking gas and had to gather wood for their kitchens. Gathering wood and brush took them as much as three hours a day, even though many women sent their children to carry out this task. Water was a problem for many rural women, too; in several areas women had to walk a mile to collect water and carry it back to their houses. Women washed laundry in nearby streams. Very few of the women I met had much time for leisure. Men, on the other hand, often were able to maintain their banana plots with time to spare for other activities. Domino matches were ubiquitous, and men spent a good deal of time at the local rum shop. Many also had the time to work on larger plantations or in some other form of wage work, such as transportation. Most men who grew their own bananas for sale to Geest thus were also wage workers for other employers. Women who worked in boxing plants were among the few women who earned a wage, and, since the work is seasonal, it was not a regular source of income.

When talking about their work on their banana plots, men emphasized the heavy labor involved and the many stages of activity in the growth and production of bananas. Men often complained about their work and their lack of leisure time, although, as noted earlier, they had more of it than women did. In spite of women's hard work, meanwhile, most rural Dominicans did not put women's work in the same category as the banana production and other wage work of men (even though many of the activities involved in banana production were actually in the hands of women). When asked what they did for a living, many women involved in subsistence agriculture, cottage industries, or marketing first mentioned their activities in banana production and only with prodding would mention the other work activities in which they were engaged on a regular basis. Women did take great pride in their work, but many connected their work as a matter of course to that of their husbands. One woman told me, "the most important part of my work is having a family, and I grow my own things; it's very expensive in the market, and having the land I can do it myself." Yet, when I asked this woman what she did for a living, she replied that she was a "housewife." Women's household-oriented work was not seen as "real" work because it did not earn women a regular wage. According to one man, "women are involved [in productive activities] in that they are helping their men." Women's work thus was seen as complementary to and not separate from men's real wage work.

Development programs in Dominica, until recently, have been aimed at banana production. Little attention has been paid to women's agricultural activities. The attempts of women to succeed in new economic areas have been often thwarted by community attitudes. For example, women's small stock production has traditionally been an important but small-scale affair. In one village a group of women decided to try their hand at raising pigs for sale to the surrounding villages on a more large-scale basis. They had received materials for the construction of a pig shelter from a local development agency, and four months later representatives from the agency came to check up on their progress. The wood and cement for the shelter's construction was in the same place it had been left four months before. The women explained that they had not been able to convince any men to help them build the shelter because the men had seen their attempts at large-scale pig raising as "childish." The women, meanwhile, had seen construction as "men's work." Furthermore, many men couldn't bring themselves to view small stock production as "work" or comprehend women's desire to raise pigs for cash and not in-kind services or goods. On the subject of small stock production one man told me: "it's not work at all! After all, it's just a matter of tethering your animal!"

Men's wage work is what counts as real work. Women's work, while made up of just as many if not more separate activities as men's, has little value attached to it and is lumped together under the term *housework* even when such work takes women miles away from the household to market, the river, or the forest and even when it has little if anything to do with the "housework," like pig farming for profit. In addition, their work is categorized as housework in spite of the fact that these activities have far-reaching effects beyond the household. Women are trapped by a mentality that accords only wage work the status of "work." According to one man, a woman is only "really working . . . when she goes out and helps her man in the field." Women's attempts to break out of this mentality are dashed by the belief that all women's activities are unimportant unless they contribute to men's wage earning.

What let me, in my original essay, to come to a critique of the public/domestic dichotomy in Caribbeanist research was that the relative levels of value attached to men's and women's work seemed not to hinge on recognized public or domestic spheres, in which real work is located only in the public. The marketing activities and small stock production of women are certainly enacted in public and, furthermore have real influence on political, social, and economic life of the island. It seemed to me that the devaluation of women's work and its lack of differentiation within the category "housework" resulted not from its location within a domestic space, the activities of which are limited to the maintenance of the household proper. Rather, this devaluation of women's work resulted from an articulation of the category "housework" to the category "woman." This is a product of the ideology of separate spheres, in which all household business is devalued. And its reiteration in a Caribbean context suggests that the doctrine of separate spheres has become hegemonic here.

It was this hegemonic character of the public/domestic dichotomy that Rosaldo called on us to grapple with. Previous researchers in the Caribbean took the dichotomy as a neutral reflection of what they observed in the field and not as part of a lived hegemony (with a few notable exceptions, especially the work of Martinez-Alier 1974, and R. T. Smith and his students; Smith 1988; Austin 1984; Alexander 1984). Thus, they did not explore further implications of the dichotomy for the devaluation of women and housework. One dimension not explored was sexuality.

Sexuality in Dominica

I was fortunate during my fieldwork in Dominica to have been nineteen years old. I was able to talk frankly with people close to me in age about sex. I could not do this easily with older people, mainly because I was afraid that raising the topic would lead people to doubt my "seriousness" as a researcher and especially to question my morals. Even with my own peers, however, I was very circumspect when trying to elicit information on some of the sexual categories I had heard tossed about in casual conversation and in jokes. People who identified with the sexual categories I list here were circumspect, too, in admitting as much to a white man from the United States who lived in Goodwill, the solidly middle-class suburb of the capital city, with an elderly woman known throughout the island as one of the bastions of "respectability" and Christian virtue. I still struggle with how to write about sexuality in Dominica. It was this struggle that led me, in 1988, to look only at "conceptual vocabularies" of sexuality and to avoid "sexual identities" or "practices" (Maurer 1991:13).

In Dominica people often label others according to their perceived sexual preferences. Men take on these labels as categories of identity. When I was in Dominica, the terms *gay, lesbian, and homosexual* were only just beginning to be used and then only in contexts that indexed the foreignness of the people and practices so labeled. AIDS had just hit the island as well, and in public forums like newspaper editorials and letters to the editor, and in the office of the Dominica Planned Parenthood Foundation (where I volunteered as a receptionist) many people expressed the belief that AIDS would not affect Dominicans since it was a "homosexual" disease and no Dominicans were homosexual.

In other contexts, however, people described men's sexuality as a spectrum. At one end are people termed *gwo gwen.* These men are considered exceptionally virile and are known for their violent sexual conquests. In English *gwo gwen* means "fat wheat," a reference to the *gwo gwen's* supposedly abnormally large penis. At the other end of the spectrum is the *anti-man,* a man who openly rejects women's advances and is loathe to engage in any sort of heterosexual union. "Anti-man" is a common insult among men. "Normal" men engage in sexual relationships with women exclusively and do not claim any special or extraordinary virility. I elicited the term *normal* only when I asked people what they would call a man who did not fit into any of the other categories discussed here. Normal men frequently work to assert their differences from *gwo gwen* and from "soft" men. A soft man is a man who has sex with one partner in a stable, monogamous relationship, a man who has fathered no children, who has fathered only female children, and who allows women to "push [him] around." I was told that I was "soft" because I allowed my landlady to bring me to church every Sunday. *Soft* is also a term used to describe male sexual dysfunction and impotence.

Three other terms refer to men who engage in sexual relationships with other men but not necessarily exclusively. All three, like *gwo gwen,* are creole terms. A *mako* is a busybody who likes to work around the house and loathes fieldwork. The line between *soft* and *mako* is indistinct, but the term *mako* indicates a possible preference, though not an exclusive preference, for male sexual partners. Often, like *anti-man, mako* is used as a term of derision but probably more because of the implication of housewifery than homosexuality.

The other two terms imply a preference exclusively for male sexual partners. *Makume* is a creole word used by a woman to refer to the godmother of her children (i.e., *ma comere*, my co-mother). *Tanti-man* is derived from the creole *tanti*, or "aunt." A *tanti-man* is so called, as one grade school boy told me, "cos he's just like your auntie." Both *tanti* and *makume*, when applied to women, suggest a sexuality linked to male partners because, as I will show, all women are presumed to be sexual only in relation to men. When people apply these terms to men, similarly, they suggest a sexuality linked to male partners and defined only in relation to other men. The fact that a *makume* or *tanti-man* may have sex with another man is not central, however, to his definition as a community member or a person. What is more important is that he is "like a woman"; he is not considered subversive, aggressive, or creepy the way an anti-man would be. To say that a man is a *makume* or *tanti-man* is to give him the same status as a woman. As a Dominican intellectual told me, people are "very accommodating" toward *makumes* and *tanti-men*.

Because *makumes* and *tanti-men* are generally accepted by others in their community, other men will sometimes pretend to be *makumes* or *tanti-men* in order to develop close relationships with women they hope later to seduce. This was a favorite strategy of some high school boys I knew. According to one of their "victims," "they put themselves in the position of women with the desire of getting them!"

All of the categories applied to women, meanwhile, imply a preference for male sexual partners as a matter of course. This is not to say that women do not have sexual experiences with other women in Dominica. Rather, men and women think about such experiences differently from the way they think about men's sexual experiences. Indeed, they do not think of them as sexual at all (cf. Elliston 1995). Dominican creole provides the term *zami* for pairs of women who form a close bond that frequently involves genital contact. *Zami* is also used to refer to any pair of very close friends, male or female (from "les ami[e]s"). Unlike special terms such as *makume*, however, *zami* does not imply an identity but a condition of being in a relationship. One can be a *makume* without necessarily being in a sexual relationship with another person; *makume* defines a condition of being, independent of one's social relationships. It is an essentialized identity. One must be in a relationship with another, however, in order for the term *zami* to apply; indeed, a creole speaker would rarely say that someone is "a" *zami* but, rather, that two people are *zami* to each other. In short, male-male and male-female relationships involving genital contact imply sexuality and special identity categories (even if only "man" and "woman,"), while female-female relationships do not.

Other words used to describe women that have sexual connotations include *streetwalker, maquel,* and *malnom.* The term *wife* is used among members of the middle and upper classes who place high value on legal marriage (see Smith 1988; Lazarus-Black 1994). A man who has sexual relationships with a woman outside of marriage will often refer to her as "my woman." Women follow this usage as well, as in "whose woman are you?"

A streetwalker is a woman who "acts like a prostitute," attempting to trap men unawares and steal them from their wives or girlfriends. A *maquel* is like the male *mako:* she is a busybody who puts her nose in other people's (sexual) business. A *malnom* is a woman who "acts like a man"— but does not engage in sexual relationships with other women. The term is supposedly derived from the French word for "bad [i.e., incomplete or improperly formed] man."[3] A *malnom* is a well-organized woman often in some position of authority. Being called *malnom* is generally a compliment: to be a *malnom* is to be able to handle "men's work" and "men's responsibilities." *Malnoms* are similar to *makumes* in that they effectively achieve the status of the opposite "biological" sex (in Dominican terms), yet, unlike *makumes,* they do not "have" sexual identities.

The public/domestic dichotomy inflects Dominican sexual categories, as in the term *mako.* Men who use *mako* as an insult stigmatize other men by associating them with the household. The terms used to describe women assume either that they do not have sexualities (*zami, malnom*) or that they depend on men for explicitly sexual expression (*streetwalker, wife*). Meanings attached to men's sexual practices, preferences, and socially sanctioned masculinity, in contrast, are constituted in identity categories. Just as women are seen as "helping men" in the arena of work and not contributing to economic production in any other meaningful way, so too women are seen as dependent on men for sexual being, expression, or identity. And both women's sexuality, when present, and women's work are understood as extensions of men's.

Waging Sex: Accounting for "Sexualities"

My analysis of 1988 stopped here, with the conclusion that Dominican "conceptual vocabularies of sex and work are similarly structured" (Maurer 1991:17). In this section of this essay, however, I will consider the public/domestic dichotomy as an analytical tool to help unravel why Dominican men got to have sexualities (and be sexual), while women, outside of their relations with men, did not.

Much of my reanalysis derives from problems I have had with the literature on sexuality that I have become familiar with since my initial fieldwork. Many of these problems are personal, though they also relate to epistemological concerns that I cannot easily separate from personal ones. Like most feminist anthropologists trained in the 1980s, I have come to articulate strong anti-essentialist accounts of gender, sexuality, and race. Yet anti-essentialist renderings of sexuality never seem satisfying to me, in part because of my own rather essentialized understanding of my sexuality and sexual identity as a gay man. Like many white gay men in the United States, I have always understood my identity to be given, stable, and perhaps "natural." Indeed, constructions of white gay male identity as natural explain not only the persistence of claims about the natural, or "genetic," causes of sexuality and the concept of "sexual orientation" itself (as opposed, perhaps, to "preference" rendered as chosen and changeable) but also the willingness with which many gay men believe scientific claims for the "discovery" of biological causes of sexuality (see Hegarty 1997). I had felt a disjuncture between my sense of identity and sexual being and my epistemological and political rejection of essentialism. The literature on sexuality from an anti-essentialist perspective never seemed to explain adequately the persistence of essentialism as a hegemonic stance in Western societies (but see Fuss 1989; Butler 1993; Sedgwick 1990; Gilroy 1993).

Historical studies of gay and lesbian identities rely on tropes of the public that do not match up with my own sense of identity (D'Emilio 1984; Freedman and D'Emilio 1988). John D'Emilio's influential "Capitalism and Gay Identity" has been especially provocative for me. In his narrative of industrialization and the transformation of family life D'Emilio argues that, as capitalism pushed men out of the home into the factory, men came to associate in groups independent of the household procreative unit and began to disarticulate sexuality from procreation. Central to D'Emilio's account is the new public world invented in industrial capitalist relations of production that separated "home" from "work." He writes that gay identity came into being when individuals interacting "outside the heterosexual family" could "construct a personal life based on attraction to one's own sex." He starts from the dubious assumption that sexuality and procreation were once articulated as a matter of course and that sexuality existed somehow as a domain of feeling and acting before the advent of capitalism, even though his argument is explicitly concerned with refuting this assumption. "By the end of the [nineteenth] century," he writes, "a class of men and women existed who recognized their erotic interest in their own sex, saw it as a trait that set them apart from the majority, and sought others like themselves" (1984:105).

D'Emilio's argument aims to upset the claims of other historians of "homosexuality," who are often taken to be essentialists, who find evidence for "gays and lesbians" throughout history, from the Greeks to the present, and in all cultures (see Boswell 1980; Cavin 1985; for critique, see Halperin 1990). D'Emilio aims to question the category of "gay identity," or homosexuality, itself. Yet he does not explore the category "sexuality" (or "identity," for that matter) and does not question whether and why certain acts are deemed sexual in any particular place and time (Elliston 1995). For instance, he writes of how World War II thrust same-sex groups together where "men and women *already gay* [found] an opportunity to meet people like themselves" and that "others could become gay because of the temporary *freedom* to explore sexuality that the war provided" (1984:107; emph. added). But how did people come to be "already gay," according to this argument, before they interacted in exclusively same-sex publics? And what constituted the sexuality that these people now had the "freedom" to explore? How did they "become gay," for that matter? D'Emilio simply writes that they made "decisions to act on their desires." This statement not only leaves desire unanalyzed, but it flies in the face of the experience of gay and lesbian people who feel they had no conscious choice in forming their sexual identities and seek out explanations in biology. D'Emilio's account falls short when we attempt to explain why many gay people's (and especially white gay men's) common-sense understandings of their sexualities are essentialist in nature.

The rhetoric of "choice" pervades D'Emilio's history: "Capitalism has created the material conditions for homosexual desire to express itself as a central component of some individuals' lives; now, our political movements are changing consciousnesses, creating the ideological conditions that make it easier for people to make that choice" (1984:109). It is not surprising, then, that he holds up the ideal of "personal autonomy" as the goal toward which gay and lesbian movements must strive. D'Emilio's stance reflects a troubling recuperation of the liberal political subject, who supposedly owes nothing to society for its identity and social standing (Collier, Maurer, and Suarez-Navaz 1995). Furthermore, by highlighting choice again, it fails to explain the hegemonic essentialisms according to which many people live their lives and forge their struggles.

Like many (but not all) gay men and lesbians, I grew up "knowing" that I was gay and was raised in relative isolation from other gay people. I did not "discover" my latent sexuality only after entering into gay public spaces. Joan Scott discusses the fetishization of experience in accounts of the discovery of identity when she analyzes Samuel Delany's autobiographical work, *The Motion of Light in Water* (Scott 1992; Delany 1988): entering St. Mark's bathhouse for the first time, Delany is overcome by the "undulating mass of naked male bodies, spread wall to wall" (1988:173), and this experience brings him to gay identity and politicized consciousness. The assumption that coming into a gay public awakens the homosexual difference within oneself creates the illusion that desires and identities are self-evident "inherent attributes of individuals" (Scott 1992:25). Where do individuals get these "inherent" attributes in the first place? How does sexuality become a thing "inside" a self, or constitutive of a self (Halperin 1990:26)? Foucault's *History of Sexuality,* volume 1, is concerned with precisely this question: how, historically, a category of acts that spoke nothing of the inner soul came to be seen as indicia of inner, immutable character—how the person who committed sodomy became the homosexual (1978:42).

D'Emilio is right to locate the emergence of gay and lesbian identities within a world in which industry separates home from work. As Marx (1844) pointed out long ago, in commodifying time and demanding its sale on the labor market, wage work leaves workers' with only their "home" life in which to develop their "real selves." The domestic sphere becomes the site of the reproduction of the labor force but also the reproduction of sentiment, feeling, preferences, interests, and identities. To Marx this separation of the public world of work from the domestic world of identity caused one of capitalism's most trenchant forms of alienation: since, in Marx's conception, to be human is to realize oneself in one's labor, the development of a sense of self outside of the context of (wage) labor was a profound alienation from humanity's true "species being." Put another way, wage labor, in offering nothing but drudgery, offered nothing to the construction of a truly human self. Marx wrote that in this context of alienated labor, people falsely craft their "true" selves from the "animal functions" they get to carry out at home: in "eating, drinking, procreating, or at most in his dwelling and dressing up, etc." (1844:74).

The construction of the domestic under capitalism is certainly more contradictory and complicated than Marx realized—and there is a lot more to dressing, eating, sleeping, and fucking than "animality." Here, however, I point out only one such contradiction (cf. Collier, Maurer, and Suarez-Navaz 1995). The domestic, in becoming the site where people realize their selves, is also the site for the formation of interests and preferences. But interests and preferences crucially shape affairs in the public realm. Indeed, through the domestic, the "private" sphere of the economy gains the abilities, preferences, and predilections it requires to function as a market. Market transactions enacted in public are still private in that they operate (supposedly) outside the sphere of state regulation and in that they emerge (supposedly) from people's natural preferences and interests.

In her coauthored essay "Is There a Family?" (1982) Rosaldo discusses how the private and the "family" came to be co-constructed in the nineteenth century. Her analysis suggests that D'Emilio's tale of capitalism and gay identity is nearly on the mark—but fundamentally backward. Rather than viewing people as "realizing" their "gay identities" in the public sphere of work, now separate from the domestic sphere of heterosexual reproduction, as D'Emilio has it, Rosaldo's insight into the mutual constitution of public, domestic, and private, together with Marx's insight into the creation of identities under capitalism, leads to the conclusion that the private sphere of individual identity formation is primary in the creation of sexualities held to be immutable, unchosen, and unchangeable.

Although she did not discuss Foucault in her work, Rosaldo's thinking in "Is There a Family?" resonates with Foucault's identification of the "great strategic unities which . . . formed specific mechanisms of knowledge and power centering on sex" in the eighteenth and nineteenth centuries (1978:103). Foucault argues that these "unities" worked to create sexualities as new modes of experience under capitalism. They included: (1) "hysterization of women's bodies," whereby the female body is first analyzed as full of sexuality then placed within the purview of medical practice and pathologized and next "placed in organic communication with the social body (whose regulated fecundity it was supposed to ensure), the family space (of which it had to be a substantial and functional element), and the life of children (which it produced and had to guarantee, by virtue of biologico-moral responsibility lasting through the entire period of the children's education"); (2) "pedagogization of children's sex" whereby children were rendered naturally sexual and at the same time their sexuality was seen as "contrary to nature"; (3) the economic, political, and medical "socialization of reproductive behavior";

and (4) a "psychiatrization of perverse pleasure," as the homosexual emerged as a "species" of being (104–5).

These strategic unities generated "four privileged objects of knowledge, which were also targets and anchorage points for the ventures of knowledge: the hysterical woman, the masturbating child, the Malthusian couple, and the perverse adult" (Foucault 1978:105). All of these came together in the construction of the family and a system of alliance—of "marriage, of fixation and development of kinship ties, of transmission of names and possessions" (106; cf. Collier 1988)—as the main site for the regulation, reproduction and deployment of sexuality:

[the family's] role is to anchor sexuality and provide it with permanent support. It ensures the production of a sexuality that is not homogeneous with the privileges of alliance, while making it possible for the systems of alliance to be imbued with a new tactic of power which they would otherwise be impervious to. The family is the interchange of sexuality and alliance: it conveys the law and the juridical dimension of the deployment of sexuality; and it conveys the economy of pleasure and the intensity of sensations in the regime of alliance. (Foucault 1978:108)

In volume 2 of *The History of Sexuality* Foucault further explores the notion of "experience" upon which sexuality as a domain of desire and identity depends. He writes that his project was to discover "how an 'experience' came to be constituted in modern Western societies, an experience that caused individuals to recognize themselves as subjects of a 'sexuality,' which was accessible to very diverse fields of knowledge and linked to a system of rules and constraints" (1985:4), and he directs his inquiry toward the following question: "What are the games of truth by which humans come to see themselves as desiring individuals?" (6). The following represents an attempt at an ideal-typic model of the "games of truth" actors engage in as they work under regimes of wage labor.

To reword Foucault in more Rosaldean terms, the domestic is the interchange of the private and the public. Under capitalism people buy and sell things in markets.[4] One of the things people sell is their labor, an abstract, objectified quality they feel they can possess and alienate. But this alienation is troubling. Notions of the individual as a proprietary subject, one who owns and controls his or her body and capacities, are central to the capitalist conception of personhood and the alienation of labor. But when people sell part of their capacities in the form of wage work, they also risk selling themselves, since the capacity to labor and to possess one's person are central to full personhood (hence the arguments that women and children were not full persons since they were possessed by others—men—and the fruits of their labor belonged not to themselves but to their husbands and fathers [see Pateman 1988]). People, in other words, not only *feel* that they can possess and alienate their labor; they are in fact *compelled* to do so, and this is an unsettling compulsion. In order to preserve the feeling of a self that capitalism encourages, labor, therefore, must be conceptualized as alienable in a way that other capacities are not. Indeed, the capitalist conception of labor calls forth supposedly intrinsically inalienable capacities (like childbearing) and objects (like babies) as well as purportedly inherent attributes (like tastes and desires) as central to personhood in a way labor supposedly is not (Radin 1987).

The public/domestic distinction handily resolves the dilemma that some parts of the self can be sold and others can not by requiring that salable items be sold freely on the open market. Aspects of personhood not related to alienable labor are relegated to the domestic sphere, but here those aspects of personhood that are not alienated are conceptualized as fundamentally inalienable—they become private, and the domestic becomes the space outside of the market, where people who would otherwise be slaves to wage labor can be free to express their real selves, those aspects of selfhood that make people who they "truly are." At the same time, those private aspects of personhood constructed in the domestic are also central to market transactions—they are also private in the economic sense—since these private capacities are what people sell on the market, and these private predilections are what determine people's purchasing. In the domestic space people forge their inner, or true, selves, and are "free" to act out their "desires." In public they sell their labor, a thing deemed inessential to their inner core yet shaped and tempered by it. Of course, these conceptions of personhood, public, domestic, and private are precisely what the labor market needs: subjects constituting themselves as individuals with natural differences in abilities and propensities, constituted in the domestic space, which tempers their laboring capacity and which can be sold in private exchanges on the free market. Markets encourage people to think of themselves as having natural differences that set them apart from others; labor markets demand such different abilities as qualifications for jobs (see Collier, Maurer, and Suarez-Navaz 1995; Macpherson 1962).

Whereas D'Emilio views the public sphere as capitalism's contribution to the creation of gay identities, I would thus place emphasis on the interchange of the domestic in activating the private as that which people hold to be the preserve of the true self. The domestic and the private in liberal market societies, in which people make "selves" for themselves, with inner capacities, inner drives, and inner desires, seems more crucial to the formation of identities deemed essential than the public.

In Dominica the model of subject formation in capitalist societies just sketched out is, of course, inflected by Caribbean colonial history. First, however, a brief review is necessary: rural Dominican men are more involved in the wage workforce than women; men think of themselves as having sexual identities; women do not "experience" sexuality except through relationships with men. Even when women engage in relationships with other women that may involve genital contact, people do not necessarily interpret this as sexual activity or as evidence of their sexuality. Men and women, meanwhile, also devalue the activities and people who spend their time within the sphere of the household (cf. Rosaldo 1974). Jane Collier has observed a similar devaluation in her work with Spanish villagers in the 1960s, who felt that "work" meant only "work for pay." As a result, she writes, "it [was] difficult for women to find words for talking about what they were doing when they clean[ed] their homes, [made] their family meals, or [grew] food for family consumption" (1992:169). Women who did not participate in the market "appear[ed] to lack the means of establishing a social identity" and instead "appear[ed] to be dependents rather than full persons" (170). Much the same could be said for the rural Dominican women discussed here.

It is significant, however, that all of the identity terms used by people to discuss and label sexualities or sexual behavior (and some relationships, like *zami*) are creole, save two: *anti-man* and *streetwalker*. The English derivation of these words speaks to Dominica's particular colonial history as a French island taken over by the English in 1792 and governed by British colonial officials well into this century. Of all the terms *anti-man* and *streetwalker* are unquestionably derogatory. There is no place in society for individuals so labeled. Not only do the terms have some origin in Dominicans' understandings about and animosities toward their English-speaking masters (Trouillot 1989) but also in English colonial capitalism's promotion of a comprador class of local rulers. To be labeled "anti-man" or "streetwalker" is to be labeled not just as outside of society but as outside of creole society, that is, to be "foreign." Ana Alonso and Maria Koreck (1993) discuss a similar construction of foreignness among men in northern Mexico who engage in genital relationships with each other but do not conceptualize themselves as gay or homosexual. As they describe, there are specific terms and identities for men who play "active" and "passive" roles in anal intercourse, but men who play both are called "internationals," "a term which indexes the 'foreignness' of practices which are more like those of American gays than the ones" they discuss in their article (119). They speculate that the internationals have been influenced by U.S. gay culture and gay liberation movements in Mexico. Similarly, the anti-man and streetwalker category may be local response to a perceived foreignness and a historical imaginary of the creation of sexualities in the context of colonial domination (as does the increasing use of the terms *gay, lesbian,* and *homosexual* in the context of the AIDS crisis).

The Dominicans I interviewed in 1987 cannot be said to have inhabited a timeless, exotic, or closed world cut off from the rest of the planet before that time. The fact that many nonderogatory sexual terms are creole points to the significance of a history of contact and interaction with the rest of the creole Caribbean. Dominica was a forgotten place to colonial capitalism in many ways, never home to profitable plantations or mercantile ports of any significance. To many Dominicans their history is one of simple peasant life, quiet and undisturbed until the advent of tourism late in this century. But during the nineteenth century many Dominicans were subject to the disciplines of the colonial state (Trouillot 1989). And from the late nineteenth century and well into the twentieth Dominicans from the predominantly creole-speaking regions in the north of the island (especially the town of Vielle Case, a sort of creole cultural center) participated in "a worldwide process of [labor] valorization in a manner independent, at least in part, from the rest of Dominica, through contacts with the French colonies" (Trouillot 1988:41). I am suggesting that these interactions generated not just a new way to think about labor but also a new way to conceive of the person and that this has encouraged the reproduction of the sexual social identities described here.[5]

Conclusion

In her last essays Michelle Rosaldo (1983, 1984) explored the Ilongot "self" as a foil to the Western self. Her work on Ilongot notions of self and feeling led her to Enlightenment and Victorian dichotomies with which she had initiated her feminist project. In the West, she argued, guilt and shame are emotions that serve to protect a self seen as interior and full of asocial passions, desires, and impulses from the often conflictual demands of a society that more often than not thwarts such desires. Guilt and shame keep inner selves in line with social order while at the same time providing a means for inner selves to maintain their integrity. The Western view of the self "holds that impulses harbored deep 'inside' our selves will ultimately be reflected in our acts"; for us guilt and shame "regulate a problematic inner self" (1983:142). For Ilongots, in contrast, guilt and shame, or what we would gloss as such, help order "a world where the resentments of the past can be resolved in a good moment's practice." For Ilongots "a person's history is thus not determinant of an identity that is continuous over time; it is instead a set of resources to be used in the establishment of a generally fluid and negotiable social life" (149).

In the same two articles Rosaldo suggested that selves and feelings vary from culture to culture. In her work with Jane Collier she attempted to map out relationships between different organizations of inequality and different conceptions of selves (Collier and Rosaldo 1981). Jane Collier has continued this project in the context of market societies. She characterizes market rationality as figuring social status based on notions of achievement through individual effort. Whether or not markets actually determine people's social status, people who think in terms of market rationality act as if they do and find it natural. Collier discusses the practices that codify "individual" characteristics and qualities—filling out application forms, submitting to performance reviews, receiving school grades, and taking job entrance exams. Judith Butler (1993) might say that these practices, which call upon the person continually to reiterate their supposedly inherent or natural attributes (including things like "sex" or "race" indicated by ticking off a box on a form), in fact are constitutive performances, creating the materiality of individual identities in the act.

The argument is not that wage work in any simple fashion "determines" the production of sexualities but that there is "a sort of ontological complicity" between identity and social world (Bourdieu 1981:306). The fact that rural men in Dominica sell their labor more often than do women does not "cause" them to possess sexualities. But wage work, the kind of private sphere it encourages, men's ideas of essentialist selves and sexualities, and women's ideas of dependency and lack of sexuality are deeply consistent and coherent within the overall structure of a colonial and postcolonial emergent capitalism as modeled here.

Markets and the liberal theories undergirding them are also related to my own contradictions in "feeling" essentially gay yet articulating anti-essentialist theories of sexuality. In her last published work Rosaldo (1984) suggested that the dichotomies of Western social thought obscure more than they reveal about the constitution of the self. Thinking about capitalism and Enlightenment social thought has helped me work through an understanding of sexuality that accounts for its "essentialness" and "naturalness" to many for whom sexuality is an aspect of lived experience. It has also suggested a politics—powerful yet unsettling. Questioning the basis of identity construction would mean taking apart the liberal subject and its capitalism, going beyond the self we currently live. I do not believe that any transcendence from our own subjectification is possible (Visweswaran 1994), but I wonder whether interrogating the construction of "real selves" can momentarily interrupt the repetitive discourses through which we make our worlds and our identities stable, fixed, and real. And I wonder whether, in spite academic and political talk of split, fragmented, and multiple subjectivities, we are truly prepared to follow Michelle Rosaldo, who called on us to move "beyond a set of classic answers that repeatedly blind our sight to the deep ways in which we are not individuals first but social persons" (1984:151).

NOTES

Fieldwork in Dominica was funded by Vassar College and the Catherine Montgomery Memorial Fieldwork Fund. For comments on earlier drafts I would like to thank Tom Boellstorff, Jane Collier, Peter Hegarty, Stefan Helmreich, Joel Streicker, and especially Alejandro Lugo. This essay bears many marks of his diligent commentary. All errors and misinterpretations are my responsibility alone.

1. Before the recent advent of Queer Theory numerous gay and lesbian scholars speculated about the capitalism/homosexual identity nexus (see, e.g., Altman 1993; Weeks 1986). D'Emilio was an important contributor to these debates. As much as this essay criticizes D'Emlio, it is also an effort to recuperate the strand of theorizing in which he participated.

2. The ethnographic present in this article is 1987. Since that time the country has undergone significant changes, particularly in light of European Community actions that changed the relationship between the United Kingdom and Caribbean banana exporters as well International Monetary Fund "structural adjustment" programs that decreased social spending and threw more peasant proprietors into new kinds of competitive market relationships. These changes have especially impacted women's agricultural production. I have not carried out fieldwork on this problem, but, for an updated account of women's agricultural work, see McAfee 1991.

3. This is according to my friends at the Dominica Planned Parenthood Association. They explained to me that the term *malnom* is a contraction of the creole for

"bad" or "imperfect" (*mal*) and "man" (*nom,* from *un homme*). According to them, it does not derive from the French term *nom* for "name."

4. Here I am engaging in the practice of model building, not the recounting of historical "truths." Part of the purpose of this essay is to provide a model of market societies that can help to explain the production of "sexualities" taken as inherent attributes of individuals. On ideal-typical model building in social analysis, see Collier 1988.

5. In a recent essay on sexuality and definitions of the good citizen in Martinique, David Murray (1996) discusses recent usages of the term *makume* that approach the U.S. definition of *gay* and that subject men so described to derision, violence, and exclusion from full participation in the "cultural" world constructed by elites to delineate Martinican from French "nationality." I would suspect a similar shift of meaning has occurred in Dominica, equating *makume* with *gay,* since the time of my fieldwork, especially given media attention to the AIDS epidemic and stereotypes of AIDS as a "homosexual" disease.

REFERENCES

Alexander, Jack
    1984   "Love, Race, Slavery, and Sexuality in Jamaican Images of the Family." In *Kinship Ideology and Practice in Latin America,* ed. R.T. Smith, 147–80. Chapel Hill: University of North Carolina Press.
Alonso, Ana María, and María Teresa Koreck
    1993   "Silences: 'Hispanics,' AIDS, and Sexual Practices." In *The Lesbian and Gay Studies Reader,* ed. H. Abelove, M. Barale, and D. Halperin, 110–26. New York: Routledge.
Altman, Dennis
    1993   [1971] *The Homosexual: Oppression and Liberation.* New York: New York University Press.
Anderson, Patricia
    1986   "Conclusion: Women in the Caribbean." *Social and Economic Studies* 35:291–324.
Austin, Diane
    1984   *Urban Life in Kingston, Jamaica.* New York: Gordon and Breach.
Austin, J. L.
    1955   *How to Do Things with Words.* Cambridge: Harvard University Press.
Barrow, Christine
    1986   "Finding the Support: Strategies for Survival." *Social and Economic Studies* 35:131–76.
Beauvoir, Simone de
    1953   *The Second Sex.* New York: Vintage Press, 1973.
Berleant-Schiller, Riva
    1977   "Production and Division of Labor in a West Indian Peasant Community." *American Ethnologist* 4:253–72.

Berleant-Schiller, Riva, and Bill Maurer
1993 "Women's Place Is Every Place: Merging Domains and Women's Roles in Barbuda and Dominica." In *Women and Change in the Caribbean*, ed. J. Momsen, 65–79. Bloomington: Indiana University Press.
Boellstorff, Tom
1996 "The Urban Archipelago: Locating the Gay and Lesbian Movement in Indonesia." Paper presented at the Thirteenth Annual Berkeley Conference on Southeast Asian Studies, "Urban Southeast Asia: Past, Present, and Future," Berkeley, February 24–25, 1996.
Boswell, John
1980 "Christianity, Social Tolerance, and Homosexuality." Chicago: University of Chicago Press.
Bourdieu, Pierre
1981 Men and Machines. In *Advances in Social Theory and Methodology: Towards an Integration of Micro- and Macro-Sociologies*, ed. K. Knorr-Cetina and A. V. Cicourel, 304–17. Boston: Routledge and Kegan Paul.
Butler, Judith
1993 *Bodies That Matter: On the Discursive Limits of "Sex."* New York: Routledge.
Cavin, Susan
1985 *Lesbian Origins.* San Francisco: Ism Press.
Collier, Jane
1988 *Marriage and Inequality in Classless Societies.* Stanford: Stanford University Press.
1992 "Negotiating Values: 'You Can't Have It Both Ways.'" In *Balancing Acts: Women and the Process of Social Change*, ed. Patricia Lyons Johnson, 163–77. Boulder: Westview Press.
Collier, Jane, Bill Maurer, and Liliana Suarez-Navaz
1995 "Sanctioned Identities: Legal Constructions of Modern Personhood." *Identities: Global Studies in Culture and Power* 2 (1–2): 1–27.
Collier, Jane, and Michelle Rosaldo
1981 "Politics and Gender in Simple Societies." In *Sexual Meanings: The Cultural Construction of Gender and Sexuality*, ed. Sherry Ortner and Harriet Whitehead, 275–329. Cambridge: Cambridge University Press.
Collier, Jane, Michelle Rosaldo, and Sylvia Yanagisako
1982 "Is There a Family? New Anthropological Views." In *Rethinking the Family: Some Feminist Questions*, ed. Barrie Thorne and Marilyn Yalom, 25–39. New York: Longman.
Delaney, Carol
1991 *The Seed and the Soil: Gender and Cosmology in Turkish Village Society.* Berkeley: University of California Press.
Delany, Samuel
1988 *The Motion of Light in Water: Sex and Science Fiction Writing in the East Village, 1957–1965.* New York: New American Library.

D'Emilio, John
1984 "Capitalism and Gay Identity." In *Powers of Desire: The Politics of Sexuality,* ed. A. Snitow, C. Stansell, and S. Thompson, 100–113. New York: Monthly Review Press.
D'Emilio, John, and Estelle Freedman
1988 *Intimate Matters: A History of Sexuality in America.* New York: Harper and Row.
de Lauretis, Teresa
1989 *Technologies of Gender: Essays on Theory, Film, and Fiction.* Bloomington: Indiana University Press.
Ellis, Pat
1986 "Introduction." In *Women of the Caribbean,* ed. P. Ellis, 1–24. London: Zed Books.
Elliston, Deborah
1995 "Erotic Anthropology: 'Ritualized Homosexuality' in Melanesia and Beyond." *American Ethnologist* 22 (4): 848–67.
Foucault, Michel
1978 *The History of Sexuality,* vol. 1: *An Introduction.* New York: Vintage Books.
1985 *The History of Sexuality,* vol. 2: *The Uses of Pleasure.* New York: Vintage Books.
Fuss, Diana
1989 *Essentially Speaking: Feminism, Nature, and Difference.* New York: Routledge.
Gilroy, Paul
1993 *The Black Atlantic: Modernity and Double Consciousness.* Cambridge: Harvard University Press.
Gussler, Judith
1980 "Adaptive Strategies and Social Networks of Women in St. Kitts." In *A World of Women: Anthropological Studies of Women in the Societies of the World,* ed. E. Bourguignon, 185–209. New York: Praeger.
Halperin, David
1990 *One Hundred Years of Homosexuality and Other Essays on Greek Love.* New York: Routledge.
Haraway, Donna
1986 "Primatology Is Politics by Other Means." In *Feminist Approaches to Science,* ed. Ruth Bleier, 77–118. New York: Pergamon Press.
Harris, Olivia, and Kate Young
1981 "Engendered Structures: Some Problems in the Analysis of Reproduction." In *The Anthropology of Pre-Capitalist Societies,* ed. Joel Kahn and Joseph Llobera, 109–47. Atlantic Highlands, N.J.
Hegarty, Peter
1997 "Materializing the Hypothalamus: A Performative Theory of the 'Gay Brain.'" *Feminism and Psychology* 7 (3): 355–72.
Lancaster, Roger
1992 *Life Is Hard: Machismo, Danger, and the Intimacy of Power in Nicaragua.* Berkeley: University of California Press.

Macpherson, C. B.
1962 *The Political Philosophy of Possessive Individualism: Hobbes to Locke.* Oxford: Oxford University Press.
Martinez-Alier, Verena
1974 *Marriage, Class and Colour in Nineteenth-Century Cuba.* London: Cambridge University Press.
Marx, Karl
1984 [1844] "The Economic and Philosophic Manuscripts of 1844." In *The Marx-Engels Reader.* 2d ed., ed. Robert Tucker, 66–125. New York: W. W. Norton.
Maurer, Bill
1991 "Symbolic Sexuality and Economic Work in Dominica, West Indies: The Naturalization of Sex and Women's Work in Development." *Review of Radical Political Economics* 23 (3–4): 1–19.
McAfee, Kathy
1991 *Storm Signals: Structural Adjustments and Development Alternatives in the Caribbean.* Boston: South End Press.
Mead, Margaret
1935 *Sex and Temperment in Three Primitive Societies.* New York: New American Library.
Morris, Rosalind
1995 "All Made Up: Performance Theory and the New Anthropology of Sex and Gender." *Annual Review of Anthropology* 24:567–92.
Murray, David
1996 "Homosexuality, Society and the State: An Ethnography of Sublime Resistance in Martinique." *Identities: Global Studies in Culture and Power* 2 (3): 249–72.
Oakley, Ann
1972 *Sex, Gender and Society.* London: Temple Smith
Pateman, Carole
1988 *The Sexual Contract.* Stanford: Stanford University Press.
Radin, Margaret
1987 "Market Inalienability." *Harvard Law Review* 100 (8): 1849–1937.
Rosaldo, Michelle
1974 "Woman, Culture and Society: A Theoretical Overview." In *Woman, Culture and Society,* ed. Michelle Rosaldo and Louise Lamphere, 17–42. Stanford: Stanford University Press.
1983 "The Shame of Headhunters and the Autonomy of Self." *Ethos* 11 (3): 135–51.
1984 "Toward an Anthropology of Self and Feeling." In *Culture Theory: Essays on Mind, Self and Emotion,* ed. R. Schweder and R. LeVine, 137–57. Cambridge: Cambridge University Press.
Safa, Helen
1986 "Economic Autonomy and Sexual Equality in Caribbean Society." *Social and Economic Studies* 35:1–21.

Scott, Joan
1992   "Experience." In *Feminists Theorize the Political,* ed. Judith Butler and Joan Scott, 22–40. New York: Routledge.
Sedgwick, Eve Kosofsky
1990   *The Epistemology of the Closet.* Berkeley: University of California Press.
Shapiro, Judith
1981   "Anthropology and the Study of Gender." *Soundings: An Interdisciplinary Journal* 64 (4): 446–65.
Smith, Raymond T.
1988   *Kinship and Class in the West Indies.* Cambridge: Cambridge University Press.
Stoler, Ann
1995   *Race and the Education of Desire: Foucault's* History of Sexuality *and the Colonial Order of Things.* Durham, N.C.: Duke University Press.
Strathern Marilyn
1992   *After Nature: English Kinship in the Late Twentieth Century.* Cambridge: Cambridge University Press.
Sutton, Constance, and Susan Makiesky-Barrow
1977   "Social Inequality and Sexual Status in Barbados." In *Sexual Stratification: A Cross-Cultural View,* ed. A. Schlegel, 292–325. New York: Columbia University Press.
Trouillot, Michel-Rolph
1988   *Peasants and Capital: Dominica in the World Economy.* Baltimore: Johns Hopkins University Press.
1989   "Discourses of Rule and the Acknowledgment of the Peasantry in Dominica, W.I., 1838–1928." *American Ethnologist* 16 (4): 704–18.
Visweswaran, Kamala
1994   *Fictions of Feminist Ethnography.* Minneapolis: University of Minnesota Press.
Weeks, Jeffrey
1986   *Sexuality.* New York: Tavistock.
Yanagisako, Sylvia, and Jane Collier
1987   "Toward a Unified Analysis of Gender and Kinship." In *Gender and Kinship: Essays Toward a Unified Analysis,* ed. J. Collier and S. Yanagisako, 14–50. Stanford: Stanford University Press.
Yankey, Joseph Bernard
1969   "A Study of the Situation in Agriculture and the Problems of Small Scale Farming in Dominica, West Indies." Ph.D. diss., Department of Agricultural Economics, University of Wisconsin.

The Domestic/Public in Mexico City: Notes on Theory, Social Movements, and the Essentializations of Everyday Life

Miguel Díaz Barriga

Yo siempre cargaba una imagen de la Virgen de Guadalupe y en cada casa en que llegaba yo, ponía mi Virgencita en mi cuarto y lo primero que hacía yo era pedirle fuerzas a ella. Y, yo con lagrimas y mucho miedo que tenía para empezar en esa casa a trabajar, decía, "Dios mío porque me hiciste tan pobre, porque tengo que soportar todo esto."

I always carried an image of Our Lady of Guadalupe and in each house that I arrived at [to work as a domestic] I placed my little Lady in my room and the first thing that I did was to ask Her for strength. And, with tears and with the fear that I had of working in this house I would say, "God why did you make me so poor, why do I have to endure all this."[1]

—Maria

In the literature on women's participation in Latin American urban movements the domestic/public has served as a basic unit of analysis of domination and resistance. By *urban movements* I broadly refer to the participation of the urban poor in grassroots organizing to demand land, housing, and other basic services. Research on women's participation in urban movements (hereafter UMs) has primarily focused on how poor women have articulated political concerns across the domestic and public domains. In this essay I outline ways to move beyond debating the merits and limitations of conceptualizing social experience in terms of the domestic/public. I start by showing how social movement researchers have conceptualized resistance in an overly restricted way—as a linear process through which inequality is recognized in the domestic and then public domains. I emphasize, in agreement with Michelle Rosaldo's 1980 position, that new modes of theorizing that move beyond conceptual dichotomies and linear narratives are needed.

As a theoretical framework, the history of the domestic/public dichotomy within anthropology is well-known. Since its appearance as a universal explanation of gender inequality (M. Rosaldo 1974) to its dismissal as essentializing (M. Rosaldo 1980), anthropologists have wavered over the dichotomy's theoretical usefulness while attempting to develop new research strategies for examining gender subordination (Collier and Yanagisako 1987; Lamphere 1993; Lugo 1992; Redclift 1997). In Michelle Rosaldo's 1980 rethinking of the dichotomy, she emphasized that its explanatory power was limited because it reinforced dominant ideologies of gender relations and relied too much on women's role in reproduction to explain gender inequality. Instead, she argued that gender relations must be interpreted both in terms of wider political inequalities and as products of concrete social practices. Since then, anthropologists have moved away from universal explanations of gender inequality to a focus on agency and the subjectivity of social actors (Ginsburg and Tsing, 1990:5; Gutmann 1996:147–48).

Research on urban social movements in Latin America has also identified the domestic/public dichotomy as being a key element of urban culture (see Jelin 1990). UM researchers have focused on how poor women, through their everyday practices, have reworked the dichotomy's meaning (Blondet 1990; Brugada 1986; Caldeira 1990; Lind 1992; Logan 1990; Martin 1990; Moser 1989).[2] Researchers have mapped the meaning of linking the domestic/public spheres onto possibilities for organizing around needs and engaging in new forms of urban development (Díaz Barriga 1998). In exploring these strategies, however, the heterogeneous perspectives of participants in UMs have been overlooked, and the wider context of debate about gender roles and identity within urban neighborhoods has been replaced by a general discussion of linking social spheres. Only recently have researchers begun to note the limitations of the domestic/public as a framework for understanding women's participation in UMs (Díaz Barriga 1998; Cubbitt and Greenslade 1997; Jelin 1997; Massolo 1994).

In what follows I purposefully contrast narratives of women's participation in UMs with the life history of María, who participated in a land takeover (commonly known as urban squatting) but was not active in grassroots organizing. Rather, María viewed her struggle for housing as a means of escape from working as a domestic (maid), a job that she hated—as reflected in the epigraph. In her life history María intertwines the themes of *telas* (fabrics) and *zapatos* (shoes) with her devotion to La

Virgen de Guadalupe (Our Lady of Guadalupe) to think about how she has succeeded in overcoming her abusive father and bosses. For María, as is true for many women active in UMs, resistance to traditional gender relations is not so much about breaking the divide between the domestic/public but, rather, about moving away from the broader inequalities and essentializations of everyday life.

My analysis is based on extended fieldwork that I conducted on the politics of urban expansion and the formation of UMs in the Ajusco area of Mexico City. This fieldwork involved interviewing a number of participants and leaders in UMs as well as examining movement documents, collecting urban planning publications, and reviewing the limited materials on *colonos'* (the urban poor's) narratives about participation in UMs.[3] While conducting this research, I lived with María, her husband, Pablo, and their two children in a small home made of *tabique* (a low-grade brick) that they themselves constructed.[4] I should note that this essay started as an attempt to reconcile my research on social movements with my everyday experiences while conducting fieldwork. While living with María and Pablo, if I was not out conducting an interview or observing a march, I would spend the day conversing with María and helping out around the house. María spent much of her day getting the kids to school, doing housework, and sewing book bags, which she sold to her neighbors on credit. On a few occasions I walked with her along the grey lava streets of the Ajusco as she delivered book bags. During these walks we talked about how she had worked as a domestic and her aspirations for the future. María also told her fourteen-year-old daughter, Rosa, about these experiences. When I asked María if she would allow Rosa to work as a domestic she curtly replied, "Pienso que para que mi hija trabaje en casa debería yo estar muerta" (I think that for my daughter to work in a house [as a domestic] I would have to be dead).[5] Indeed, María perceives her struggles not in terms of interlocking social spheres but as overcoming the limitations of "what she was," a poor domestic from the countryside.

The Domestic/Public in Urban Movements Research

During the 1960s and 1970s, in response to massive urbanization and widespread poverty, urban social movements erupted throughout Latin America (Canel 1992; Castells 1983; Perlman 1976; Perló and Schteingart 1984). In many cases the emergence of UMs was linked to the formation of irregular settlements such as "squatter" neighborhoods and shantytowns.

Because land tenure in such settlements was not legal, and they lacked urban services, the urban poor organized protests and marches to pressure the state to recognize their rights to housing and services. This grassroots organizing was linked to the work of political parties, Christian groups influenced by liberation theology, and activist groups working outside official party structures (Mainwaring 1987). While the main goals of UMs were gaining urban services and land tenure, they were also responsible for organizing collective kitchens, food cooperatives, and health care centers (Andreas 1985; Castells 1983).

Initially, research on UMs emphasized the structural factors behind the political marginalization of the poor and the lack of services and housing (Alonso 1980; Castells 1977; Epstein 1973; Perlman 1976). This research described in detail the land tenure conflicts and urban service issues that conditioned the emergence of UMs. By the 1980s urban researchers began shifting their focus to the production of urban meaning and new cultural identities (Alvarez 1992; Bennett 1992, 1993; Blondet 1990; Canel 1992; Castells 1983; Díaz Barriga 1995a, 1996; Velez-Ibañez 1983). This shift was both a result of the widening of the projects of UMs, to include both urban planning and gender issues and the rise of new theoretical concerns in social movement research (Hiernaux 1988; Lind 1992; Ramírez-Saiz 1986, 1990). On the one hand, UMs began to organize national and even international councils to better coordinate their political projects. On the other, urban poor women began to organize around gender issues, such as child care and domestic violence. These efforts included attempts to challenge and transform traditional gender ideologies through the organization of workshops and regional conferences on gender issues (Andreas 1985; Brugada 1986; Hernández 1987; Sternbach 1992; Tamayo 1989).

During the 1980s researchers sought to devise a conceptual framework for understanding the barriers—including traditional notions of women's role in the domestic sphere—that had limited women's participation in grassroots organizing. This understanding of the domestic/public dichotomy, as an aspect of dominant culture, was strikingly similar to that outlined in Michelle Rosaldo's early work (1974). For example, Elizabeth Jelin, a noted expert on women's participation in social movements, characterized the subordination of women in the following terms:

In the Latin American cultural tradition, the subordination of women is anchored to the strongly cohesive family group that constitutes the base of the whole system of social relations. The patriarchal family is seen as the natural unit around which daily life revolves. The household is the basic unit of reproduction. Within it, the relations between the genders and generations are hierarchical, involving a clear division of labour and areas of activity. Women are in charge of the domestic tasks associated with the private sphere of reproduction and maintenance of the family; men are responsible for tasks relating to the public sphere of social and political life. (1990:2)

This characterization of dominant notions of gender relations was common throughout the literature on Latin American social movements (Brugada 1986:13; Chaney 1979:19–20; Blondet 1990:13; Martin 1990:471; Stephen, 1992:74; Sternbach et al. 1992:210). For the most part notions of the domestic and public have relied on the opposition between male/wage-work/factory/money/corruption/violence and female/nonwage-work/family/love/honesty/cooperation (Blondet 1990; Caldeira 1990; Collier and Yanagisako 1987).

By the early 1990s research on UMs had identified several strategies that poor women employed to break the domestic/public divide, including organizing around needs and devising grassroots urban development projects. In examining women's participation, Carolyn Moser, following the lead of Maxine Molyneux (1985), focused on how women's organizations within UMs have expanded their agendas from basic or practical needs to strategic needs. "Strategic needs," according to Moser, are based on using gender identity to challenge the sexual division of labor (1989:1803). Similarly, Amy Conger Lind, in her overview of women's organizations in Ecuador, shows how "poor women in urban areas often base their politics on a certain set of 'needs' derived from their reproductive roles" (Lind 1992:139). Lind demonstrates how these women's groups integrate practical and strategic needs in their struggle for housing, services, and gender equality. In her research on the experiences of poor women in the *pueblos jovenes* (low-income neighborhoods) of Lima, Cecilia Blondet (1990) looks at a series of articulations between the domestic and public spheres. Blondet describes an initial pattern, usually following migration to the city, in which women's lives are focused on domestic activities. According to her informants, this initial period was followed by increasing activity in the public economic sphere. With the series of recessions starting in the 1970s, however, poor women became involved in new survival strategies including the organization of food clubs and collective kitchens. These attempts to pool resources were part of wider community efforts to gain services and make demands on the state. According to Blondet, the creation of this "public collective domestic sphere" represents a creative attempt to generate new forms of social organization. Attempts by women in low-income neighborhoods to form cooperatives and popular kitchens, which has happened throughout Latin America, thus represent a new articulation of the domestic/public spheres that is based upon satisfying basic needs (Brugada 1986; Canel 1992).

The writings of Moser, Lind, and Blondet explore the participation of women in grassroots organizing in terms of the processes by which the recognition of basic needs and participation in struggles for land and housing lead to a questioning of traditional gender relations in both the domestic and public domains. Recently, social movement researchers have begun to explore the limitations of describing women's resistance in terms of the domestic/public. Alejandra Massolo (1994), for example, has criticized the ways that researchers have conceptualized resistance mainly in terms of women's roles as mothers and housewives (*madres y amas de casa*). Massolo argues that women's participation in UMs represents a struggle for citizenship (*ciudadanía*) and an ethical position for defending life (*defensa de la vida*). In the volume *Gender Politics in Latin America: Debates in Theory and Practice* (1997) Elizabeth Jelin also argues that notions of women's empowerment that are based upon participation in the public domain (social movements and the workforce) have to be modified:

If oppression was grounded in the domestic-patriarchal domain, breaking the divide between the private and the public world and learning to express their needs and demands in work and in collective action could become the means of shattering it. Experience showed that at times these practices were liberating, but that they could also reinforce subordination. Women's community work in collective dining halls, in cooperative child care efforts, or in neighborhood activities is not remunerated. Indeed, it often ends up reproducing subordination and clientelism. And entering the world of paid work generally means a double (or triple, if there is also community work to do), day's work, which suggests not liberation but rather exhaustion, fatigue, and overwork. (74–75)

Similarly, in their overview of urban movement research in Mexico City, Tessa Cubitt and Helen Greenslade argue that women's participation in grassroots organizing has led to both empowerment and continued subordination. Because of these complexities, a model of social life based on the domestic/public only serves to limit analysis and reinforce oppressive ideological constructs (1997:60–61).

At a general level UM researchers' understanding of the domestic/public has converged with Michelle Rosaldo's 1980 rethinking of the dichotomy. As in Rosaldo's 1974 work, UM researchers initially conceptualized both domination and resistance in terms of the domestic/public. As women became active in grassroots organizing, the limitations of the dichotomy as a conceptual tool became evident. Although Rosaldo's work is not usually cited, the reasons that researchers have questioned the dichotomy are similar to those outlined in her 1980 article: its application both limits understandings of how women negotiate and challenge sexism as well as reinforces dominant gender ideologies. And, as in the case of Rosaldo's 1980 article, researchers have just started to outline new ways to rethink gender identities and domination.

Researching Urban Movements in the Ajusco

In my own research I have examined how understandings of needs and urban development have transcended notions of the domestic/public (Díaz Barriga 1996, 1998). I have noted that in conceptualizing resistance around the domestic and public, UM research has tended to condense the experiences of *colonas* into one broad narrative. For the most part research on women in low-income neighborhoods has treated them as a homogeneous group—*faveladas, colonas,* etc.—without looking at the multivalent and contradictory aspects of activism and transformations in gender identity.[6] In short I have argued that focusing on resistance in terms of the domestic/public dichotomy has de-emphasized the variety of ways in which poor women have conceptualized the politics of channeling needs, gaining land, and challenging sexism.

The area where I conducted research, the Ajusco, was well suited for looking at differing perspectives and outcomes of women's participation in UMs. Located on the southwestern edge of Mexico City, the urbanized section of the Ajusco region (which includes the Ajusco foothills) covers an area of about five square miles and has a population of about 250,000 (Díaz Barriga 1995b:377). The urbanization of this area was rapid. Starting in the late 1960s, the urban poor began to settle on and consequently to urbanize *ejidos*[7] and private property located in the Ajusco. The irregular land tenure situation in the Ajusco foothills generated political conflict between landholders, the urban poor, and the state, ultimately leading to the emergence of several UMs. Indeed, the Ajusco foothills were the site of some of the most well-organized UMs in Mexico City.[8] During the late 1970s and early 1980s a number of UMs in the zone were organized following a series of land takeovers and rent strikes against illicit subdividers. Participants in UMs organized marches with up to 3,000 participants to pressure the government for land tenure rights and basic services like schools, running water, sewage, etc. They were also responsible for paving streets, constructing primary schools and other public buildings, and devising grassroots development projects (Díaz Barriga 1995a, b; Pezzoli 1987, 1994; Schteingart 1987).

I began my research by focusing on the experiences of two women who were leaders in their neighborhoods, Remedios and Ursula. Both women were poor migrants who became involved in grassroots organizing as a result of participating in a land takeover. To be sure, both Remedios's and Ursula's experiences could be understood in terms of the expansion of basic needs to strategic needs, from domestic to public concerns. For example, Remedios's husband initially opposed her participation in a land takeover and attendance at evening meetings. As settlers became involved in violent confrontations with the police, Remedios's husband argued that the family should move to another part of the city. Remedios opposed this move, demanding that her husband struggle with her to gain a home. When her husband beat her to prevent her from participating in meetings, Remedios forced him to move out. Working as a janitor in a local school and participating in urban organizing, she raised their three children in a small four-room self-constructed house.

This mechanical understanding of needs, however, does not capture the full range of meanings that Remedios articulated around the concept. Remedios's understanding of needs was part of a wider chain of discourses through which hierarchical social relations were challenged and resisted (Díaz Barriga 1996). Remedios herself identified needs as conditioning understandings of power:

We [the poor] speak with the words that *necesidad* gives us. More than anything, this [the words of *necesidad*] is what defended us. We do not speak with *palabras rebuscadas* [complicated words] that we are not able to understand because we do not have an education. All of the people that participated in this struggle, all of the people who remained are people of scarce resources, poor![9]

My goal, following Remedios's lead, was to show how poor women's understandings challenge and reinforce a wider series of discourses about needs. These discourses, as I show in a previous work, are articulated around the state's bureaucratic approach to needs, urban activists' attempts to mobilize the poor around needs, and the poor's emphasis on needs in descriptions of urban politics and poverty (Díaz Barriga 1996).

With this focus on "needs talk'" in mind, I began to look at a number of personal accounts of poor women's participation in grassroots organizing. I looked at the experiences of three women, Ursula (Díaz Barriga 1995a, 1998), Doña Jovita (MRP n.d.), and Pilar (Massolo 1992), all of whom participated in land takeovers and were key players in struggles for land tenure and urban services (Díaz Barriga 1998). Ursula's need for housing moved her into wider conflicts and broader participation in organizing. She became a political pragmatist, eventually taking leadership of the urban movement in her neighborhood, Lomas de Padierna, and then in the early 1980s cooperating with the ruling party, the Partido Revolucionario Institucional (PRI, or Institutional Revolutionary Party). Doña Jovita's discussion of needs was tied to providing for her children and, in religious terms, creating the promised land on earth. Doña Jovita was active in citywide councils of UMs and in the Ajusco neighborhood (distinct from the Ajusco region), where she organized protests to demand land tenure. Finally, Pilar discussed wider gender issues, such as abortion rights, in terms of recognizing women's needs. Pilar, who was active in the neighborhood Campamento 2 de octubre, neither emphasized needs as informing pragmatic choices nor focused on providing for her children but, rather, discussed her activism as questioning all forms of gender inequality—as becoming a "rebellious" woman.

In recounting their experiences, each woman discussed the ways she sought to impact community politics and development projects. For example, Ursula, with the support of a large number of poor women, became the leader of her neighborhood, replacing male leaders whom she viewed as ineffective. When she began to cooperate with the PRI in the early 1980s (according to many, she was co-opted) she relied on this base of support to maintain her leadership position and to criticize outside activists who she felt were too ideological and not focused on gaining services.[10] Doña Jovita was involved with Catholic religious groups and organizing women in her neighborhood while criticizing male leaders for being corrupt. Her discussion of women being the major participants in the movement focuses on their attempts to play a role in the development of the neighborhood, including decisions about plot sizes, prices for land, layout of streets, parks, etc. In contrast, Pilar stresses the ways in which the state and church teach women to be submissive. While active in both a UM and a leftist political party, she pushed for the inclusion of issues such as abortion rights. She was also active in the organization of popular kitchens and schools until the police burned the neighborhood and the major leader of the movement was co-opted. During the 1980s she shifted the focus of her activism to participating in political campaigns for a leftist party.[11]

The particulars of each woman's experiences neither fit into a smooth narrative of linking the domestic and public domains nor do their understandings of needs mechanically push them into questioning gender inequality and participating in public politics. Rather, the meanings that they associate with needs are both linked to wider political discourses and are contextualized in terms of their experiences in grassroots organizing. In exploring these wider meanings, however, I neglected to discuss the experiences of women not active in UMs. Indeed, discourses of needs also formed part of the understandings of politics and gender relations of residents of the Ajusco not active in UMs. María, for example, contextualized needs in terms of escaping rural poverty and overcoming the humiliation she suffered working as a domestic. Even though María's understanding of needs did not lead her into grassroots organizing, her account also points to the importance of moving beyond the domestic/public framework.

María's Account

When I asked María why she participated in a land takeover she replied, "Out of *need,* out of the desire to have a plot of land—more than anything for our children" (emph. added).[12] Like Doña Jovita, María sees needs and family concerns as major elements of participation in land takeovers. María's participation in a land takeover, however, does not represent a key moment in bridging the domestic/public and becoming active in grassroots organizing. Rather, she sees this participation as part of her struggle to ensure that she and her daughter do not have to work as domestics. At the time of our conversations (spring 1987 and summer 1989), María felt that her family had indeed "moved ahead." When I asked María about her current situation, she spoke of becoming a new person: "for me everything now is like a dream, everything is like a dream, that I have *left what I was before*" (emph. added).[13] When I asked her why it seemed like a dream she answered:

> Because, well . . . I wanted to have a husband that respected me and even if we lived in a shack, that we would be happy. We [my husband and I] have both struggled. We now have what I never dreamed of having, our own house, two kids. And now I plan to keep moving ahead—with more determination—while I am able to see, my eyes still feel fine, my arms. I feel strong enough to continue struggling, much stronger than before because everything I have is mine. Before everything was somebody else's and they [the bosses] paid me whatever they wished. Thanks mainly to God everything is going to be different as long as no one in the family, my husband, my children, do not become sick. This is what I am presently thinking.[14]

María's insistence on moving ahead speaks to her sense of having overcome abusive bosses and family. She emphasized how she was even mistreated by her parents when they lived in an impoverished *rancho* (small village) before migrating to Mexico City.

María's recounting of life in the *rancho* goes against an idealized version of the domestic domain (love, nonwage work, etc.), since her father was so violent and she, as one of the older children, was immediately put to work to help support the family. María neither attempted to embellish

TABLE 1.   Chronology

1948	Born in Charcas, the state of Guanajuato
1956	As an eight-year-old she works in a house taking care of a baby as well as tending sheep, collecting firewood, etc.
1960	Gets her first pair of shoes when she is twelve years old
1964	Arrives in Mexico City to work as a domestic
1970	Works as a domestic in United States
1972	Returns to Mexico City, works in a factory making cables at a telephone company and as a street vendor
1975	Marries Pablo, lives with godmother, daughter born, participates in land takeover
1976	Works in a factory
1979	Son born, tries working as domestic again
1982	Begins to sell fabric
1990	Pablo injured
1991	Attempts to migrate to United States

this past nor highlight traditional notions of women in the domestic domain (caring, nurturing, supportive, etc.). Rather, María focused on her parents' reliance on the income of their older children and the lack of options for escaping rural poverty. In describing her experiences growing up in the *rancho*, María emphasized how she helped out by tending sheep (which she remembers as a difficult and lonely task) and, even though she was only eight years old, caring for an infant. María also talked about her father's drunken fits and how on a number of occasions she had challenged his authority. In summing up her childhood, María mentioned her awareness of being poor and her fantasies about having decent clothing:

> I never knew what a doll was, never. I envied people that wore clothing that was not torn, a complete outfit. Sometimes when I went to mass, when all of the people were kneeling at their pews, I would look around and think, "why don't I bring a pair of scissors to cut a piece of fabric from each outfit." Their clothing was full, when they kneeled it spread out. I said to myself, "discreetly I could cut a piece of cloth from each one (outfit) . . . what beautiful fabric."[15]

Similarly, María described not having shoes until she was twelve years old. When she saved money to purchase shoes her father accused her of holding money back from the family and took the shoes away. These experiences in the *rancho* conditioned María's understanding of needs. She responded to my question about the pervasiveness of needs in Mexico by focusing on rural poverty:

> In the different villages surrounding Mexico City, they don't have—or we don't have anything to eat, nothing, not even a tortilla. At times one is told, "let's go to Mexico City, there nobody lacks anything . . . one can sell *elotes* [grilled corn] or candy to earn money."[16]

María said this with a slight grin, knowing that the experiences of migrants to Mexico City were much more difficult.

María was first brought to Mexico City by her parents when she was sixteen years old. After they left her at a house to work as a domestic, María only saw her parents once a month, when they collected her pay. Her discussion of working as a domestic follows the same narrative format described by Mary Goldsmith in her research on domestic workers in Mexico City. It is worth citing Goldsmith at length here:

The attitudes of domestic workers also vary according to life stages. Initially, when a young woman migrates to the city, she regards domestic service essentially as a means of assisting her family or acquiring at least a primary education. She does not have a clear view of future aspirations such as marriage, a different job, or further studies . . . For women with children, particularly older workers, domestic service represents a permanent phenomenon. Usually, such a worker dreams of her children's future rather than her own. Not surprisingly, she does not want her daughter to repeat her life history and instead envisions for her a job in accounting or typing. (1989:229)

These two goals of providing for one's parents and ensuring her children's future inform María's experiences. María, however, criticizes her parents for taking her salary. In the end, however, she points out that she had little choice because she wanted to help her brothers and sisters:

No, I have never liked it [working as a domestic] but my parents brought me [to work] and they would leave me there by force . . . in the house that they chose, without knowing the people with whom they left me and [not considering] whether I wanted to stay or not. They went there to collect my pay at the beginning of each month and I had to be the slave of my patrones . . . Well, I did not feel this [obligation to my parents], but I saw all of my brothers and sisters so poor, without shoes or clothing. I was ashamed and sad to see them like that and there was nothing else I could do but help them.[17]

For María these years of working as a domestic were just as difficult as living in her *rancho*. She still talked about her loneliness and lack of shoes and decent clothing: "I did not know anyone and I barely had clothes and shoes . . . they [the *patrones*] humiliated me often and I had to endure all of this because there was no other option."[18] Later in the interview she explained that because of their rural backgrounds domestics rarely challenge their *patrones:*

Because one is very timid upon arriving from the countryside, very timid. They do not treat one well because one is timid—one does not have schooling, nothing. The *Señor* and *Señora* make false accusations. We [the domestics] know that we are innocent of robbery, we say to ourselves, "well, I am very poor but not a thief." We swear that this is the truth but they, with their words—they are better able to talk—and with their money, according to them, they win. But we strongly believe in God, we leave everything to God and God gives us strength to move ahead . . . He gives us the strength to continue another day, one more day, months and months.[19]

She attempted to improve her plight by going to Los Angeles, through a contact provided by a patron, to work as a domestic. Her parents pressured her to send them her earnings by threatening to move the family, which had recently migrated to Mexico City, back to the *rancho*. The thought of her brothers and sisters living in the *rancho* was enough to convince María to send back her earnings.

Upon returning to Mexico City, she worked in a factory and as a street vendor selling soft drinks and coffee. One of her favorite places to sell was near a quarry because the soldiers who worked there were good customers. One of these soldiers, Pablo, eventually asked María out. Both María and Pablo described how they became close friends before deciding to marry. María was especially impressed by Pablo's courteous and "simple" (*sencillo*) bearing. Both in their mid-twenties, they considered it especially fortunate that they had met, since they had both given up on marrying. María's parents strongly opposed their relationship because, according to Maria, this meant that her parents would not have claims to her earnings. No one in her family attended their civil wedding, and they had their wedding dinner (three Pepsis and two roasted chickens) with their godparents.[20]

María and Pablo lived with their godparents until later that year, 1975, when they participated in the land takeover in the Ajusco. When they arrived they staked out a plot that had already been demarcated by an illegal subdivider. Neither María nor Pablo knew exactly who owned the plot. The part of the Ajusco where María and Pablo settled was especially conflictual since illegal subdividers were selling land, the urban poor were taking over land, PRI-backed leaders were claiming that they could provide titles, and university-based activists were organizing a UM.[21] In this area activists were not able to consolidate a UM as they had done in parts of the Ajusco that were formerly *ejidos*.[22] In the one private property area in the Ajusco where a UM did form, the level of violence, including murders, was ferocious.[23] When I was in the field in 1987 a government initiative to regularize land titles, which included residents making more payments, led to widespread protests. María and Pablo, who had already obtained title to their land under an earlier regularization program, did not participate.

María's understanding of needs motivating participation in land takeovers was contextualized in terms of this corruption and violence. She differentiated between people who moved in because of need and those who were involved in taking over and selling plots. When I asked her why there were so many confrontations, including families being removed by force, she replied:

> Because many people do it [take over land] out of need, and others ambition. It is still like that now, higher up [the Ajusco foothills] they do it out of ambition. There are many people that have up to three plots, they are doing it as a business, and many others—*we do it with great need.* (Emph. added)[24]

Like Remedios and others, María's participation in a land takeover led to conflicts with her husband. María, for example, described how Pablo was hesitant to participate:

> We decided among ourselves that nobody was going to remove us, well, at least I told Pablo that nobody was going to remove us because, like it or not, I was not going to leave. I would only leave dead because we are going to struggle; I am going to struggle, for our children . . . We made ourselves very strong and I think that God gave us strength to act in this way because we had never been so intimidated. Yes, we felt very afraid but we had to move ahead for our children.[25]

When I asked María about an incident in which she scolded Pablo for wanting to leave the area she replied:

> Yes, everything that I said hurt him. My desperation was so great that I told our neighbor (she was the one who told me about this plot of land): "well, yes but this is for men who truly desire to take over a plot of land but my husband, no, for this [fighting for land], no." I wanted to come here to work. My hands longed to begin to clear [the plot]. But this hurt my husband so much that he said, "That's fine if this is what you want, if you want to suffer, come on let's go look for a plot."[26]

María's narrative is similar to that of Remedios and Doña Jovita, who had conflicts with their husbands over enduring the hardships of participating in a land takeover. As mentioned, Remedios forced her husband to leave when he resorted to violence against her. Ursula and Pilar both participated in land takeovers as heads of their households.

According to María, she did not participate in community politics because she had just given birth to her first child. María spoke about how Pablo "protected" her from having to go to meetings and participate in community work projects (*faenas*). *Faenas* to clear streets and provide basic services are an important, if not somewhat romanticized, element of land takeovers. In some areas of the Ajusco, including where María and Pablo lived, residents organized *faenas* to clear streets and build schools and other public buildings. María and Pablo, like many residents of the Ajusco, were critical of *faenas*. Remedios, for example, pointed out how tiring it was to work all week and then spend all day Sunday clearing a street instead of resting. She was critical of the way that some men would celebrate the end of the *faena* by going on a drinking binge. María also mentioned these binges but was proud that Pablo did not participate. She also noted, with a touch of irony, that Pablo would not allow her to engage in the backbreaking work of clearing streets.

> No, because Pablo was, I don't know, a gentleman. He never allows me to mistreat myself. It is a very beautiful detail for me because until I married him I had worked like an animal. He never allowed me to [mistreat myself] . . . he carried the baby and the diaper bag, he never let me carry anything, even now . . . I feel *overly* protected [*demasiado protegida*] by him. (Emph. added)[27]

After establishing themselves on their plot by clearing it and constructing a room, María returned to work assembling cables. She described how happy she was working because she could afford decent clothing and shoes. Her boss, however, ridiculed her for bringing her daughter to work, and she was later forced to leave this job. After giving birth to her son in 1979, María tried working as a domestic again:

> I tried working in a house [as a domestic] where I had worked years before, before I was married, many years ago. The house was so elegant that wherever you looked there were delicate things. My son began to

touch these elegant things and I was afraid that he was going to break something. I thought it over and decided not to return.[28]

Her attempts to work, however, were limited because she would not allow anyone else to care for her children. In recounting these experiences, María never questioned taking primary responsibility for child care. Rather she talked about how ashamed Pablo felt that he could not earn more and how she would never let anyone else care for her children—not even family members.

Her "decision," however, made it difficult to earn an income. In her desperation she came upon the idea of selling *tela* (fabric) from a woman she saw working on a street corner:

> I saw a lady, an old lady, I had seen her many years ago selling bits [of fabric] and I always thought about doing this but I did not know where they were sold . . . My dream was to sell a lot of curtains from these [snippets].
>
> I dreamed that my neighbor had acquired my thoughts about selling fabric . . . that she had an enormous mountain of snippets. I grabbed a bucket of water and hid myself in back of the mountain of snippets. I submerged them in the bucket of water (in the bucket of water they sink, they do not rise because the water weighs them down).
>
> I thought about this for days—that I wanted to sell snippets and this nightmare scared me.[29]

María went on to describe the difficulty of finding a place downtown where she could buy *tela* and emphasized how difficult it was moving about the city with the kids while wearing shoes that did not fit properly.

As she dragged the *tela* home, her feet bleeding, she thought about how her husband was going to criticize her for starting her own business. She explained how she had to prove that she could be successful:

> I said, "I am going to show him." I cried a lot, but I was going to show him, and I showed him. He finally had to give in. He said, "How do you do it *vieja* [old woman], how do you do it?" He felt humiliated because at the time I earned more than him, a lot more, twice as much . . . This made him angry and ashamed. He felt humiliated. He asked, "how is it possible that a woman earns more than him?"[30]

As in the case of the land takeover, María frankly noted how Pablo had to overcome the humiliation he felt. When I talked to Pablo, he mentioned how lucky he was to have a woman who knows how to struggle. He also noted that María was forced to work out of need. In his discussion of men's attitudes toward gender relations, Matthew Gutmann notes in passing that men's understandings of need often mask that they are being forced/influenced by their wives to change (1996:156). Indeed, Pablo's discussion of María working fits this pattern.

Throughout the 1980s María successfully sold curtains, book bags for school children, and clothes from her home. She talked about her limited success in terms of her devotion to La Virgen de Guadalupe and her belief in God. For example, María described how she prayed while sewing, "At times when I am sewing I pray, 'God, illuminate me, I want to learn more,' I learned how to sew by myself, to cut [patterns], I started to cut [patterns] myself and so blessed is God that I made these dresses without ever having made any before!"[31] When I asked about having other economic options she replied that she did not have any: only her two sewing machines, her faith in God, and her desire that her daughter continue studying. Indeed, while María was proud of her family's accomplishments, she recognized the fragility of their economic situation. She talked, for example, about the fear she had of Pablo being in an accident:

> I see that Pablo is not going to be able to work [much longer]. One might think that I am very happy because he works and I receive his money but this is mistaken. I see how he [Pablo] comes home with his feet very swollen and at times, you saw this week, with blows to his head. Soon bad news arrives about what happened at work, the men go to work and one does not know if they are going to return in good health, one does not know.[32]

María's words, spoken in the spring of 1987, were an accurate portrayal of her situation. On a return visit in 1991 I learned that one of Pablo's legs had been crushed at work and that an infection had set in.[33] Pablo had been working for a contracting firm that was replacing large drainage pipes on a throughway near University City when a pipe fell on him. He was attempting to collect compensation from his employer, but in the meantime he had been "working" as a beggar downtown. In desperation María traveled with a sister to Tijuana, but each time they attempted to cross the border they were caught by agents from the Immigration and Naturalization Service. María told me about the abuse they suffered from the *coyotes* and the humiliation of being captured. She also told me that her brothers and sisters were all moving to Los Angeles, and she hoped to move her family there soon. We read letters sent by her brothers and sisters now in the United States. María was sure she could get work as a domestic in the United States.

Later I taped this conversation as an interview. María's daughter, Rosa, dutifully listened, helping to fill in some of the details. Although she was a good student, Rosa had been forced to drop out of school to help María sew book bags. When Pablo arrived, with a crutch and one leg dangling, we talked about his seemingly poor prospects for receiving compensation. While talking about moving to the United States (though Pablo was contemplating staying behind), they both emphasized that the decision was based on need.

María's understanding of needs centered on her attempts to escape rural poverty and move ahead and justified her decision not to become involved in grassroots organizing. María neither reflected on the relation of needs to class dynamics, like Remedios, nor linked them to wider gender issues, as did Pilar. Instead, María contextualized her struggles in terms of how she suffered working as a domestic and how her faith in La Virgen de Guadalupe enabled her to endure. These struggles do not fit into a smooth narrative of maintaining or creating continuities between the domestic and public spheres. To be sure, María criticized Pablo's attempts to prevent her from participating in a land takeover and starting her own business, yet she also partially challenged other essentializations of identity, such as being poor, a timid migrant, a domestic. Indeed, notions of gender identity based upon the domestic/public represent only one strand of María's struggle to "leave what she was before."

Conclusions

In Michelle Rosaldo's rethinking of the domestic/public dichotomy she challenged us "to provide new ways of linking the particulars of women's lives, activities, and goals to inequalities wherever they exist" (1980:417). Thus, she argued against essentialized notions of gender identity because they limited understandings of inequality and women's resistance. Her aim was to show that gender hierarchy and concepts such as the domestic/public were social constructs tied to wider systems of inequality. In the study of urban movements in Latin America the functioning of the domestic/ public has been linked to activism around needs and the articulation of development alternatives. In moving beyond the domestic/public framework, I have looked at the social relations that define needs by contextualizing them both in terms of wider relations of power and the particulars of women's experiences (Díaz Barriga 1996, 1998). In doing so, I have suggested that Michelle Rosaldo's 1980 rethinking of the domestic/public model is a useful point of departure and comparison for attempts to reconceptualize women's participation in UMs.

In the conclusion to *Gender Politics in Latin America* Nanneke Redclift ironically titles her essay "Post Binary Bliss: Towards a New Materialist Synthesis." The title is meant to capture the difficulties in moving beyond dichotomies such as the domestic/public and devising new ways of representing gender politics. She points out: "The post-binary world is still an uncertain one, if indeed it is where we are" (1997:232). Redclift is right to emphasize uncertainty. For María her brief moment of leaving behind "what she was before" represents neither experiencing blissful empowerment nor completely adhering to a dominant ideology based on overarching social spheres. Rather, her vision of struggling speaks to the importance of understanding the creative ways in which poor women have conceptualized the politics of needs and land takeovers. For urban movement researchers these experiences highlight the possibilities for contextualizing activism in terms of the heterogeneous struggles of poor women— from becoming rebellious to exploring the power of one's devotion to La Virgen de Guadalupe and telling one's daughter about the humiliation of working as a domestic. Whether or not "postbinary" theories are able to express the range of these experiences and memories, the desperation of attempting to cross into the United States, and the harshness of once again being forced to work as a domestic remains to be seen.

NOTES

1. Taped interview with María, May 10, 1987.
2. Researchers have also focused on the integration of political concerns across these spheres as a response to the failure of modernist development paradigms and widespread political corruption (Alvarez and Escobar 1992; Escobar 1992).
3. This essay is part of a larger study on urban movements and the politics of urban expansion in the Ajusco foothills. I spent the year 1987 in the Ajusco collecting data on the history of urban movements in the region. During follow-up

visits in 1989, 1991, and 1993 I updated my research to include data on the formation of irregular settlements in the newly formed ecological conservation area. I have interviewed both *colonos* (residents of low-income neighborhoods) and activists about the historical development of the region and their participation in urban movements. The total number of persons interviewed was forty-four, including in-depth interviews with six political activists, five leaders of urban movements, and thirteen *colonos*. I also observed marches and meetings in which a much larger number of colonos were involved. Information on political activism in the Ajusco foothills is based upon interviews with activists, materials published by activists organizations, and general works on the history of the Left in Mexico. Finally, research on specific urban movements is based upon interviews with both activists and *colonos* as well as internal documents and public announcements. Document sources include urban zoning and development plans, historical archives, academic articles and theses, and a collection of over six hundred newspaper articles about urban politics in the region.

4. I lived with María, Pablo, and their two children for nine months while conducting field research in 1987.

5. Taped interview with María, May 10, 1987.

6. Social movement researchers have just begun to rethink notions of activism by emphasizing the ways in which women involved in grassroots organizing might retreat back into the domestic to take a break from activism. As Judith Hellman points out: "In reality, women may not only emerge from the isolation of the patriarchal family to work together with others in a soup kitchen; they may also retreat back into the private sphere of the family—however oppressive—when relationships with coactivists become too difficult to manage or even bear" (1997:16–17). Hellman is right to point out that social movement research has yet to look at activism in this more nuanced way.

7. *Ejidos* were agricultural lands granted to peasant communities as part of the agrarian reform program of the Mexican government. *Ejidatarios* (peasants who have land rights on *ejidos*) usually held pasture and woodland in common, but cropland was farmed individually (Hansen 1971:31–32). When *ejidos* were created in the Ajusco, mainly in the 1930s, government officials had not anticipated that Mexico City would expand into neighboring villages and rural areas. Because land tenure on *ejidos* was based on usufruct, the urbanization of *ejidos* generated conflicts over political jurisdiction, land use and tenure, and issues concerning urban zoning. These political dynamics changed dramatically on November 7, 1991, when the *ejido* system was abolished. For a detailed discussion of the process of *ejido* urbanization in the Ajusco, see Díaz Barriga 1995.

8. The historical significance of urban movements in Ajusco is well noted. Perló and Schteingart (1984), for example, list urban movements in Ajusco as among the most visible in making demands on the state. Detailed chronologies of urban movements, such as that found in a recent edition of the journal *Estudios Políticos* (1986), constantly refer to the activities of urban movements in southern Ajusco. From 1980 to 1990 I collected over six hundred newspaper articles about urban conflict in the zone from seven Mexican newspapers.

9. Taped interview with Remedios, May 27, 1987.

10. The presence of university activists was key for the organization of many urban movements; see Bennett 1992, 1993; Díaz Barriga 1995a, 1996.

11. Pilar was active in the United Socialist Party of Mexico (PSUM), which joined with the Mexican Workers' Party (PMT) to form the Mexican Socialist Party (PMS). The PMS was part of the National Democratic Front (FDN) for the 1988 elections and later formed part of the Party of the Democratic Revolution (PRD).

12. Interview with María, June 11, 1989.

13. Taped interview with María, May 10, 1987.

14. Taped interview with María, May 10, 1987.

15. Taped interview with María, May 10, 1987.

16. Interview with María, June 11, 1989.

17. Interview with María, June 11, 1989.

18. Interview with María, June 11, 1989.

19. Interview with María, June 11, 1989.

20. Their marriage licence is dated January 10, 1975.

21. In other works I have documented the range of conflicts over land that occurred in the region; see Díaz Barriga 1995a, b.

22. In a 1984 report written by social workers from the district offices, the land tenure situation was listed as ambiguous and the leadership situation of the neighborhood chaotic, with different individuals, including "outsiders," interfering with the progress of the community (Tlalpan 1984:1–2). The same report lists two thousand inhabitants in the area with 66.46 percent of those working earning the minimum wage or less. The majority of plots were under 250 square meters, and, while residents had a variety of documents, including sales receipts and contracts, less than 9 percent had legal titles. The great majority of the housing was constructed out of *tabique* (a low-grade brick) with prefabricated roofs of bituminized cardboard or asbestos.

23. Leaders of the UM in Belvedere attempted to organize a payment strike to protest the lack of a clear government initiative to provide land titles. I did not conduct field research in Belvedere because of the area's reputation for violence and also widespread corruption.

24. Interview with María, June 11, 1989. Pablo, whose main interest was obtaining a legal land title, went to a variety of meetings before deciding to work with a group of leaders who identified with the PRI. The concern of the urban poor with gaining legal titles and the PRI's ability to manipulate this issue, I should point out, is well recognized in the literature (Díaz Barriga 1995b; Gilbert and Ward 1982; Velez-Ibañez 1983; Ward 1990).

25. Taped interview with María, May 10, 1987.

26. Taped interview with María, May 10, 1987.

27. Taped interview with María, May 10, 1987.

28. Taped interview with María, May 10, 1987.

29. Taped interview with María, May 10, 1987.

30. Taped interview with María, May 10, 1987.

31. Taped interview with María, May 10, 1987.
32. Taped interview with María, May 10, 1987.
33. Interview with María and Pablo, July 31, 1991.

REFERENCES

Alonso, Jorge, ed.
1980   *Lucha Urbana y Acumulación de Capital.* Mexico City: Casa Chata.
Alvarez, Sonia E., and Arturo Escobar
1992   "Conclusion: Theoretical and Political Horizons of Change in Contemporary Latin American Social Movements." In *The Making of Social Movements in Latin America: Identity, Strategy, and Democracy,* ed. Arturo Escobar and Sonia E. Alvarez, 317–29. Boulder: Westview Press.
Andreas, Carol
1985   *When Women Rebel: The Rise of Popular Feminism in Peru.* Westport, Conn.: L. Hill.
Bennett, Vivienne
1992   "The Evolution of Urban Popular Movements in Mexico between 1968 and 1988." In *The Making of Social Movements in Latin America,* ed. Arturo Escobar and Sonia E. Alvarez, 240–59. Boulder: Westview Press.
1993   "Orígenes del Movimiento Urbano Popular Mexicano: Pensamiento Político y Organizaciones Políticas Clandestinas, 1960–1980." *Revista Mexicana de Sociología* 3:89–102.
Blondet, Cecilia
1990   "Establishing an Identity: Women Settlers in a Poor Lima Neighborhood." In *Women and Social Change in Latin America,* ed. E. Jelin; trans. A. Zammit and M. Thomson, 12–46. London: Zed Books.
Brugada, Clara
1986   *La Mujer en la Lucha Urbana y El Estado.* Mexico City: Equipo Mujeres en Acción Solidaria.
Caldeira, Teresa
1990   "Women, Daily Life and Politics." In *Women and Social Change in Latin America,* ed. E. Jelin; trans. A. Zammit and M. Thomson, 47–78. London: Zed Books.
Canel, Eduardo
1992   "Democratization and the Decline of Urban Social Movements in Uruguay: A Political-Institutional Account." In *The Making of Social Movements in Latin America: Identity, Strategy, and Democracy,* ed. Arturo Escobar and Sonia E. Alvarez, 276–90. Boulder: Westview Press.
Castells, Manuel
1977   *The Urban Question: A Marxist Approach.* Trans. Alan Sheridan. London: E. Arnold.
1983   *The City and the Grassroots: A Cross-Cultural Theory of Urban Social Movements.* Berkeley: University of California Press.

Chaney, Elsa
1979   *Supermadre: Women in Politics in Latin America.* Austin: University of Texas Press.
Collier, Jane Fishburne, and Sylvia Junko Yanagisako, eds.
1987   *Gender and Kinship: Essays toward a Unified Analysis.* Stanford: Stanford University Press.
Cubitt, Tessa, and Helen Greenslade
1997   "Public and Private Spheres: The End of Dichotomy." In *Gender Politics in Latin America: Debates in Theory and Practice,* ed. Elizabeth Dore, 52–64. New York: Monthly Review Press.
Del Castillo, Adelaida
1993   "Covert Cultural Norms and Sex/Gender Meaning: A Mexico City Case." *Urban Anthropology* 22 (3–4): 237–58.
Díaz Barriga
1995a   "Urban Movements in Mexico City: A Case Study of Urban Expansion, Ecology, and Development in the Ajusco Region, 1970–1990." MS.
1995b   "The Politics of Urban Expansion in Mexico City: A Case Study of *Ejido* Urbanization in the Ajusco Foothills, 1938–1990." *Urban Anthropology* 24 (3–4): 363–96.
1996   "*Necesidad:* Notes on the Discourses of Urban Politics in the Ajusco Foothills of Mexico City." *American Ethnologist* 23 (2): 291–310.
1998   "Beyond the Domestic and Public: *Colonas* Participation in Urban Movements in Mexico City." In *Cultures of Politics / Politics of Culture: Revisioning Latin American Social Movements,* ed. Sonia E. Alvarez, Evalino Dagnino, and Arturo Escobar, 252–77. Boulder: Westview Press.
Estudios Políticos
1985   *Cronología* 4:102–8.
Epstein, David
1973   *Brasilia, Plan and Reality.* Berkeley: University of California Press.
Escobar, Arturo
1992   "Culture, Economics, and Politics in Latin American Social Movements Theory and Research." In *The Making of Social Movements in Latin America: Identity, Strategy, and Democracy,* ed. Arturo Escobar and Sonia E. Alvarez, 62–85. Boulder: Westview Press.
Gilbert, Alan, and Peter Ward
1982   "Low-Income Housing and the State." In *Urbanization in Contemporary Latin America,* ed. A. Gilbert, 79–127. New York: John Wiley.
Ginsburg, Faye, and Anna Lowenhaupt Tsing, eds.
1990   *Uncertain Terms: Negotiating Gender in American Culture.* Boston: Beacon Press.
Goldsmith, Mary
1989   "Politics and Programs of Domestic Worker's Organizations in Mexico." In *Muchachas No More: Household Workers in Latin America and the Caribbean,* ed. Elsa M. Chaney and Mary Garcia Castro, 221–43. Philadelphia: Temple University Press.

Gutmann, Matthew C.
1996   *The Meanings of Macho: Being a Man in Mexico City.* Berkeley: University of California Press.

Hansen, Roger D.
1971   *The Politics of Mexican Development.* Baltimore: Johns Hopkins University Press.

Hellman, Judith Adler
1997   "Anniversary Essay on Social Movements: Revolution, Reform, and Reaction." *NACLA: Report on the Americas* 30 (6): 13–18.

Hernández, Ricardo
1987   *La Coordinadora Nacional del Movimiento Urbano Popular; CONAMUP.* Mexico City: Equipo Pueblo.

Hiernaux, Daniel
1988   "Planificación y Gestión: El Caso de la Ciudad de México." In *Política y Movimientos Sociales en la Ciudad de México,* ed. Alfonso Iracheta Cenecorta and Alberto Villar Calvo, 59–76. Mexico City: Departamento del Distrito Federal.

Jelin, Elizabeth
1997   "Engendering Human Rights." In *Gender Politics in Latin America: Debates in Theory and Practice,* ed. Elizabeth Dore, 65–83. New York: Monthly Review Press.

Jelin, Elizabeth, ed.
1990   *Women and Social Change in Latin America.* Trans. A. Zammit and M. Thomson. London: Zed Books.

Lamphere, Louise
1993   "The Domestic Sphere of Women and the Public World of Men: The Strengths and Limitations of an Anthropological Dichotomy." In *Gender in Cross-Cultural Perspective,* ed. Caroline B. Brettell and Carolyn F. Sargent, 67–77. Englewood Cliffs, N.J.: Prentice-Hall.

Lind, Amy C.
1992   "Power, Gender, and Development: Popular Women's Organizations and the Politics of Needs in Ecuador." In *The Making of Social Movements in Latin America: Identity, Strategy, and Democracy,* ed. A. Escobar and S. Alvarez, 134–49. Boulder: Westview Press.

Logan, Kathleen
1990   "Women's Participation in Urban Protest." In *Popular Movements and Political Change in Mexico,* ed. Joe Foweraker and Ann L. Craig, 150–59. Boulder: Lynne Rienner.

Lugo, Alejandro
1992   "The Use and Abuse of M. Rosaldo's Feminist Understanding." Paper presented at American Anthropological Association meetings, Papers in Honor and Memory of M. Rosaldo: Toward New and Different Readings, San Francisco, December 2–6, 1992.

Mainwaring, Scott
1987   "Urban Popular Movements, Identity, and Democratization in Brazil." *Comparative Political Studies* 20 (2): 131–59.

Martin, Joann
1990 "Motherhood and Power: The Production of a Women's Culture of Politics in a Mexican Community." *American Ethnologist* 17 (1): 470–90.
Massolo, Alejandra
1992 *Por Amor y Coraje: Mujeres en Movimientos Urbanos de la Ciudad de México.* Mexico City: El Colegio de México.
1994 "Vecinas y Ciudadanas." Disensos 35. http://www.iztapalapa. uam.mx/ iztapalapa.www.topodrilo/35/td35_06.html.
Molyneux, Maxine
1985 "Mobilisation without Emancipation: Women's Interests, the State and Revolution in Nicaragua." *Feminist Studies* 11 (2): 227–54.
Monsivais, Carlos
1992 *Entrada Libre: Crónicas de la Sociedad que se Organiza.* Mexico City: Ediciones Era.
Moser, Carolyn
1989 "Gender Planning in the Third World: Meeting Practical and Strategic Gender Needs." *World Development* 17 (11): 1799–1825.
Movimiento Revolucionario del Pueblo (MRP)
N.d. *Doña. Jovita; un Testimonio de la Participación de las Mujeres en las Luchas Urbanas.* Mexico City. Mimeo.
Perlman, Janice E.
1976 *The Myth of Marginality: Urban Poverty and Politics in Rio de Janeiro.* Berkeley: University of California Press.
Perló, Manuel, and Martha Schteingart
1984 "Movimientos Sociales Urbanos en México." *Revista Méxicana de Sociología* 4:105–27.
Pezzoli, Keith
1987 "The Urban Land Problem and Popular Sector Housing Development in Mexico City." *Environment and Behavior* 19 (3): 371–97.
1994 "Human Settlements and Planning for Ecological Sustainability in Mexico City." MS.
Ramírez-Saiz, Juan Manuel
1986 *El Movimiento Urbano Popular en México.* Mexico City: Siglo XXI.
1990 "Urban Struggles and their Political Consequences." In *Popular Movements and Political Change in Mexico,* ed. Joe Foweraker and Ann L. Craig, 234–46. Boulder: Lynne Rienner.
Redclift, Nanneke
1997 "Post Binary Bliss: Towards a New Materialist Synthesis?" In *Gender Politics in Latin America: Debates in Theory and Practice,* ed. Elizabeth Dore, 222–36. New York: Monthly Review Press.
Rosaldo, Michelle
1974 Introduction. In *Woman, Culture, and Society,* ed. Michelle Rosaldo, 1–42, Stanford: Stanford University Press.
1980 "The Use and Abuse of Anthropology: Reflections on Feminism and Cross-Cultural Understanding." *Signs: Journal of Women in Culture and Society* 5 (5): 389–415.

Sandoval, Juan Manuel
  1991 "Los Nuevos Movimientos Sociales y el Medio Ambiente en México." In *Servicios Urbanos, Gestión Local, y Medio Ambiente*, ed. Martha Schteingart and Luciano d' Andrea, 305–35. Mexico City: El Colegio de México.
Schteingart, Martha
  1987 "Expansión Urbana, Conflictos Sociales y Deterioro Ambiental en la Ciudad de México." *Estudios Demográficos y Urbanos* 2 (3): 449–77.
Selby, Henry A., Arthur D. Murphy, and Stephen A. Lorenzeno
  1990 *The Mexican Urban Household: Organizing for Self-Defense*. Austin: University of Texas Press.
Stephen, Lynn
  1992 "Women in Mexico's Popular Movements: Survival Strategies against Ecological and Economic Impoverishment." *Latin American Perspectives* 72 (19): 73–96.
Sternbach, Nancy, Marysa Navarro-Aranguren, Patricia Chuchryk, and Sonia E. Alvarez
  1992 "Feminisms in Latin America: From Bogotá to San Bernardo." In *The Making of Social Movements in Latin America: Identity, Strategy, and Democracy*, ed. Arturo Escobar and Sonia E. Alvarez, 207–39. Boulder: Westview Press.
Tamayo, Sergio
  1989 *Vida Digna en Las Ciudades: El Movimiento Urbano Popular en México 1980–1985*. Mexico City: Ediciones Gernika.
Tlalpan
  1984 "Delegación del Departamento de Distrito Federal en Tlalpan: Oficina de Trabajo Social." Mimeo.
Velez-Ibañez, Carlos
  1983 *Rituals of Marginality: Politics, Process, and Culture in Central Urban Mexico, 1969–1974*. Berkeley: University of California Press.
Ward, Peter
  1990 *Mexico City: The Production and Reproduction of an Urban Environment*. New York: G. K. Hall.

History, the State, and Class

Victorian Visions

Jane F. Collier

A project that Michelle Z. Rosaldo hoped to pursue, had she lived, was to conduct a feminist reexamination of nineteenth-century social theory. Although some of her published works contain references to this project (e.g., Rosaldo 1980; Collier, Rosaldo, and Yanagisako 1982), the most complete record of Shelly's thoughts and plans are contained in the notes and lectures from a course that she designed and taught at Stanford University in 1978–79 along with historian Ellen Dubois and myself and with the participation of three other faculty members, Myra Strober, Mollie Rosenhan, and Marilyn Yalom. The course was planned as the second half of a two-quarter sequence on the "The Female Experience: Victorian Heritage." The first course, designed and taught primarily by historians, focused on the condition and experiences of women during the Victorian period in the United States, France, and England (see Bell and Offen 1983). The second course, in which Shelly Rosaldo participated, focused on turn-of-the-century social theory. Both courses were designed to explore the social and cultural resources that we, as late-twentieth-century feminists, inherited from those who came before us.

Shelly, in particular, wanted to study late-nineteenth-century social theory in order to understand the implicit and explicit assumptions about society that informed and limited the ideas of feminist anthropologists writing in the 1970s. In the minutes she wrote after one of the early planning sessions for the course—known as "Victorian Heritage II"—she observed that "we" (the course planners) were "interested in a number of perspectives: positive roots of contemporary theory; gaps in contemporary theory which can be traced to turn of the century assumptions; feminist insights and thinkers who were important at their time but have been 'lost' through subsequent developments; feminist thinkers who should have been important but were not" (minutes from September 7, 1978).

Here I plan to focus on two characteristics of mid-twentieth-century social theory that Shelly hoped to understand by studying the Victorians:

(1) the domestic/public conceptual opposition that we share with nineteenth-century social theorists; and (2) their recognition that families were not universal, unchanging units, an insight that twentieth-century functionalists seem to have forgotten. In the 1982 article that Shelly coauthored with Sylvia Yanagisako and me, she observed that, although twentieth-century thinkers dismissed many Victorian ideas, "Victorian assumptions about gender and the relationship between competitive male markets and peace-loving female homes were not abandoned in later functionalist schools of thought." She also noted that the Victorians "understood, as we do not today, that families—like religions, economies, governments, or courts of law—are *not* unchanging but the product of various social forms, that the relationships of spouses and parents to their young are apt to be different things in different social orders" (Collier, Rosaldo, and Yanagisako 1982:32).

Late-nineteenth-century evolutionists, for example, commonly argued that primitives lacked families. Herbert Spencer, writing about human evolution, observed, "We have thus to begin with a state in which the family as we understand it, does not exist" (1893:602):

> The lowest groups of primitive men, without political organization, are also without anything worthy to be called family organization: the relations between the sexes and the relations between parents and offspring are scarcely above those of brutes. (610)

But, if nineteenth-century evolutionists characterized primitives as lacking "families," they nevertheless read their own experiences of gender relations back into the past. Primitive men, like Victorian capitalists, competed with one another for possessions: "The males of gregarious animals usually fight for possession of the females; and primitive men do not in this respect differ from other gregarious animals" (601). And primitive women were angels in the home. Bachofen, writing earlier in the century, observed that "at the lowest, darkest stages of human existence the love between the mother and her offspring is the bright spot in life, the only light in the moral darkness, the only joy amid profound misery." Just as men "naturally" competed with one another for property, so women "naturally" loved their children. For Bachofen mother love was "that mysterious power which equally permeates all earthly creatures," in contrast to father love, which requires "a far higher degree of moral development than mother love" (1973:79).

Early in the twentieth century Malinowski (1913) effectively demolished the Victorian idea that families were recent accomplishments when he distinguished between marriage and mating. Evidence of promiscuity, he argued, did not mean that primitives lacked marriage. Rather, all humans, despite their mating practices, recognize a culturally constructed bond between a man and a woman that establishes a special relationship between a husband and the children his wife bears. But twentieth-century functionalists who rejected the notion of Victorian evolutionists that primitives lacked families nevertheless kept Victorian assumptions about "natural" gender roles. Robin Fox, writing in the middle of the twentieth century, for example, reproduced the Victorian opposition between loving female homes and competitive male markets in his statement that, "for the greater part of human history, women were getting on with their highly specialized task of bearing and rearing the children. It was the men who hunted the game, fought the enemies, and made the decisions" (1967:31–32).

Shelly Rosaldo used the Victorian Heritage II course as a context for exploring Victorian notions of gender and the family. The intellectual framework for the course was provided primarily by historian Ellen Dubois. Ellen argued that Victorian social theory came out of nineteenth-century concerns over an apparent breakdown of morality in public life. Focusing on the women's suffrage movement, Ellen explained that debates over "women's place" were part of larger arguments about where to find authority and ethical standards in a social world in which kings and fathers no longer had the unquestioned right to rule over those they "sired." As Shelly phrased these Victorian concerns in one of her lectures: "if authority doesn't come from the top down (i.e., from the king through officials to heads of families), where does it come from? And if authority is not moral (i.e., does not restrain self-interest and competition in favor of the social good), where does morality come from?"[1]

We who taught the course stressed political and economic causes for the crisis in authority. Ellen Dubois focused on political theories of natural rights, using the women's suffrage movement as lens for contrasting different approaches to justifying "men's" right to rule themselves rather than submit to divinely ordained monarchs. She compared equal rights feminism, which based women's right to vote on women's equal capacity for "reason," with domestic feminism, which emphasized women's unique moral capacities. And she contrasted both types of feminism with the antifeminist political arguments invoked by those who wanted to deny women the vote. Shelly and I, on the other hand, tended to focus on economic factors to understand the apparent crisis in morality. We emphasized the role of triumphant capitalism in undermining the economic security of families and the authority of husbands/fathers. We also credited capitalism with the creation of new social problems, such as urban slums and industrial pollution. And we stressed the apparent amorality of capitalism, which seemed to champion individual selfishness over concern for the welfare of others and the social good.

In the first half of the Victorian Heritage II course Ellen Dubois and the other three instructors focused on women's issues—the women's suffrage movement, women's participation in communist revolutionary movements, their participation in the paid workforce, including prostitution, and portrayals of women in literature. They did so in order to explore how arguments about women's place intersected with ongoing political debates over the morality of democracy, capitalism, and science. In the second half of the course Shelly reversed this emphasis. Instead of exploring how women's issues intersected ongoing political debates, she asked why intellectuals debating political issues, such as John Stuart Mill and John Ruskin, were so interested in women. Everyone has heard of Mill's concern for the position of women, but conservative thinkers also addressed the woman-question. When Ruskin, for example, lectured on the ability of a "noble education" to confer "kingly authority" on men, he also considered "what special portion or kind of this royal authority . . . may rightly be possessed by women; and how far they also are called to a true queenly power" (1907:49). Not surprisingly, given his antifeminist sentiments, he concluded that a woman needed to be "wise, not for self-development, but for self-renunciation; wise not that she may set herself above her husband, but that she may never fail from his side" (1907:60).

Shelly also asked why social scientists in the late nineteenth century seemed so interested in women, the family, and sexuality. She observed that arguments over women's place, the separation of public and domestic spheres, and family roles were raised not just by female suffragists and male political theorists but also by statisticians studying the poor, psychologists studying "deviance," and anthropologists studying "primitives." "Why," Shelly asked, were women, the family, and sexuality so salient at the time?

To answer this question Shelly focused on the role of capitalism in undermining the economic security of families. She observed that families who depended on capital investments or on wages earned in the marketplace, rather than on the food family members grew on lands they controlled, could be destroyed by a single unwise investment or by the death or departure of a male "breadwinner." Moreover, once a husband/father became a breadwinner, rather than the manager of a family's estate, his authority depended on his ability to provide for his dependents. Should he lose his capital or his job, he lost his justification for demanding their obedience. Shelly also explored the role of capitalism in apparently freeing those who earned their own money to make individual decisions about how to spend it. Men, the Victorians worried, might waste their money on prostitutes and drink rather than spend it on supporting their families. The Victorians also worried that young women who earned wages might be able to escape parental authority. Given the apparent fragility of the family, particularly among the middle classes, educated Victorians had good reason to be concerned about drawing and policing the boundary between the family and the outside world. Political theorists understandably wanted to distinguish domestic spheres based on selfless "love" from public spheres based on social and political contracts negotiated among self-interested individuals. And social scientists understandably credited the poor, deviant, or primitive "others" they studied with the unbridled greed and sexuality that they defined as outside of their own "pure" families.

When Shelly asked, for example, why nineteenth-century evolutionary theorists, such as Morgan, Bachofen, Marx, Engels, and even Durkheim, thought that "primitives" practiced incest, were promiscuous, and had matriarchies, when none of these assumptions was true, she pointed out that, despite their very real differences, all the evolutionists cast progress in terms of a move from a state of nature to a state of culture. Having defined their own monogamous, pure families at one end of their evolutionary continuums, nineteenth-century social theorists understandably needed to discover incestuous, promiscuous hordes at the beginning. And having located moral orders constructed by men at the end of their evolutionary schemes, nineteenth-century social theorists had to find natural orders, based on unrestrained male greed and natural mother-child bonds, at the beginning. Social evolutionists, Shelly observed, sought in primitive others the familial and sexual customs that allowed them to chart "our" progress from nature to culture, from savagery to civilization, and from emotion to reason.[2]

Although Shelly hoped to continue her exploration of Victorian social theory, she was never able to undertake the project. By studying the Victorians, she wanted to uncover the gendered assumptions embedded in the apparently genderless analytical concepts that late-twentieth-century feminists had inherited from the founders of modern social theory: Marx, Durkheim, Weber, and Freud. Everyone recognizes how easy it is to fall into the trap of mapping Marx's distinction between "production" and "reproduction" onto a male/female distinction between the social production of goods and the biological reproduction of human beings (Harris and Young 1981). But Shelly wanted to emphasize that all nineteenth-century contrasts between opposite ends of imagined evolutionary continuums, however genderless they might appear, encode similar Victorian gender assumptions of a natural female sphere and a culturally constructed male one.

The Marxist distinction between production for use and production for exchange, for example, may appear gender neutral but easily slips into the capitalist distinction between women's unpaid "domestic" work, apparently done to fulfill "biological" needs, and the paid work of male breadwinners, which responds to social market forces. Similarly, Durkheim's apparently genderless distinction between mechanical and organic solidarity maps onto a Victorian gender difference between women, who—like primitives—all think alike because they all perform the same task (i.e., homemaking), and men, who have developed modern individuality and large brains because they perform different roles in an increasing division of labor. By studying the Victorians, Shelly hoped to explore further how their experiences of gender differences within capitalism were encoded, albeit implicitly, into the central concepts that Victorian social scientists developed—and that we have inherited—for studying and understanding social and historical processes.

Shelly also wanted to study the invention of functionalism at the beginning of the twentieth century in order to figure out why functionalists, who rejected and ridiculed their predecessor's imagined evolutionary progress from nature to culture, nevertheless retained their deeply gendered nature/culture distinction—simply putting natural and moral bonds side by side, as unchanging domestic spheres encompassed by historically changing public ones. Why, she wondered, had functionalists limited their recognition that primitives had "culture" to the imagined public sphere of relationships between domestic units, leaving domestic arrangements themselves in the realm of nature? When Malinowski (1913), for example, argued for the universality of "the Family" against earlier evolutionists who had portrayed families as a recent triumph of human culture over brute nature, he did so by stressing the biological need of human children for long-term care. Even as he distinguished marriage as a cultural contract from mating as a biological act, Malinowski continued to treat relationships within domestic units as regulated by the natural bonds of affection that develop among humans involved in the long-term process of rearing children. Malinowski thus paved the way for later functionalists, such as Evans-Pritchard, to distinguish domestic relations, based on supposedly natural bonds of affection (1951), from "kinship," defined in terms of political relations based on marriage contracts negotiated between male-headed groups (1940).

Shelly also wanted to explore the Victorian gender assumptions implicit in modern social theory in order to reflect critically on her own work and to contribute to developing a feminist anthropology that could build on Victorian insights about changing families while avoiding Victorian assumptions about natural gender differences.

By 1978 many colleagues had criticized Shelly's 1974 introductory essay in the edited collection *Woman, Culture, and Society* for arguing that "gender asymmetry" favoring men is universal and can be attributed to an equally universal structural opposition between domestic spheres organized around mothers and their children and public spheres dominated by men. Feminists understandably objected to what they perceived as Shelly's assertion of "universal male dominance." Such an assertion appears to support antifeminist arguments that women's subordination is a natural and inevitable result of women's biological capacity to give birth to children.

Shelly had developed her argument about universal gender asymmetry in the process of planning and teaching an anthropology course at Stanford on "Women in Cross-Cultural Perspective." In 1970–71, seven years before the Victorian Heritage II course was taught, Shelly and I, who were then faculty wives, joined five women graduate students (Janet Fjellman, Julia Howell, Kim Kramer, Ellen Lewin, and Ann Rosenthal) to plan a course that drew on the ethnographic record to explore the range of what women actually did. Professor Peggy Golde served as our faculty sponsor. We who developed the course wanted to challenge the dominant idea in anthropology at the time that women everywhere did the same thing—that they were all wives and mothers whose interests and activities varied little from society to society or from historical period to historical period (Evans-Pritchard 1965; Fox 1967). Our group thus read ethnographies from around the world in order to discover examples of all the varied things that women had done and were doing. When we taught the course in the spring of 1971 we enthusiastically told our students about women who were queens, priestesses, farmers, traders, and healers.

At the end of the course, however, our students complained that, whatever wonderful things women did, women's contributions seemed to be less valued than the contributions of men. This complaint led Shelly and me to rethink how we taught the course in subsequent years, after we had both been hired as part-time assistant professors and had to teach the course by ourselves. We decided to focus not just on documenting the wide variety of women's roles and activities but also on exploring the cultural concepts that people used to evaluate women's and men's contributions to society as a whole. Through doing so, we hoped to find an answer to the question raised by the students of why, whatever varied and useful things women did, their activities seemed to be accorded less cultural value, and to bestow less publicly recognized authority on those who performed them, than the activities culturally assigned to men. In short, Shelly wanted to answer the question raised by Margaret Mead when she observed that

> in every known society, the male's need for achievement can be recognized. Men may cook, or weave, or dress dolls or hunt hummingbirds, but if such activities are appropriate occupations of men, then the whole society, men and women alike, votes them as important. When the same occupations are performed by women, they are regarded as less important. (1949)

In contrast to Mead, however, who had offered a psychological explanation for male privilege, Shelly wanted to find a social explanation. She was not convinced by Mead's suggestion that men everywhere need to be compensated by the fact that they are not able to give birth to babies. Shelly thus drew on her training in symbolic anthropology and particularly on Clifford Geertz's insight that culture is created and negotiated in public settings. Culture, Geertz had argued, exists not as rules inside the heads of individuals but, rather, as concepts that people use in communicating with one another (1973). Shelly thus suggested that men's activities and contributions—whatever these might be—tended to be accorded more cultural value than women's because women's obligation to care for small children made it more difficult for women to participate in the public interactions in which people developed, negotiated, and contested the concepts that constituted their culture.

In developing this structural explanation for universal sexual asymmetry, Shelly and I were influenced not only by our readings of anthropological theory but also by our experiences as faculty members. After becoming assistant professors, we discovered how much an ability to control our interactions with others, simply by closing our office doors, contributed to our ability to articulate our ideas in a coherent and forceful fashion. We thus came to recognize how men's ability to hand small children over to female caretakers might help men to acquire and maintain the air of distance that facilitates authority. Women forced to contend with crying or demanding children understandably had fewer opportunities than men to make their voices heard in public settings among other adults.

Because Shelly developed her ideas about the domestic/public opposition in the context of teaching about women's varied activities, she never took seriously those critiques of her 1974 article that were based on variants of the argument "but women in the society I studied are not confined to the home." Not only had Shelly never argued that women were confined to the home; she had never argued that women lacked access to the public sphere. She had merely observed that, "universally," men tended to have greater access to participating in public discussions than women because men could more easily turn noisy and misbehaving children over to female caretakers.

Shelly also never took seriously the critiques of her essay that were based on variants of the argument that "motherhood in the society I studied is a source of power and authority for women." Shelly recognized that in many, if not most, of the societies studied by anthropologists women gained autonomy, power, and prestige by becoming mothers. She merely observed that motherhood, however highly valued, tended to confer less publicly recognized authority and prestige on women than the religious or political roles commonly assigned to men.

On a deeper level Shelly dismissed both the "women are not confined to the home" and the "motherhood confers value" critiques on the grounds that proponents of both arguments had misread her 1974 essay as implying that it was the activity of mothering that determined women's "inferior" status. Shelly always avoided succumbing to the commonsense capitalist assumption that activities have value in and of themselves. Rather, as a cultural anthropologist and a Marxist, she started from the assumption that humans, in their interactions, attribute value to activities.

Finally, Shelly never took seriously critiques of her 1974 article based on demonstrating that women in a particular society enjoyed considerable power. She was always careful to distinguish between *power,* defined as one person's ability to affect the conduct of others, and *authority,* defined as the culturally validated right to tell others what to do (whether others obeyed or not). Shelly readily agreed that women could, and often did, enjoy considerable power, particularly if they were older or belonged to high-ranking families. But she argued that women rarely enjoyed as much culturally sanctioned authority as men of similar age and rank. One of her favorite examples of how women could enjoy power, while powerless men enjoyed only prestige, was drawn from an ethnography of Jewish ghetto communities in Eastern Europe (Zborowski and Herzog 1955). Shelly observed that, while the women ran family businesses and participated in political decisions, wives would nevertheless "defer to their husbands, and their greatest joy in life was to have a male child" who became a Talmudic scholar (Rosaldo 1974:20).

There was one critique of her 1974 essay, however, that Shelly did take seriously. This was the observation that the domestic/public structural opposition, which Shelly argued could be applied universally, was, in fact, a product of recent Western thought (Rapp 1978; Lewis 1977). Because Shelly had always argued that cultural concepts, including analytical ones, do not reflect some acultural reality but are, instead, produced and propagated through human interactions, she was sensitive to the observation that her own domestic/public opposition was a product of social interactions organized by capitalism.

As Shelly came to accept the idea that the domestic/public opposition she posited as universal was a historical legacy of the European Enlightenment, she turned to exploring the source of her ideas. Many cultures, she realized, make a domestic/public cultural contrast, but the particular version she had been using, which imagined domestic spheres based on emotion in contrast to public spheres based on self-interested political contracts, was culturally specific. It derived from late-nineteenth-century political and economic theories, particularly from natural rights political theory, which cast public and domestic spheres as organized on different principles, and from capitalism, which created a distinction between paid work and unpaid activities.

Shelly also came to recognize that the Marxist-feminists who had criticized her domestic/public opposition as a modern Western construct were not themselves free from Victorian gender conceptions. Shelly's use of the domestic/public opposition may have been a particularly egregious example of the nineteenth-century doctrine of "separate spheres," but Marxists who argued that the distinction between domestic and public spheres did not exist before the invention of private property also used conceptual oppositions that encoded Victorian gender conceptions. For example, Marxist-feminists who contrasted "production for use" with "production for exchange" tended to reproduce the Victorian opposition between peace-loving female homes, in which people of different ages and sexes cooperated in fulfilling biological needs, and competitive male markets, in which men struggled for advantage. Even Gayle Rubin, in her brilliant essay on "The Traffic in Women" (1975), tended to reproduce Victorian gender oppositions by trying to separate a "sex-gender system" dealing with biological reproduction from a socially organized system of production, even though she portrayed both as historically produced and changeable.

Once Shelly came to realize that the central concepts of modern social theory encoded Victorian gender assumptions associated with natural rights political theory and capitalist economic relations, she turned from focusing on similarities among cultures to exploring differences. Returning to data she had collected among the Ilongot of the Philippines, she became interested in the fact that Ilongot, in contrast to many peoples around the world, seemed to lack a developed concept of femininity, particularly a concept of "woman the life-giver" to balance and oppose their well-developed concept of "man the hunter and life-taker" (see Rosaldo and Atkinson 1975). Following Shelly's insight that cultural concepts are created, negotiated, and spread in interactions, I suggested a reason for the lack: in foraging or hunting-horticultural groups, such as Ilongot, in which men marry with "brideservice," people tend to handle conflicts between men over women by staging "contests" that focus everyone's attention on the bravery of the male contestants rather than on the qualities of the woman they are fighting over. Perhaps, I suggested, the Ilongot lacked a developed concept of femininity because they lacked occasions for developing such concepts. Shelly and I thus began to explore political processes in hunter-gatherer and hunter-horticultural societies, a project that resulted in our joint paper on "Politics and Gender in 'Simple' Societies" (1981).

Shelly's suggestions for future directions in feminist anthropology are best expressed in her 1980 article in *SIGNS*. She began the essay by declaring—in contrast to what many feminists of the time were arguing—that we do not need more ethnographic data on what women around the world are saying and doing. "We have," she observed, "plenty of data 'on women';

but when it comes to writing about them, all too few of us know what to say." What we need, she argued, is new theoretical frameworks. Because "what we know is constrained by interpretive frameworks which, of course, limit out thinking; what we *can* know will be determined by the kinds of questions we learn to ask" (1980:390). Writing for a general audience of feminist scholars, Shelly focused on anthropology's role in supplying information about the "origins" of women's subordination. Because searches for origins, she observed, tended to discover that "women elsewhere are, it seems, the image of ourselves undressed" (392), she drew on her experiences teaching the Victorian Heritage II course to uncover the culturally specific gender assumptions inherent in contemporary feminist scholarship:

I would suggest that the typically flat and unilluminating picture of women that appears in most conventional accounts is bound up with theoretical difficulties that emerge whenever we assume that feminine or domestic spheres can be distinguished from the larger world of men because of their presumably panhuman functions. And insofar as feminists are willing to accept this virtually presocial and unchanging base for women's lives, their explorations of the worlds of women will remain a mere addition—and not a fundamental challenge—to traditional ways of understanding social forms as the creation of the lives and needs of men. (409)

Shelly suggested that the popular feminist model for human evolution at that time—"Woman the Gatherer" (Slocum 1975; Zihlman 1976, 1978)—fell into this trap. While she praised the model for challenging the dominant, sexist view of human evolution, which credited "Man the Hunter" with all human advances, Shelly observed that Woman the Gatherer nevertheless tended to reproduce Victorian assumptions about women's roles as dictated by their biological capacity to bear children. "The problem," she suggested, "lay in an attempt to understand the forms of female action and the woman's role by asking, 'What did early woman do?' and not, 'What kinds of bonds and expectations shaped her life.'" As an alternative, Shelly proposed the analysis of gender in "simple" societies that she and I were developing. She observed that we had "been concerned to stress not the activities of women—or of men—alone; instead we [were] attempting to convey the ways in which a sexual division of labor in all human social groups is bound up with extremely complex forms of interdependence, politics, and hierarchy" (1980:414).

At the very end of her 1980 article Shelly suggested that the same kind of political and economic analysis she and I had proposed for understanding the gender conceptions of foragers and hunter-horticulturalists should be used to study contemporary gender stereotypes:

I cannot begin here to add to the fast-growing literature on women's place in our contemporary social form. It seems relevant to my argument, however, to observe that one way gender is bound up with modern capitalist social life is that a central quality we believe that women lack, aggression, figures overwhelmingly in popular accounts of how it is that some men fail and some succeed. (1980:416)

Shelly's untimely death prevented her from carrying out the sustained analysis of Western capitalism that she hoped would help her to understand why Westerners tended to imagine the gender difference as one between emotional, self-sacrificing women and aggressive, competitive men. She was particularly interested in this question, given that our joint teaching about "Sex-Roles in Cross-Cultural Perspective" had convinced us that in many, if not most, of the world's societies women are cast as selfish and cunning, in contrast to self-sacrificing and morally sensitive men. It is usually men, not women, who are imagined to put the interests of others, and of society as a whole, over their own desires for food, sex, and self-advancement (Strathern 1981). Following the analytical strategy she had laid out in our 1981 article, in which she argued that "gender conceptions are to be understood as functioning aspects of a cultural system through which actors manipulate, interpret, legitimize, and reproduce the patterns of cooperation and conflict that order their social world" (1981:311), Shelly wanted to explore capitalism as a cultural system that shaped the goals and experiences of modern men and women. She hoped to understand not only Western gender stereotypes but also why feminist anthropologists kept reproducing Western stereotypes about loving female homes and competitive male markets despite our knowledge, as anthropologists, that Western families are not universal and despite our experiences, as women living within capitalism, that homes can be sites of struggle and competition while workplaces can encourage cooperation and caring.

NOTES

I would like to thank Bill Maurer and Alejandro Lugo for their helpful comments and suggestions for revising the earlier version of this essay.

1. This quotation is from notes I took when Shelly Rosaldo lectured on May 9, 1979.

2. Although Shelly may have gotten this point from reading Foucault (1978), she did not mention Foucault when lecturing about evolutionary theories in the nineteenth century. Foucault's work was discussed later in the course, primarily in the lectures.

REFERENCES

Bachofen, J. J.
1973 *Myth, Religion, and Mother Right.* Bollingen Series, 84. Princeton: Princeton University Press.
Bell, Susan Groag, and Karen Offen, eds.
1983 *Women, the Family, and Freedom: The Debate in the Documents.* Stanford: Stanford University Press.
Collier, Jane F., and Michelle Z. Rosaldo
1981 "Politics and Gender in 'Simple' Societies." In *Sexual Meanings,* ed. Sherry Ortner and Harriet Whitehead, 275–329. New York: Cambridge University Press.
Collier, Jane F., Michelle Z. Rosaldo and Sylvia J. Yanagisako
1982 "Is There a Family? New Anthropological Views." In *Rethinking the Family: Some Feminist Questions,* ed. Barrie Thorne with Marilyn Yalom, 25–39. New York: Longman.
Evans-Pritchard, E. E.
1940 *The Nuer.* Oxford: Clarendon Press.
1951 *Kinship and Marriage among the Nuer.* Oxford: Clarendon Press.
1965 "The Position of Women in Primitive Societies and in Our Own." *The Position of Women in Primitive Societies and Other Essays in Social Anthropology,* 37–58. London: Faber and Faber.
Foucault, Michel
1978 *The History of Sexuality,* vol. 1: *An Introduction.* New York: Random House.
Fox, Robin
1967 *Kinship and Marriage.* Baltimore: Penguin Books.
Geertz, Clifford
1973 "Thick Description: Toward an Interpretive Theory of Culture." *The Interpretation of Cultures,* 3–30. New York: Basic Books.
Harris, Olivia, and Kate Young
1981 "Engendered Structures: Some Problems in the Analysis of Reproduction." In *The Anthropology of Pre-Capitalist Societies,* ed. Joel S. Kahn and Josep R. Llobera, 109–47. London: Macmillan.
Lewis, Diane K.
1977 "A Response to Inequality: Black Women, Racism, and Sexism." *SIGNS: Journal of Women in Culture and Society* 3 (2): 339–61.

Malinowski, Bronislaw
  1913 *The Family among the Australian Aborigines.* London: University of London Press.
Mead, Margaret
  1949 *Male and Female.* New York: William Morrow.
Rapp, Rayna R.
  1978 "Family and Class in Contemporary America: Notes toward an Understanding of Ideology." *Science and Society* 42 (3): 278–300.
Reiter, Rayna Rapp, ed.
  1975 *Toward an Anthropology of Women.* New York: Monthly Review Press.
Rosaldo, Michelle Z.
  1974 "Woman, Culture, and Society: A Theoretical Overview." In *Woman, Culture, and Society,* ed. Michelle Z. Rosaldo and Louise Lamphere, 17–42. Stanford: Stanford University Press.
  1980 "The Use and Abuse of Anthropology: Reflections on Feminism and Cross-Cultural Understanding." *SIGNS: Journal of Women in Culture and Society* 5 (3): 389–417.
Rosaldo, Michelle Z., and Jane Atkinson
  1975 "Man the Hunter and Woman." In *Interpretation of Symbolism,* ed. R. Willis, 43–75. London: Malaby Press.
Rubin, Gayle
  1975 "The Traffic in Women: Notes on the 'Political Economy' of Sex." In *Toward an Anthropology of Women,* ed. Rayna Reiter, 157–210. New York: Monthly Review Press.
Ruskin, John
  1907 "Of Queens' Gardens." *Sesame and Lilies,* 48–79. London: J. M. Dent.
Slocum, Sally
  1975 "Woman the Gatherer: Male Bias in Anthropology." In *Toward an Anthropology of Women,* ed. Rayna Reiter, 36–50. New York: Monthly Review Press.
Spencer, Herbert
  1893 *The Principles of Sociology,* vol. 1. New York: D. Appleton.
Strathern, Marilyn
  1981 "Self-Interest and the Social Good: Some Implications of Hagen Gender Imagery." In *Sexual Meanings,* ed. Sherry Ortner and Harriet Whitehead, 166–91. New York: Cambridge University Press.
Zborowski, Mary, and Elizabeth Herzog
  1955 *Life Is with People.* New York: International Universities Press.
Zihlman, Adrienne
  1976 "Women in Evolution, Part I: Innovation and Selection in Human Origins." *SIGNS: Journal of Women in Culture and Society* 1 (3): 585–608.
  1978 "Women in Evolution, Part II: Subsistence and Social Organization among Early Hominids." *SIGNS: Journal of Women in Culture and Society* 4 (1): 4–20.

A (Short) Cultural History of Mexican Machos and Hombres

Matthew C. Gutmann

> Haven't you also lost something
> for following your father?
> —Rodolfo Usigli, *El gesticulador*

Machos and Hombres

"Are any of you married?" I asked the *muchachos.*

"No, *todos solteritos,* all young and single," said Felipe.

"That bozo's got two little squirts. He's the *macho mexicano,*" said Rodrigo, pointing to Celso, the father of two children who lived with their mother in another city.

"What does that mean?" I inquired.

"Macho? That you've got kids all over," said Esteban.

"That your ideology is very closed," said Pancho. "The ideology of the *macho mexicano* is very closed. He doesn't think about what might happen later, but mainly focuses on the present, on satisfaction, on pleasure, on desire. But now that's disappearing a little."

"You're not machos?" I asked.

"No, *somos hombres,* we're men."[1]

My discussions with these young men, the *muchachos,* took place in May 1993, in the working-class neighborhood of Santo Domingo, on the south side of Mexico City, where I was living and conducting ethnographic fieldwork on changing male identities.[2] Similar to other poor areas of the Mexican capital, men and women of all ages in Colonia Santo Domingo have experienced dramatic transformations in recent years in terms of what it means to be men and women, including with regard to parenting, participation in political movements, paid work, education, sexuality, and more.

At the same time, because the *colonia* was founded by land invasion and has been largely self-built and because women have played a prominent role in this history, residents of Santo Domingo have also been challenging gender relations inherited from the past even more than in many other parts of Mexico.

With so many men working outside Santo Domingo during the day, from its inception much of the daytime responsibility to construct and defend the *colonia* fell largely upon women. They were the ones in charge of communications during the early days in the 1970s, when private and police-connected goons swept through the community trying to extort or evict less than vigilant squatters. With wooden poles, clods of dirt, rocks, and shovels the women physically had to guard their new properties and those of neighbors. Such exploits on the part of many women became emblematic of the invasion, not simply because of the courage and determination they evinced but because women throughout the area were coming to be widely regarded as key decision makers and leaders.

This essay takes as its point of departure Michelle Rosaldo's insight that, with regard to the study of women, "what is needed . . . is not so much data as questions" (1980:390). Certainly, the most conscientious of data-gathering ethnographers, Rosaldo nonetheless was never satisfied with merely expanding anthropology's storehouse of empirical knowledge. In a similar fashion, in the study of masculinities, while we have much to learn about men *as men,* it is even more true that we need new ways of studying and interpreting and not simply gathering more raw information. Most specifically, I wish to apply Michelle Rosaldo's emphasis on the need for new approaches to feminist theory and method to an examination of how men in Mexico have recently been characterized by different anthropologists and other scholars.

Why, for example, have so many writers seemed intent on discovering a ubiquitous, virulent, and "typically Mexican" machismo among men in that country? In this chapter I trace the roots of such stereotyping in part to earlier national character studies in anthropology as well as to the imposition by the media and by other social scientists in the United States of totalizing cultural histories, including with respect to gender, on countries like Mexico.

In many respects Rosaldo anticipated the critical feminist analysis represented by what Nancy Fraser calls the "shift from 'differences among women' to 'multiple intersecting differences'" (1997:180). It was precisely such differences that Michelle Rosaldo saw as elemental to the creative activities of men and women to develop new social formations and relations (1980:416). Only by employing a critical feminist analysis and exploring multiple intersecting differences can we adequately record and understand emerging and diverging gender politics in societies such as Mexico's today. For example, although it is common to hear women and men in Colonia Santo Domingo say that while there used to be a lot of macho men, many will add that they are not as prevalent today. Some older men like to divide the world of males into machos and *mandilones* (meaning female-dominated men), where the term *macho* connotes a man who is responsible in providing financially and otherwise for his family. For older men to be macho more often means to be *un hombre de honor,* "an honorable man."[3]

It is far more common for younger married men in Colonia Santo Domingo to define themselves as belonging to a third category, the "non-macho" group. "*Ni macho, ni mandilón,*" (neither macho nor *mandilón*) is how many men describe themselves.[4] Others may define a friend as "your typical *macho mexicano,*" but the same man will often reject the label, describing all the things he does to help his wife around the home or pointing out that he does not beat his wife (one of the few generally agreed on attributes of machos). What is most significant is not simply how the terms *macho, machismo,* and *machista* are variously defined—there is little consensus on their meanings—but, more, that today the terms are so widely regarded by working-class men in Colonia Santo Domingo, Mexico City, as pejorative and not worthy of emulation. The same could be noted with regard to the semantic opposite of *el macho mexicano,* that is, *la mujer abnegada,* "the self-sacrificing woman." These twin, reified images of gender identity are frequently and explicitly contrasted in popular discourses in and about Mexico.

For both material and ideological reasons *los hombres* (men) and *los machos* are indeed valid anthropological categories in Mexico today. Often, though not always, these terms are popularly conceived of in contradistinction to *las mujeres* (women) and *las mujeres abnegadas.* Yet in line with Behar's call to "go beyond first world representations of third world women as passive, subservient, and lacking in creativity" (1993:272), we should recognize that there is always both acquiescence and dissension with regard to these concepts and that no category is popularly regarded—or should be seen—as homogeneous. Nor is the following discussion based on a structuralist binary opposition, in this case that of man/woman or *macho/abnegada.* "Manliness" and "womanliness" are not original, natural, or embalmed states of being; they are gender categories whose precise meanings constantly shift, transform into each other, and ultimately make themselves into whole new entities.

For younger men like the *muchachos,* then, the present period is largely distinguished by its liminal character with respect to male gender identities: as neither-macho-nor-*mandilón* these men are precisely betwixt and between marked cultural positions. This is a clear illustration that, like other cultural identities, notions of masculinity and femininity must be historically understood in relation to other divergent cultural trajectories such as those involving class, ethnicity, and generation.

Anthropologists and the Creation of Mexican Machismo

Because of his crispness, scope, and vigor in presentation, Oscar Lewis (1951, 1959, 1961) is a central anthropological ancestor for the contemporary study of Mexican machismo. Although he contradicts himself on occasion, his descriptions in *The Children of Sánchez* (1961) and other books are still a constant point of reference for all contemporary students of the changes and continuities of life between and among women and men in Mexico. His theoretical formulations are also still delightfully provoking, if unfortunately too often insufficiently developed, including with regard to the concept of machismo.

In trying to understand Mexican men, however, some scholars have utilized details from Oscar Lewis's ethnographic studies to promote sensationalist generalities that go far beyond anything Lewis himself wrote. For instance, in David Gilmore's (1990) widely read survey of the Ubiquitous (if not Universal) Male in the world, machismo is discussed as an extreme form of manly images and codes. Modern urban Mexican men are useful to Gilmore mainly as exaggerated archetypes; with other Latin men they constitute the negative pole on a continuum—from machismo to androgyny—of male cultural identities around the world. Mexican machos are thus employed as a foil against which other men less concerned with virility are compared. Gilmore cites Lewis in making his ethnographic points about Mexican men:

In urban Latin America, for example, as described by Oscar Lewis (1961:38), a man must prove his manhood every day by standing up to challenges and insults, even though he goes to his death "smiling." As well as being tough and brave, ready to defend his family's honor at the drop of a hat, the urban Mexican . . . must also perform adequately in sex and father many children. (1990:16)

To be sure, such a characterization of "the urban Mexican [male]" does find echoes in popular culture—for instance, in the line from the hit song of 1948 "Traigo mi 45" (I'm Carrying My 45): "¿Quién dijo miedo, muchachos, si para morir nacimos?" (Who's talking scared, boys, if we were born to die?).[5] But, even if Lewis's ethnographic descriptions, compiled in the 1950s, were just as valid decades later, Lewis did not usually generalize in this fashion about the lives of Jesús Sánchez and his children. His anthropology was often artfully composed, and some of his theories were naive, but Lewis generally tried to keep "mere" romance and fancy out of his ethnographic descriptions.[6]

Before proceeding further, three general points bear mentioning here. First, *macho* (in its modern sense) and *machismo* (in any sense) have remarkably short word histories. Indeed, tracing the historical permutations and modulations of these words is critical to understanding the ongoing discrepancies that exist popularly and in the social sciences regarding their meanings. Carlos Monsiváis (1981, 1992) in particular has linked the emergence of the ethos of machismo especially to the Golden Age of Mexican cinema in the 1940s and 1950s.

Second, *machismo* as discussed here is not reducible to a coherent set of sexist ideas. It is not simply male chauvinism. As Roger Lancaster stresses in his astute and pioneering study of Nicaragua, "machismo is resilient because it constitutes not simply a form of 'consciousness,' not 'ideology' in the classical understanding of the concept, but a field of productive relations" (1992:19).[7] Determining the systemic character of machismo is predicated on following the historical tracks of the term. As these lead in various directions in different times and circumstances in Mexico and Nicaragua, for instance, the structural and material content of *machismo* must be kept in mind.

Finally, I would point to another central, recurring focal point in many if not most meanings of *machismo:* bodily functions. These refer to beatings, sexual episodes, consumption of alcohol, defiance of death, and the not so simple problem of defining the categories of "men" and "women." Regardless of how confusing gender identities may seem, they usually share relations of mutual dependence with these somatic realms.

As for some of the characteristics frequently cited as manifesting machismo on the part of men—wife beating, alcoholism, infidelity, gambling, abandonment of children, and bullying behavior in general—many men, and more than a few women, exhibit certain of these qualities and not others, at certain times and not others. There are historic, systemic, and bodily facets of machismo. Figuring out how exactly the pieces fit together is the problem.

Cowboys and Racism

In Mexican newspapers, academic literature, and dictionary entries the terms *macho* and *machismo* have been used in contradictory ways. The definitions employed or implied in such official circles reveal not only a diversity of views regarding the substance of the terms but also widely disparate conjectures about the origins of the words and their meanings. Emphasizing sexuality, in a frequently quoted essay, Stevens calls machismo "the cult of virility," adding that "the chief characteristics of this cult are exaggerated aggressiveness and intransigence in male-to-male interpersonal relationships and arrogance and sexual aggression in male-to-female relationships" (1973:90). Greenberg captures some of the ambivalence of machismo when he describes an episode in which Fortino, the protagonist of his study, "was being very macho, in a nonconfrontational, almost womanly manner" (1989:227). *Macho* may thus be identified with nonaggressive ("womanly") behavior.[8] Many anthropologists and psychologists writing about machismo utilize characterizations like *manly, unmanly,* and *manliness* without defining them. They seem to assume, incorrectly in my estimation, that all their readers share a common definition and understanding of such qualities.[9]

In a brilliant essay published in English in 1971 Américo Paredes provides several clues about the word history of *machismo* and in the process draws clear connections between the advent of machismo and nationalism, racism, and international relations. Paredes finds that prior to the 1930s and 1940s in Mexican folklore—a good indication today of popular speech at the time—the terms *macho* and *machismo* do not appear. The word *macho* existed but almost as an obscenity, similar to later connotations of *machismo.* Other words, some also semantically related to men, were far more common at the time of the Mexican Revolution: *hombrismo, hombría, muy hombre, hombre de verdad* (all relating to *hombre,* man), and *valentía, muy valiente,* etc. (relating to valor, courage).[10] Despite the fact that during the Mexican Revolution the phrase *muy hombre* was used to describe courageous women as well as men, the special association of such a quality with men then and now indicates certain points in common regardless of whether the words *macho* and *machismo* were employed. Making a connection between courage and men during times of war— in which men are the main, though assuredly not the only, combatants—is nevertheless not the same thing as noting the full-blown "machismo syndrome," as it is sometimes called. To oversimplify, if courage was valued during the Revolution, this was true for both men and women, though the terms used to refer to courage carried a heavy male accent. Beginning especially in the 1940s, the male accent itself came to prominence as a national(ist) symbol. For better or worse Mexico came to mean machismo and machismo to mean Mexico, providing an illustration of what Mary Louise Pratt shows to be the "androcentrism of the modern national imaginings" in Latin America (1990:50).[11]

The consolidation of the nation-state and party machinery throughout the Mexican Republic and the development of the country's modern national cultural identity took place on a grand scale during the presidencies of Lázaro Cárdenas and Manuel Avila Camacho (1934–46). After the turbulent years of the Revolution and the 1920s, and following six years of national unification under the populist presidency of Lázaro Cárdenas, the national election campaign of 1940 opened an era of unparalleled industrial growth and demagogic rule in Mexico. Coincidentally, one of the campaign slogans of the ultimately successful presidential candidate Avila Camacho was: "Ca . . . MACHO!" As Paredes points out, the president was not responsible for the use of the term *macho,* but "we must remember that names lend reality to things" (1971:23).

Searching for *a* national identity is a very modern project in Mexico, as elsewhere. Often remembered for his blunt diagnosis of the country's "inferiority complex," Samuel Ramos (1962) is also frequently cited as the original critic of Mexican machismo. Once again, however, Ramos never used the terms *macho* or *machismo.* Yet the connections between *lo mexicano* and manliness (however defined) were striking in Ramos. He centered his account of the nation's inferiority around the "well-known Mexican type, the *pelado,"* whose conduct was one of "virile protest" (1962:9). The *pelado* is a male proletarian, vulgar and poorly educated, Ramos reports, who himself associates "his concept of virility with that of nationality, creating thereby the illusion that personal valor is the Mexican's particular characteristic" (63). The particular association by Ramos of negative male qualities with the urban working class has been a prominent theme in writings on "Latin American masculinity" and machismo ever since his study was published in 1934.

Notions of machismo in Mexico are connected by many scholars to discussions of social class. Stevens calls the popular acceptance of a stereotyped Latin American macho "ubiquitous in every social class" (1973:94), a summation which has led some scholars whose geographical interests lie outside the region to utilize the concept of machismo in their own studies and made *machos* and *machismo* standard terms in the social sciences for labeling a host of negative male characteristics in cultures around the world.[12] In contrast, Paredes links *machismo* especially to Mexico's middle classes, while Limón (1994), writing about working-class Chicanos in south Texas, effectively critiques the class prejudices of Ramos regarding machos *pelados*.[13]

The word history of *machismo* is but a piece of the larger puzzle regarding the outlooks and practices codified in tautological fashion as instances of machismo. For Paredes the peculiar history of U.S.-Mexican relations has produced a marked antipathy on the part of Mexicans for their northern neighbors. The image of the frontier and the (Wild) West has in turn played a special role in this tempestuous relationship, with the annexation of two-fifths of the Mexican nation to the United States in 1848, and repeated U.S. economic and military incursions into Mexico since then, putting the lie to proclamations of respect for national sovereignty.

Trade between the two countries initially included the export of the Mexican *vaquero*-cowboy to the United States, Paredes reminds us. In the early nineteenth century the frontiersmen of Texas and further west were running point for the expanding Jacksonian empire, and their combination of individualism and sacrifice for the higher national good came to embody the machismo ethos. Together with the pistol, the supreme macho symbol, such an ethos came to play a similar role in the consolidation of the Mexican nation, which is one reason why "*machismo* betrays a certain element of nostalgia; it is cultivated by those who feel they have been born too late" (1971:37).

On the other side of the border, in the United States, I would argue that the term *machismo* has a rather explicitly racist history; from its first appearance in print in English (Griffith 1948:50) *machismo* has been associated with negative stereotypes of Mexicans, Mexican-Americans, and Latin American men.[14] Contemporary popular usage of the term *machismo* in the United States often serves to rank men according to their supposedly inherent national and racial characters, as in, "My boyfriend may not be perfect, but at least he's no Mexican macho." Such analysis utilizes nonsexist pretensions to make denigrating generalizations about fictitious Mexican male culture traits.

Jorge Negrete and *Lo Mexicano*

The consolidation of the Mexican nation, ideologically and materially, was fostered early on not only in the gun battles on the wild frontier, not only in the voting rituals of presidential politics, but also in the imagining and inventing of *lo mexicano, mexicanidad,* in the national cinema. And of all the movie stars of this era one stood out as "a macho among machos." Ever the handsome and pistol-packing *charro*, singing cowboy, with his melodious and eminently male tenor, Jorge Negrete came to epitomize the swaggering Mexican nation, singing:

I am a Mexican, and this wild land is mine.
On the word of a macho, there's no land lovelier
and wilder of its kind.
I am a Mexican, and of this I am proud.
I was born scorning life and death,
And while I have bragged, I have never been cowed.[15]

In the rural cantinas, the manly temples of the Golden Age of Mexican Cinema, the macho mood was forged. Mexico appeared on screen as a single entity, however internally incongruent, while within the nation the figures of Mexican Man and Mexican Woman loomed large. The former,

> untamed, generous, cruel, womanizing, romantic, obscene, at one with family and friends, subjugated and restless . . . [the latter] obedient, seductive, resigned, obliging, devoted to her own and slave to her husband, to her lover, to her children, and to her essential failure. (Monsiváis 1992:18)

The distinctions between being a macho and being a man were starting to come into clearer focus in the Mexican cinema of the 1940s:

> To be macho is now part of the scenery. To be macho is an attitude. There are gestures, movements. It is the belief that genital potency holds the key

to the universe, all that. It goes from the notion of danger to the notion of bragging; that's the difference between macho and man [*hombre*]. As the song says, "If you've got to kill me tomorrow, why don't you get it over with now." That is being very manly [*ser muy hombre*]. "I have four wives." That is being very macho [*ser muy macho*]. (Carlos Monsiváis)[16]

Then, at the end of the 1940s, Mexican machismo underwent a most refined dissection by Octavio Paz. Despite Paz's wish to speak only to a small group, "made up of those who are conscious of themselves, for one reason or another, as Mexicans" (1961:11), this work more than any other has come to represent the official view of essential Mexican attributes, like machismo, loneliness, and mother worship. When Paz writes, "The Mexican is always remote, from the world and from other people. And also from himself," he should not be taken literally but *literarily* (29). It is a beautifully written book, and part of the reason for its elegance may be that Paz was creating as much as he was reflecting on qualities of *mexicanidad.* As he put it in his "Return to the Labyrinth of Solitude," "The book is part of the attempt of literally marginal countries to regain consciousness: to become subjects again" (1985:330).

Paz writes with regard to men and women in Mexico, "In a world made in man's image, woman is only a reflection of masculine will and desire" (1961:35). In Mexico "woman is always vulnerable. Her social situation—as a repository of honor, in the Spanish sense—and the misfortune of her 'open' anatomy expose her to all kinds of dangers" (38). Biology as destiny? But there is nothing inherently passive, or private, about vaginas in Mexico or anywhere else. Continuing with Paz, just as "the essential attribute of the *macho*"—or what the macho seeks to display anyway—is power, so too with "the Mexican people." Thus, *mexicanidad,* Paz tells us, is concentrated in the macho forms of "caciques, feudal lords, hacienda owners, politicians, generals, captains of industry" (82).

Many Mexican men are curious about what it means to be a Mexican and what it means to be a man. One is not born knowing these things; nor are they truly discovered. They are learned and relearned. For some this involves the quest for one's patrimony. "Pedro Páramo is my father too," declares one of Mexico's bastard sons (Rulfo 1959:3). Even if he is an infamous brute, a father is a father. For the Mexican macho and for the nation it is better to have one than to be fatherless.

In Paz and much of the literature of cultural nationalism in Mexico in recent decades, the problem of national identity was thus presented primarily as a problem of *male* identity, and it was male authors who debated its defects and psychoanalyzed the nation. In national allegories, women became the territory over which the quest for (male) national identity passed. (Franco 1989:131)

Mandilones and Dominating Women

In Colonia Santo Domingo, in addition to Paz, another authoritative source of information about machismo and national identity that people use in the stories they tell about themselves is Oscar Lewis—or at least what people have heard about his anthropological writings (Lewis is "remembered" far more than he is read).

In the social sciences Lewis continues to be the most cited reference with regard to conclusions about Mexican masculinity. In fact, three particular sentences from his book *Children of Sánchez* (1961) are employed with astonishing frequency in anthropological texts to represent all Mexican males past, present, and future:

In a fight I would never give up or say, "Enough," even though the other was killing me. I would try to go to my death smiling. That is what we mean by being "macho," by being manly. (38)

This specific passage is cited, for example, by Marshall in his discussion of machismo in Micronesia (1979:89); by Madsen and Madsen in an essay on alcohol consumption in Mexico (1969:712); and, as quoted here, by Gilmore in his comparative survey of the images of masculinity (1990:16). A few sentences on page 38 of *Children of Sánchez* have thus come to shoulder an immense responsibility in anthropology: to provide a quotable sound bite defining Mexican masculinity/machismo.

Is this quotation really such a good and accurate concentration of Mexican male identity? If it were, as if by ethnographic decree, every male soul who finds himself south of the shallows of the Rio Grande and north of the highlands of Guatemala must at least try to go to his death smiling if he wishes to retain his Mexican male credentials. I doubt very much if Lewis's intention was to summarize the life experiences and desires of all Mexican men in this short passage. Perhaps most revealing of all, the sentences in question are not even Lewis's own but are actually part of a monologue by Manuel Sánchez, one of the Sánchez children. Manuel is nonetheless the man whose ideologically charged comments to Lewis on one particular day in the mid-1950s have frequently come to speak for all Mexican men since that time.[17] We anthropologists may well ask where this need to see pervasive machismo comes from and why so many have used Lewis to prove their own preconceptions and prejudices.

In Colonia Santo Domingo in Mexico City there are significant differences in the uses and meanings of the terms *macho* and *machismo.* These reflect, and often concentrate, contrasting urban and rural experiences, generational differences, class stratification, stages within individuals' lives, and, in the age of television satellites, the impact on people throughout Mexico of what others around the world say about them and their national peculiarities.

Returning to the term *mandilón,* stronger than *henpecked* but not nearly as vulgar as *pussy-whipped* in English, we see by its common daily use that it is an expression produced by a machista system and that it is at the same time a response to machismo.[18] Angela and I were walking through the *sobre ruedas* open-air markets one day in October 1992, shortly after we first met, and she remarked that maybe my wife, Michelle, should buy a *mandil,* an apron, "in Mateo's size," so I could be a proper *mandilón.* Angela added that her son Noé, whom I had not yet met, was a *mandilón.* I asked her why, and she responded by saying that Noé washed dishes, cooked, and took care of his daughter. I wanted to know how Noé had come to do these things. "*No lo crié para ser macho mexicano*" (I didn't raise him to be a *macho mexicano*), came the answer. I wondered aloud if Noé would accept this appellation. Angela insisted that he would.

In early November I asked Noé about being a *mandilón.* "*No soy mandilón,*" corrected Noé; "I'm not a *mandilón.* It doesn't bother me at all to help my wife. I share everything with her." But Noé rejected the title of *mandilón,* which he defined as, "he who is dominated by women."

Noé's younger sister Norma came by our apartment in January because her husband, Miguel, had not come home, and I was the last person to have seen him. After a *futbol* playoff Miguel and I had gone over to the coach's house for tacos, beans, and beer. I had left hours earlier, but by 8 P.M. Mie still had not returned, and Norma was worried. Yet she could not go looking for him herself, she said, because that might make him look like a *mandilón* in front of the other young men: a wife coming to fetch her (presumably) drunk husband.

Not labeling a man a *mandilón* is not merely a matter of helping him save face, however, because for many women as well as men it carries negative connotations. That is, being a *mandilón* is seen as a positive opposite of macho to some like Angela, but to others it is but an inverse form of the macho's empty boasting. In both cases the definitions of *mandilón* reflect awareness of power differences between men and women, that is, a contradictory consciousness, to engage Gramsci's formulation (1929–35:333), with respect to male identities.

"I don't want a man who's either macho or *mandilón*," one young woman told me.

"Why not *mandilón?*" I asked.

"Because who wants someone who can't stick up for himself, who's used to getting bossed around and likes it that way." In other words, life is hard enough as it is, and a young woman can ill afford depending on a *mandilón* for her husband. Instead, one needs a partner who can make things happen and not just wait for orders from others, his wife added.

Among men in their twenties and thirties in Colonia Santo Domingo it was rare to hear anyone claim the title of *macho* for himself. "Why, I wash dishes and cook," some would protest when called macho by a friend. Machos do neither of these things, nor do they spend a lot of time with their children, many felt. Even more than these activities, however, the most common reason for *not* accepting the name of *macho* was, "I don't beat my wife." A grandfather of sixty-seven explained to me that he was no macho and that his own father before him had not been either. "Why, he never drank a beer in front of the kids," my friend told me, "and he never beat his wife."

Today among the young in Mexico City the model of aggressive masculinity is no longer the pistol-packing *charro* cowboy of yore looking for a tranquil rancho where he can hang his sombrero. He has been replaced by the submachine gun–spraying Rambo launching assaults on the Vietnams or Afghanistans of the moment. No one would argue that Rambo is a product of Mexico, yet there and in his land of origin is he not known as the ultimate macho? Local symbols become globalized and then relocalized and reglobalized.

For some men today "the macho" is also a playful role they can perform on demand. I stifled my displeasure one evening when, at her three-year-old granddaughter's birthday party and in her capacity of patron saint of my research project, Angela took me by the hand and introduced me to several men whom she said were "genuine representatives of Mexican machismo." After being so presented to one young man, Angela demanded of him, "Where's your wife?" A sly smile crossed the man's face, "I sent her to the bathroom." His wife was seven months pregnant, the man added, so, like the good macho Angela accused him of being, he had to send her to the bathroom a lot. Often such jokes were followed by remarks that revealed an acute sensitivity to the cultural beliefs about Mexican men that many in Mexico think are held by North Americans. "That's really what you gringos believe about us, isn't it?" people would sometimes comment when I raised the image of Mexican men preferring to go their death smiling than lose face.

The ethnographic authority of anthropologists to expound on issues of supposed "national character traits" has a long history in Mexico and elsewhere, stemming back to World War II and the need at the time to place clear national labels on enemy and allied characters (see Fabian 1983). Not only is such a quest for national characteristics premised upon the notion that cultures are in some reasonable sense "whole" and sealed, but anthropology in particular has been instrumental in "discovering" common cultural beliefs and practices, thus linking nation-states to particular ideas and behaviors. Hence were born theories of cultural difference and national otherness. Of course, if this starting point of dividing the world into national others is found wanting—that is, if with Michelle Rosaldo we insist on asking the right questions and not simply gathering more documentation for evident truths—then the whole framework of Mexican male attributes collapses in a heap of national(ist) essentializing.[19]

In the dramas that people in *colonias populares* offer about their own and others' marriages, the parts played by self-designated machos are not all playful by any means. "We cheat on our wives because we're men," said one acquaintance. "We want to be macho." What does this mean, "we want to be macho," except that "to be macho" is an ideological stance that can only be sanctified by others—men and women—and by oneself? In my discussion with the *muchachos,* while one of them said that they were not machos but, rather, they were *hombres,* men, Celso insisted that, as men, by definition they were machos. He said that, if they needed to call themselves something, *mandilón* and *marica* (queer) were obviously inappropriate. So what else did this leave except *macho?*[20]

The description provided by Celso makes it appear that the youths rummage around in an identity grab bag, pulling out whatever they happen to seize upon, as long as it is culturally distinct. One minute these *muchachos* identify themselves as machos who enjoy bragging about controlling women and morally and physically weaker men. The next minute the same young men express bitterness at being the ones on the bottom.

Redefinitions

Delineating cultural identities and defining cultural categories, one's own and those of others, is not simply the pastime of ethnographers. Despite the fact that creating typologies of Mexican masculinity can result in parodies without living referents and overlooking for the moment the not unimportant issue of how men and women in Colonia Santo Domingo understand manliness and define what *ser hombre,* "to be a man," means, there is purpose to the social science quest for better ways to categorize men in Mexico.

So, while no one in Santo Domingo might explicitly divide the population of men this way, I think most would recognize the following four male gender groups: the macho, the *mandilón,* the neither-macho-nor-*mandilón,* and the broad category of men who have sex with other men. But the fact that few men or women do or would care to divide the male population in this manner reveals more than simply a lack of familiarity with the methods of Weberian ideal typologizing. Masculinity, like other cultural identities, is not confined so neatly in boxlike categories like "macho" or "mandilón." Identities only make sense in relation to other identities, and they are never firmly established for individuals or groups. Further, consensus will rarely be found about whether a particular man deserves a label such as neither-macho-nor-*mandilón.* He will likely think of himself as a man in a variety of ways, none of which necessarily coincides with the views of his family and friends.

In terms of the group of men who have sex with other men, this includes among others the male prostitute *putos,* who have sex for money with other men and always play the "active role," and the *homosexuales* (*maricas, maricones,* and so on), who are marked not only by their preference for male sex partners but more generally by the low cultural esteem in which they are held by many in society. Men who have sex with other men are by some people's definition outside the bounds of masculinity altogether and would not even constitute a separate male gender type.

Yet, while this taxonomy may indicate some important lines of demarcation, like all ideal typologizing it hopelessly obscures salient differences that are so numerous that they can hardly be considered exceptions. And this is undoubtedly all the more true during liminal moments historically in which cultural categories lack clearly circumscribed boundaries. No man today in Santo Domingo neatly fits into any of the four categories, either at specific moments or throughout the course of his life. Further, definitions such as these resist other relevant but complicating factors such as class, ethnicity, and historical epoch. "*El mexicano es muy hablador; habla mucho y no cumple*" (The Mexican man is a big talker; he talks a lot but doesn't come through), one of the *muchachos* told me at the end of our discussion. So who represents the more archetypal *macho mexicano:* the man who wants many (male) offspring and later abandons them or the man who wants few, works hard to earn money for them, and calls these his manly duties?

To unravel these stereotyped social roles we must return to the point raised by Lancaster (1992): machismo, in whatever guise, is not simply a matter of ideology.[21] Machismo in Colonia Santo Domingo has been challenged ideologically, especially by grassroots feminism and more indirectly by the mainly middle-class feminist and gay rights movements (see Massolo 1992; Stephen 1997). But it has also faced real if usually ambiguous challenge in the forms of the strains of migration, falling birthrates, exposure to alternative cultures on TV, and so on. These economic and sociocultural changes have not automatically led to corresponding shifts in male domination, in the home, the workplace, or society at large. But many men's authority has been undermined in material, if limited, ways, and this changing position for men as husbands and fathers, breadwinners and masters, has in turn had real consequences for machismo in Santo Domingo.

To be a macho for most people in Colonia Santo Domingo involves qualities of personal belligerence, especially though not only as directed toward women, and in this sense it is very tied to appearances and style. In substance this veneer of arrogance and hostility derives on the part of some men from feelings of superiority—and repeated and regular actions to back up these sentiments. At the same time, in Santo Domingo some men may seek to hide deep fears of physical inadequacy and losing male prerogative behind the guise of the macho. Women in particular talk of men who match the second description, referring to them in terms of disdain, ridicule, and even pity.

Mexican Machismo: The Use and Abuse of Anthropology

The words *macho* and *machismo* have become a form of calumny, shorthand terms in social science and journalistic writing for labeling a host of negative male characteristics in cultures around the world. A researcher at the Center for Gender Studies in Moscow told a reporter in 1994: "Before the view of Russian men were as creatures without willpower who drink too much. Now they have the ability to make money, they want everything in this life. They have that macho feeling" (qtd. in Stanley 1994:7). This is illuminating: men who drink too much are not called macho, yet those who have money more easily acquire "that macho feeling." In earlier examples cited here male sexual conquest and procreation are central themes, as are bragging and defiance of death.

And the writings of Oscar Lewis continue to be cited by anthropologists as the empirical source for more recent analysis of Mexican masculinity. The use of Lewis to prove alleged "national" traits like machismo seems particularly abusive because, despite the fact that Lewis was writing at the high tide of national character studies in anthropology, in contrast to the homogenizing portraits created by other ethnographers, Lewis consistently emphasized the diversity of cultural life along the lines of class, ethnicity, and age, in Mexico as in all countries where he conducted his research. Yet, in spite of these efforts, to this day, one way or another, the prevalent assumption in anthropology and more popularly continues to be that we all know what *machismo* means and what machos do and that the task of social scientists after Oscar Lewis is principally to find cultures in which machos flourish as much as they supposedly do in Mexico.

An equation of machismo with Mexican culture as a whole has occurred well beyond the confines of mere social science, of course; it has also been common in the stories Mexicans tell about themselves, both in daily discussions among Mexicans as well as in the grand proclamations of the scholarly elite. Stereotypes about machismo are critical ingredients in the symbolic capital operated by ordinary Mexicans. Even if verbally denigrated by many, machismo is widely regarded in Mexico as constituting part of the national patrimony in the same way as the country's oil deposits are a source of national if not necessarily individual self-identity. In this manner machismo has become part of the more general political economy of cultural values in Mexico.

Authoritative discussions of machismo in Mexico, or what later came to be known as machismo in some form (Ramos 1962; Paz 1961), have all made connections between the macho who "represents the masculine pole of life" (Paz 1961:81) and the broader social and political world of twentieth century Mexico.[22] Just as Lafaye (1976) has shown with regard to the Virgen de Guadalupe, so too with Mexican masculinity: it has not always represented the same kind of national symbol but, rather, has been used for different purposes at various times to emphasize particular cultural nationalist qualities by a vast array of social forces.[23]

In Colonia Santo Domingo, as elsewhere in the republic, the fate of machismo as an archetype of masculinity has always been closely tied to Mexican cultural nationalism. My good friend César commented to me one day about drinking in his youth: "More than anything we consumed tequila. We liked it, maybe because we felt more like Mexicans, more like *lugareños* [equivalent to *homeboys*]."

For better or for worse Ramos and Paz gave tequila-swilling machismo pride of place in the panoply of national character traits. Through their efforts and those of journalists and social scientists on both sides of the Rio Bravo / Grande, the macho became "the Mexican." This is ironic, for it represents the product of a cultural nationalist invention: you note something (machismo) as existing and in the process help foster its very existence. Mexican machismo as national artifact was in this sense partially declared into being.

And from the beginning the portrayal of machismo (or its *pelado* forerunner) has been uniquely linked to the poor, unsophisticated, uncosmopolitan, and un–North American. From the 1920s on in Mexico the bourgeoisie and the middle classes were, in Monsiváis's words, "obstinate in seeing nationalism as the most fruitful for their progress and internal coherence" (1976:194). The macho-*pelado,* always eminently male, was either like Jorge Negrete, the homespun figure from Mexico's rural past, or he was the essential backwardness of the nation, rural and urban, which needed to be exposed and eradicated. On the other side of the class ledger nearly all union leaders and many leftist intellectuals in Mexico for much of this century have championed the cause of national progress by promoting the heroic figure of the proletarian male militant. In all versions Mexican masculinity has been at the heart of defining a Mexican nation, its past and its future.

Defining the words *macho* and *machismo* must not be done arbitrarily. Is macho to be considered brutish, gallant, or cowardly? These things change over time for various sectors of Mexican society, and we must not ignore the often elusive and mutually exclusive ways in which these catchwords are today employed in Mexico. And, needless to say, social scientists in the United States must not assume that they are privy to the sole legitimate understanding of the terms. Nor should we forget that masculinity, like the family, is not simply a precondition but is a product of men and women's cultural efforts. Michelle Rosaldo made this clear in writing that "to claim that family shapes women is, ultimately, to forget that families themselves are things that men and women actively create and that these vary with particulars of social context" (1980:416).

Like religiousness, individualism, modernity, and other convenient concepts, machismo is used and understood in many ways. And history in the form of nationalism, feminism, and socioeconomic conjunctures impinges directly on gender identities in Mexico, including on what *masculinity* and *machismo* mean and how they are variously regarded. We either accept the multiple and shifting meanings of *macho* and *machismo,* or we essentialize what were already reified generalizations about Mexican men in the first place. Like any identity, male identities in Mexico City do not reveal anything intrinsic about men there. Their sense and experience of being *hombres* and machos is but part of the reigning chaos of the lives of men in Colonia Santo Domingo at least as much as the imagined national coherence imposed from without.

NOTES

1. The word *hombre* may have special resonance for aficionados of Hollywood Westerns. Expressions like "He's a tough *hombre*" are regularly used to conjure up images of Mexican bandits for whom life means little, and sexual conquest is but part of daily life. Historically, there is more than a coincidental relationship between Mexican male identities and cowboys.

2. Fieldwork was conducted in 1992–93 with grants from Fulbright-Hays DDRA, Wenner-Gren, National Science Foundation, Institute for Intercultural Studies, UC MEXUS, and the Center for Latin American Studies and Department of Anthropology at University of California at Berkeley; and in 1993–95 under a grant from the National Institute of Mental Health. My gratitude to the Centro de Estudios Sociológicos and the Programa Interdisciplinario de Estudios de la Mujer, both at El Colegio de México, and to the Departamento de Antropología, Universidad Autónoma Metropolitana–Iztapalapa, for providing institutional support during fieldwork in Mexico City. Portions of this essay were presented at the 1994 Latin American Studies Association Congress; the University of California at Davis; and a 1994 colloquium on Oscar Lewis in Mexico City. My thanks to those who offered commentaries and to those who read earlier drafts of this essay, especially Stanley Brandes, Teresita de Barbieri, Mary Goldsmith, M. Patricia Fernández Kelly, Michael Herzfeld, Gwen Kirkpatrick, Louise Lamphere, Margarita Melville, Eduardo Nivón, Ben Orlove, Nancy Scheper-Hughes, and Carol Smith. I have also greatly benefited from discussions on machismo with Carlos Monsiváis and Roger Lancaster. Portions of this essay are excerpted with permission from my book *The Meanings of Macho: Being a Man in Mexico City* (1996).

3. Behar cites an incident several decades ago involving a woman who denounced her husband in front of municipal authorities in a village in San Luis Potosí using these words: "The fact is that he's no man. He's no man because he's not responsible for his family. He never treats his family well. He treats them worse than animals!" (1993:40).

4. *Mandilón* comes from *mandil* (apron) and translates literally as "aproner."

5. See Monsiváis 1981:108.

6. Although Lewis did include *machismo* on his list of over sixty possible traits illustrative of the "culture of poverty" (see Rigdon 1988:114–15), he seemed ambivalent about the efficacy of using the term, inserting and deleting it in his publications (see Gutmann 1994).

7. Machismo is not necessarily the same beast in every cultural context, however, as we will see.

8. For a psychological-anthropological analysis of machismo, see also Gilmore and Gilmore 1979. The role of the press and popular writings in the United States have not been incidental in popularizing the terms *macho* and *machismo,* for instance in national character studies and their progeny. For the earliest published references in English to *macho,* see Beals 1928:233; and Mailer 1959:19, 483–84.

9. Dictionaries are in conflict over the term, tracing the etymological roots of *macho* to Latin and Portuguese words for masculine and mule and tracing the cultural ancestry of *macho* to Andalusian soldiers of the Conquest or certain indigenous peoples of the Americas or Yankee gringo invaders in the early part of this century. On the etymology of *macho,* see Gómez de Silva 1988:427; and Moliner 1991:2:299–300. On diverse and contradictory aspects of the cultural history of *machismo,* see Mendoza 1962; Santamaría 1959:677; and Hodges 1986:114.

10. Even though the classic novel of the Mexican Revolution, *Los de abajo* (first published in 1915) at one point uses the expression *machito* (translated as simply "a man" in Azuela 1962:79), this does not constitute the widespread use of the word *macho* or even familiarity with the term in the sense of *machismo* or any of its derivatives.

11. See Bolton 1979, on machismo among Peruvian truckers for a recent study of these imaginings.

12. On the former Yugoslavia, see, for example, Simic 1969:100; 1983; on modern Muslin society, see Mernissi 1975:5; and on Micronesia, see Marshall 1979:90.

13. A review of recent literature regarding machismo and Chicanos is outside the scope of this essay, but, beyond Limón 1989 and 1994, interested readers may profitably consult Baca Zinn 1982; Almaguer 1991; and Mirandé 1997.

14. Representative examples of popular stereotyping of Mexican and Latin American men in the United States media are Reston 1967; and McDowell 1984.

15. *Yo soy mexicano, mi tierra es bravía.*
Palabra de macho, que no hay otra tierra más linda
y más brava que la tierra mía.
Yo soy mexicano, y orgullo lo tengo.
Nací despreciando la vida y la muerte,
Y si he hecho bravatas, también las sostengo.
(From the song *"Yo soy mexicano"*)

16. Interview, 20 February 1993.

17. Another U.S.-born writer, Ernest Hemingway, is perhaps more responsible for popularizing ideas about Latin heroics, also known as machismo, in the United

States; see the discussion of defiance in the face of death on the part of Hemingway's characters in Capellán 1985.

18. Another way to refer to a man-as-*mandilón*, is "*El es muy dejado*" (He's very put upon).

19. An illustration of the influence of the United States on macho self-perceptions among Mexicans was provided for me on July 5, 1993, when I participated in the Mexico City–based, nationally televised talk show "María Victoria Llamas." I was invited to speak to the theme "A lo macho" and asked to make two points: (1) machismo is not just a problem in Mexico; and (2) based on my research, it was clear that not all men in Mexico were machos. I was informed that this would sound especially convincing coming from a North American anthropologist.

20. On the issue of men's sexuality, and especially sex between men, see Gutmann 1996:chap. 5.

21. It includes this aspect, however, as Fernández Kelly (1976) makes clear in an essay on some of the ideological foundations of the notion of machismo.

22. On Mexican national identity, nationalism, *mexicanidad*, and *lo mexicano*, most recently, see Bartra 1992; and Lomnitz-Adler 1992.

23. See also Bushnell 1958; Wolf 1958; and Alarcón 1990.

REFERENCES

Alarcón, Norma
1990   "Traddutora, Traditora: A Paradigmatic Figure of Chicana Feminism."
        Cultural Critique 13:57–87.
Almaguer, Tomás
1991   "Chicano Men: A Cartography of Homosexual Identity and Behavior."
        differences 3 (2): 75–100.
Azuela, Mariano
1958   [1915] *Los de abajo.* Mexico City: Fondo de Cultura Económica.
1962   *The Underdogs.* Trans. E. Munguía Jr. New York: Signet.
Baca Zinn, Maxine
1982   "Chicano Men and Masculinity." *Journal of Ethnic Studies* 10 (2): 29–44.
Bartra, Roger
1992   *The Cage of Melancholy: Identity and Metamorphosis in the Mexican
        Character.* Trans. Christopher J. Hall. New Brunswick: Rutgers University Press.
Beals, Carleton
1928   "With Sandino in Nicaragua. II. On the Sandino Front." *Nation* 126
        (326): 232–33, February 29.
Behar, Ruth
1993   *Translated Woman: Crossing the Border with Esperanza's Story.* Boston:
        Beacon.

Bolton, Ralph
1979 "Machismo in Motion: The Ethos of Peruvian Truckers." *Ethos* 7 (4): 312–42.
Bushnell, John
1958 "La Virgen de Guadalupe as Surrogate Mother in San Juan Atzingo." *American Anthropologist* 60 (2): 261–65.
Capellán, Angel
1985 *Hemingway and the Hispanic World.* Ann Arbor: UMI Research Press.
Fabian, Johannes
1983 *Time and the Other: How Anthropology Makes Its Object.* New York: Columbia University Press.
Fernández Kelly, M. Patricia
1976 "Ideology of Sex in Latin America: The Case of Mexican Machismo." MS, Rutgers University, Department of Anthropology.
Franco, Jean
1989 *Plotting Women: Gender and Representation in Mexico.* New York: Columbia University Press.
Fraser, Nancy
1997 *Justice Interruptus: Critical Reflections on the Postsocialist Condition.* New York: Routledge.
Gilmore, David
1990 *Manhood in the Making: Cultural Concepts of Masculinity.* New Haven: Yale University Press.
Gilmore, Margaret M., and David D. Gilmore
1979 "'Machismo': A Psychodynamic Approach (Spain)." *Journal of Psychological Anthropology* 2 (3): 281–99.
Gómez de Silva, Guido
1988 *Breve diccionario etimológico de la lengua española.* Mexico City: El Colegio de México / Fondo de Cultura Económica.
Gramsci, Antonio
1971 [1929–35] *Selections from the Prison Notebooks.* New York: International.
Greenberg, James
1989 *Blood Ties: Life and Violence in Rural Mexico.* Tucson: University of Arizona Press.
Griffith, Beatrice
1973 [1948] *American Me.* Westport, Conn.: Greenwood.
Gutmann, Matthew C.
1994 "Los hijos de Lewis: La sensibilidad antropológica y el caso de los pobres machos." *Alteridades* (Mexico) 4 (7): 9–19.
1996 *The Meanings of Macho: Being a Man in Mexico City.* Berkeley: University of California Press.
Hodges, Donald C.
1986 *Intellectual Foundations of the Nicaraguan Revolution.* Austin: University of Texas Press.

Lafaye, Jacques
1976 *Quetzalcóatl and Guadalupe: The Formation of Mexican National Consciousness, 1531–1813.* Trans. Benjamin Keen. Chicago: University of Chicago Press.

Lancaster, Roger
1992 *Life Is Hard: Machismo, Danger, and the Intimacy of Power in Nicaragua.* Berkeley: University of California Press.

Lewis, Oscar
1963 [1951] *Life in a Mexican Village: Tepoztlán Restudied.* Urbana: University of Illinois Press.
1959 *Five Families: Mexican Case Studies in the Culture of Poverty.* New York: Basic Books.
1961 *The Children of Sanchez: Autobiography of a Mexican Family.* New York: Vintage.

Limón, José
1989 "Carne, Carnales, and the Carnivalesque: Bakhtinian Batos, Disorder, and Narrative Discourses." *American Ethnologist* 16 (3): 471–86.
1994 *Dancing with the Devil: Society and Cultural Poetics in Mexican-American South Texas.* Madison: University of Wisconsin Press.

Lomnitz-Adler, Claudio
1992 *Exits from the Labyrinth: Culture and Ideology in the Mexican National Space.* Berkeley: University of California Press.

Madsen, William, and Claudia Madsen
1969 "The Cultural Structure of Mexican Drinking Behavior." *Quarterly Journal of Studies on Alcohol* 30 (3): 701–18.

Mailer, Norman
1959 *Advertisements for Myself.* New York: G. P. Putnam's Sons.

Marshall, Mac
1979 *Weekend Warriors: Alcohol in a Micronesian Culture.* Palo Alto, Calif.: Mayfield.

Massolo, Alejandra
1992 *Por amor y coraje: Mujeres en movimientos urbanos de la ciudad de México.* Mexico City: El Colegio de México.

McDowell, Bart
1984 "Mexico City: An Alarming Giant." *National Geographic* 166 (2): 138–78.

Mendoza, Vicente T.
1962 "El machismo en México." *Cuadernos del Instituto Nacional de Investigaciones Folklóricas* (Buenos Aires) 3:75–86.

Mernissi, Fatima
1987 [1987] *Beyond the Veil: Male-Female Dynamics in Modern Muslim Society.* Bloomington: University of Indiana Press.

Mirandé, Alfredo
1997 *Hombres y Machos: Masculinity and Latino Culture.* Boulder, Colo.: Westview.

Moliner, María
1991   *Diccionario de uso del español.* 2 vols. Madrid: Gredos.
Monsiváis, Carlos
1983   [1976] "La nación de unos cuantos y las esperanzas románticas (Notas sobre la historia del término 'Cultura Nacional' en México)." In *En torno a la cultura nacional,* ed. Héctor Aguilar Camín, 159–221. Mexico City: Instituto Nacional Indigenista / SepOchentas.
1981   *Escenas de pudor y liviandad.* Mexico City: Grijalbo.
1992   "Las mitologías del cine mexicano." *Intermedios* 2:12–23.
Paredes, Américo
1971   "The United States, Mexico, and Machismo." Trans. Marcy Steen. *Journal of the Folklore Institute* 8 (1): 17–37.
Paz, Octavio
1961   *The Labyrinth of Solitude: Life and Thought in Mexico.* Trans. Lysander Kemp. New York: Grove.
1985   "Return to the Labyrinth of Solitude." *The Labyrinth of Solitude and Other Writings,* 327–53. Trans. Yara Milos. New York: Grove.
Pratt, Mary Louise
1990   "Women, Literature, and National Brotherhood." *Women, Culture and Politics in Latin America,* 48–73. Seminar on Feminism and Culture in Latin America. Berkeley: University of California Press.
Ramos, Samuel
1962   *Profile of Man and Culture in Mexico.* Trans. Peter G. Earle. Austin: University of Texas Press.
Reston, James
1967   "Santiago: The Cult of Virility in Latin America." *New York Times,* April 9, sec. 4, p. 12.
Rigdon, Susan M.
1988   *The Culture Facade: Art, Science, and Politics in the Work of Oscar Lewis.* Urbana: University of Illinois Press.
Rosaldo, Michelle Z.
1980   "The Use and Abuse of Anthropology: Reflections on Feminism and Cross-Cultural Understanding." *Signs* 5 (3): 389–417.
Rulfo, Juan
1959   *Pedro Páramo.* Trans. Lysander Kemp. New York: Grove.
Santamaría, Francisco J.
1959   *Diccionario de mejicanismos.* Mexico City: Porrúa.
Simic, Andrei
1969   "Management of the Male Image in Yugoslavia." *Anthropological Quarterly* 42:89–10.
Stanley, Alessandra
1994   "Sexual Harassment Thrives in the New Russian Climate." *New York Times,* April 17, sec. 1, pp. 1, 7.
Stephen, Lynn
1997   *Women and Social Movements in Latin America: Power from Below.* Austin: University of Texas Press.

Stevens, Evelyn
1973 "Marianismo: The Other Face of Machismo in Latin America." In *Male and Female in Latin America,* ed. Ann Pescatello, 89–101. Pittsburgh: University of Pittsburgh Press.
Usigli, Rodolfo
1985 [1947] *El gesticulador.* Mexico City: Editores Mexicanos Unidos.
Wolf, Eric
1958 "The Virgin of Guadalupe: A Mexican National Symbol." *Journal of American Folklore* 71:34–39.

Myths of the Bourgeois Woman: Rethinking Race, Class, and Gender

Christine E. Gray

> The reconciliation of irrational forms in which certain economic relations appear and assert themselves in practice does not concern the active agents of these relations in their everyday life . . . [T]hat which seems irrational to ordinary common sense is rational, and that which seems rational to it is itself irrational.
>
> —Karl Marx, *Capital*

> I wish I were Barbie. That bitch has everything.
>
> —License plate holder, California

> F—— Barbie!
>
> —Graffiti in Olecko, Poland, 1993

The image of the bourgeois woman is one of the most powerful and least recognized components of capitalist ideology, critical to its export abroad and essential to capital accumulation on a global scale. Trivialization of bourgeois women is often effected through automatic "class leaping" comparative strategies that juxtapose the circumstances of the lives of middle-class women, particularly those who are upwardly mobile, against those of poor or working-class people as a silencing technique. This epistemological strategy deserves serious scrutiny since, in both scholarship and social life, it shifts the terms of the argument at precisely the point at which significant insights arise about race, class, gender, health, and the hidden entitlements of bourgeois men.

The argument that the problems of "privileged" women are significant, different, and in some respects more severe than those of working-class people causes universal discomfort; in U.S. society it is almost automatically characterized as selfish. The trivialization of bourgeois women, the "Barbie attack" discussed throughout this essay, protects forbidden areas of discourse. Like racism, it has many forms, the most potent of which are unspoken assumptions, silent value judgments, and lack of recognition and outrage at the circumstances of people's lives.

The first part of this piece describes my growing awareness of the naturalized hostility toward bourgeois women as a young university professor. The second critiques the notion of class from a bourgeois feminist perspective. The third part locates common myths, caricatures, and contradictions regarding bourgeois women in three leading feminist works: Emily Martin's *The Woman in the Body* (1987), Rayna Rapp's "Family and Class in Contemporary America" (1982), which heavily influences Martin's text, and Karen Sacks' review article "Toward a Unified Theory of Class, Race, and Gender" (1989). The conclusion proposes a postmodern definition of bourgeois women. Modifying Bourdieu's (1984) work on class and aesthetics, it suggests a gendered framework for class analysis that places the image of the bourgeois women at the center of capital accumulation. Finally, it considers the effects of "bourgeois bashing" on students of any race or class.

For the most part this essay reflects the sensibilities of the 1980s, the Reagan years, marked by startling affluence/Wall Street greed and the optimism of a new generation of "postliberation" women. In this second decade since the publication of *Woman, Culture, and Society* images of the "displaced homemaker" faded quietly from public view, and the professional "superwoman" became a mainstay of popular media. "thirtysomething," a television program depicting the work and lives of young urban professionals, achieved phenomenal popularity. The first wave of undergraduates mentored by Rosaldo entered the academic job market, and Barbie (the doll), *the* bimbo in American culture, "a seminal figure in the life of modern American women and some of the stranger modern American men" (Plunket 1993), celebrated her thirtieth birthday.[1]

Bashing Barbie

I first became aware of the hostility toward bourgeois women when I observed the extreme and varied nature of the hostility expressed by students toward Barbie dolls, which I used to introduce the idea of commodity fetishism. This led me to collect "Barbie stories," some funny, some not. I became sensitive to the fact that Barbie has a dark side, which, while widely recognized, operates at the edges of social awareness.

An engineer in his thirties reminisced about lining up his sisters' Barbies and shooting them with a .22-caliber rifle. A student in his twenties described a playmate microwaving his sister's Barbie. A technician for National Public Radio recalled laying his sister's Barbie doll on a railroad track and watching a train run over it.[2] Barbie's impassioned reception in my gender classes recalls Mies's discussion about the disproportionate symbolic weight given to housewives, bourgeois women, in advertising and other public media in Third World nations (1986:206–9).[3]

My awareness of this hostility increased as I compared notes with other young female professors on the odd reversals of authority we encountered inside and outside the classroom. I discovered that, more than anything, women at the large urban university where I taught dreaded the designation *bourgeois feminist.* Any remaining illusions I had about the power and authority of highly educated professional women were dispelled by the shock of a divorce and the staggering demands of raising an infant alone.

The bashing of bourgeois women in its theoretical form was first brought to my attention by graduate students who summarily dismissed Rosaldo and Lamphere's *Woman, Culture, and Society* (1974) as "bourgeois feminist" and "essentialist"—often without having ever read it. A colleague summarized the book's central argument as "all women are alike." And he and another colleague, both trained at elite universities, were pitting the work of bourgeois feminists against those of "Marxist feminists" in their classrooms (see MacKinnon 1989:47). Somewhere along the way issues of child care and domestic responsibilities that were so central to Rosaldo's theoretical position disappeared into the woodwork.

Why would an early 1970s critique of androcentric bias in anthropology, posed as an alternative to biological reductionism, elicit such antagonism in the late 1980s and early 1990s? I regarded the theories of Rosaldo and her co-contributors as just that, theories—long since tested, rejected, and/or extended (see di Leonardo 1991). The essays, in fact, helped students analyze connections between gender and political economy. The work was easy to update in light of contemporary feminist work and to adapt to historical analysis (see Chodorow 1979). In fact, once one recognizes that Rosaldo's work is an almost perfect theoretical rendition of capitalist gender ideologies and practices,[4] it provides a useful perspective for exploring the subtleties of capitalist accumulation in non-Western societies, for ferreting out the symbolic structures that generate the myths and antagonisms of Western capitalism. How are Western ideologies of public/domestic space and the idea of the bourgeois woman who "does it all" without messing up her hair being imposed on non-Western societies (see Lutz 1992)? Why the lack of emphasis on reconciling Marxist and cultural approaches, as was occurring elsewhere in anthropology? And why, always, the undercurrent of hostility? The answer, I believe, lies less in the debates themselves than in the academic environments that produced them.

At some point I began to sense that class designations for women are not merely wrong but actively misleading: forms of capitalist mystification that are perpetuated by mainstream American culture, Marxists, and white feminists alike. After several years of studying rationales for bashing Barbie, I began to suspect that hostility toward bourgeois women is an unexamined mainstay of the U.S. capitalist emotional repertoire.

There are several reasons why it is okay to bash Barbie. First, she is neotenized, or childlike, and inherently trivial. Second, Barbie embodies the cultural maxim that *men act and women appear,* a key organizing principle of gender relations in Western capitalist society (see Berger 1972:47). Third, the doll embodies the vacuousness attributed to bourgeois women as primary agents of consumption rather than production or work, highly prized male attributes (see Hartmann 1981a; Donovan 1991:83–84). This, combined with powerlessness, makes her a perfect target for class antagonism.

The following section explores the hegemony that derives from systematic ambiguities in the use of class and how these ambiguities relate to processes of capital accumulation. Although I draw heavily from this literature, my purpose is not to rehash debates about the "unhappy marriage" of Marxism and feminism (Hartmann 1981a; Sargent 1981; MacKinnon 1989). Rather, my intent is to illustrate ways in which class analyses operate as hidden carriers of capitalist gender ideology in order to stimulate new ways of thinking about race, class, and gender.

Following Rayna Rapp (1982:170–71) I use *class* to mean a process "by which different social relations to the means of production are inherited and reproduced under capitalism," one that dichotomizes rich and poor. Unlike Ehrenreich (1989:3–6), who discusses middle-class women in relation to the new professional middle class in America (i.e., primarily in terms of education and occupation), I use *middle-class* to refer to women in the two cultural senses embodied by Barbie: as glamour-bourgeois (housewife) and professional-bourgeois. These terms more accurately describe women's options and images in capitalist society.[5] I also use *class* in a new sense, as a linguistic shifter, a term whose meanings shift when applied to men and women. Ideology—and postmodernism—aside, once women bear children in capitalist societies, their class or cultural positions rarely if ever compare to men's.

Against Defining Women by Class

Class Illogic: A Theoretical Overview

As a native of a capitalist society, I intuitively feel that class is an accurate way of differentiating people. When I view the issue analytically, however, I can only conclude that use of class obscures more than it clarifies about women and, hence, society. Men and women, certainly bourgeois men and women, are not analogous by almost any criterion of class, either by the classical Marxist definition as relation to the means of production (see Donovan 1991: chap. 3, 67 ff., p. 83), by Weberian definitions of class and status (1946:180–95), or by specific descriptive criteria (see Quest 1981: pt. 3). The nature of marriage and kinship obligations for women in American society is such that class criteria do not apply equally to them and their male counterparts.

The specific arguments leading to these conclusions are certainly not news to feminists (Flax 1981; MacKinnon 1989) or to feminist anthropologists.[6] Nonetheless, they run counter to unexamined assumptions in work that attempts to analyze race, class, and gender simultaneously. Let us examine the most general features of class analysis, those that most seriously distort women's position in society.

First, most class analyses, Marxist or not, reflect the fictions of civil contracts. The primary categories of analysis, production (from the classical Marxist tradition) and occupation (from the American sociological tradition), are male defined and reflect male viewpoints. The subject of analysis, groups or individuals, are often generically male.[7] The voice of the author, like that of the law, is generally "objective" and classless. Most studies, especially those of the lower class, carry assumptions of benevolence, that is, that the people written about are less privileged and insightful than the author.

Second, Marxist approaches to class, and thus Marxist praxis and theories of resistance, are based on the dominant ideology thesis, the idea that "the class which has the means of material production at its disposal, has control at the same time over the means of mental production, so that thereby, generally speaking, the ideas of those who lack the means of mental production are subject to it" (Marx and Engels 1970:64). By no stretch of the imagination are middle- or upper-class women the "ruling material force of society," merely its adjuncts. As citizens, workers, kinfolk, household members, and/or heads of households, they have limited or convoluted access to capital. They control neither the means of material nor mental production. Nevertheless, the dominant ideology thesis and dominant capitalist ideologies have one thing in common: both define bourgeois women in ways that serve capitalist interests by attributing to them powers that they probably lack, systematically misrepresenting their ability to achieve and maintain upper-class positions. This misrepresentation justifies their oppression as a privileged class while maintaining them as a motivated/mystified reserve labor force; it drives the beauty market, the production and consumption of necessary inessentials that sustain the illusion of upper-class status (see Frye 1981; Hartmann 1981a; Russell 1981; Mies 1986:205–9; Donovan 1991:83).

Third, the meaning of class as a communal relationship and an individual calculation systematically shifts when referring to men and women, and both scholarly and popular uses of class accept dissonant and even contradictory meanings as being "natural." For men class is identified primarily as an achieved status, as a relation to capital or to the means of production. Men's class position is calculated primarily in terms of occupational, economic, and cultural capital, usually in that order. For women class is presented more as an ascribed status. Most often, it refers to social status as determined by relationships to men, by their fathers' and/or husbands' class position, with their own education and occupations considered last (see Ostrander 1984). Women's "class position," unlike men's, has little pertinence, however, to establishing a direct relationship to capital. For certain categories of wealthy women it may have the opposite effect.

The idea that bourgeois women can be identified primarily by class is a form of false consciousness. This idea not only serves capitalist interests by implying that bourgeois women have an economic base that they lack; it also disguises striking similarities between bourgeois women and women of other classes (cf. Ostrander 1984: chap. 3, p. 64; Rubin 1976). For bourgeois women, more than any other group, an emphasis on class difference conceals similarities to people who are most subordinated under capitalism, disguising the system's genuine dynamics.

Taking a cue from Rosaldo, let us analyze class labels from a symbolic perspective, as ideology. Class designations for women are based on idioms of emotion and appearance. They imply fear of women of other classes and horror of taking on their supposed characteristics: the cold-heartedness, disdain, and/or silliness of upper-class women, the unrestrained sexuality, unkept houses, and unruly children of poor and working-class women (see Ehrenreich 1989:7). Class designations by nature are inherently antagonistic, but class designations for bourgeois women are hyperantagonistic. This anomaly bears serious scrutiny since supposed disdain of the lower classes operates as a class marker that establishes bourgeois women, be they university professors or society hostesses, as legitimate targets of class and race antagonism (see Ostrander 1984:32; Stoler 1991).

At issue is the fact that the dualism inherent in Marxist thought, the "creative negativity" implied by the dialectical method (McLellan 1980: 153), has radically different consequences for men and women, especially bourgeois women. For Marx "a class only existed when it was conscious of itself as such, and this always implied common hostility to another social group" (qtd. in Donovan 1991:67). As visible representatives of "their" class, however, bourgeois women are identified in politics, feminism, and the popular imagination with commodity consumption and self-indulgence—as the "parasites of the parasites" of the social body (Luxemburg 1971:219–20; cf. Friedan 1963)—whereas bourgeois men are identified more with commodity production, work, and a work ethic. As a consequence, bourgeois women are safer and more accessible targets of social hostility than their more powerful partners. Both high-profile society women and high-profile professional women provide socially acceptable outlets for diffuse hostility at social inequities, certainly more than their male counterparts.

Thus, while the dualism inherent in Marxist thought may seem intuitively right for analyzing capitalist societies, it provides no effective means for analyzing significant differences or similarities of women by class. Certainly, it provides no means of analyzing the disadvantages of bourgeois women in relation to working-class women, an idea that is anathema to both Marxist and capitalist thought.

The most telling criticism of Marxist-inspired class analyses, however, is that it is virtually impossible to reconcile the commonsense insights of feminism with ideologically loaded, commonsense notions about women in class analyses. Compare, for example, statements that poverty is a women's issue (see Fraser 1991:267), women rank last in the allocation of household resources, households are the loci of abuse and exploitation for

women, and women are members of the reserve labor force with stereotypes of Marxist analysis and popular culture: that housewives and rich
women live a life of leisure (see Ostrander 1984:1), are primary conspicu-
ous commodity consumers in their households, oppress the women who
work for "them," and pursue lucrative careers at will. This discrepancy
stems from a central contradiction of Marxist analysis: insistence on the
centrality of a labor theory of value coupled with the refusal to acknowledge women's unwaged domestic labor as the fundamental source of surplus value.[8]

Marxist theories of value are generated by the same cultural codes that
organize other domains of capitalist culture. They prize male over female
labor and assume that men act (work) and women appear (or disappear
into the home). They assume that men produce valued commodities
whereas women produce little or nothing of value and that the separation
of public and private domains, a subtle marker of prestige, is more actuality than ideology (see Fraser 1991:257).

Thus, few feminist scholars would quarrel with the assertion that
women are subordinated under capitalism (or socialism, communism, and
military dictatorships), that they are a dependent rank in capitalist societies and in the emerging global economy. These statements imply, however, that women's class position is inherently ambiguous. To assign a
woman the same class position of her husband is like assigning a factory
manager and worker the same class position should they share the same
residence, with the worker averaging an additional daily six-hour shift.
Definitions of class by occupation or relation to capital are moot.[9]

If class is defined in terms of occupation, then whose occupation is
being discussed? The woman's, her husband's, or her father's? What if
wealthy women divorce or marry socially undesirable spouses? What if
they have sex with the gardener? Their relatively "secure resource base"
and class privileges vanish. And, like other disenfranchised people, women
who work outside the home, regardless of occupation, are by history and
custom members of the reserve army of labor: the last to be hired and first
to be fired, a rule that operates in the factory, the board room (see Lewis
1989:237), and the university.

As Berger (1972: chap. 3) points out, women's symbolic presence is
inherently ambiguous. As many feminist scholars have pointed out,
women are regarded as property in capitalist systems, explicitly and
implicitly (see Mies 1986; Pateman 1988: chap. 5). As a consequence,
women never enter contracts, the basis of a free-market economy and the

ability to sell one's labor in the marketplace, totally independently. As one student pointed out, the dialogues in the feminist film classic *Rosie the Riveter* (1980) are not about women working, the film's explicit motif. Rather, they are about whether women are qualified to enter into contracts. Do women need permission from husbands, fathers, or the government in order to work? Do women require male protectors from the union or management to sign contracts? Should they even be considered for men's jobs, or high-paying jobs?

Once a woman of any "class" enters the workplace, much of the resulting dialogue is framed in an idiom of appearance ("What's a pretty girl like you . . . ?") or reproductive status. This is true of jobs at all levels in society. Lest the point about *Rosie the Riveter* be lost on present generations, in the late 1980s I attended a seminar in which female faculty and graduate students representing every stage in the reproductive cycle related stories about rationales for discrimination in hiring in academia. Young unmarried women might get married and leave. Married women might have children. Pregnant women should not even be applying for jobs, and how could women with young children perform an academic job adequately? Although these types of dialogues are ostensibly about reproduction, and we accepted them as such, they also carry a fundamental message about women's inherent unfitness to enter into contracts (see Hartsock 1981:11–12).

Women have more in common than biology or subordination through biological idioms. All women, from housewives to secretaries, presidents' wives to university professors, are subject to various and shifting forms of learned incompetence and cultural idiocy in order to keep their jobs or maintain their social positions—asking questions to which they know the answers, mastering culturally devalued restricted codes of small talk, baby talk, personal morality (see Bernstein 1971; Gilligan 1982; Martin 1987: 195–96)—although discourse positions and forms of erasure compound differently by class (Stoler 1991).[10] This sort of cultural idiocy provides a fundamental rationale for denying women systematic access to capital in which women are trained to be complicit.[11]

Upclassing and Other Irrationalities

All women have greater fluidity of status, verging on the dramatic, than men through marriage (see MacKinnon 1989:34–35). This makes the assignment of class labels difficult, if not irrelevant, but gives life to the characterization of the bourgeoisie as imitating the imagined mannerisms of the upper classes. Marrying up is the theme of *Cinderella,* that mainstay of female socialization. In many families marrying up often takes on overtones of duty or family obligation; indeed, it is the number-one precept in the cult of domesticity. This theme permeates decades of American films, from *Gentlemen Prefer Blondes* (1953), in which a scheming show girl plots to marry a millionaire, to *Pretty Woman* (1990), in which an ingenue prostitute captivates a ruthless businessman, to *The Little Mermaid* (1991), in which a member of the under(water)class aspires to marry a human/ prince. It permeates television programs, popular romance novels, national political dramas, and the social dramas of royalty. Yet marrying up is also dangerous and degrading: in the original Hans Christian Andersen version the little mermaid (like Diana, princess of Wales) dies. Upclassing may be an ideal for women, but, as Bourdieu's work indicates, class societies have a horror of upclassing in the way that non-class-based societies have a horror of wrong-group or wrong-caste marriages.

In actuality, what exceptional leaps in social class through marriage achieve is a superdependent rank (Ortner and Whitehead 1981). Women who make these class leaps automatically become objects of suspicion and denigration and arouse the ire of women of all classes, especially the "catty" women of the upper classes, as caricatured by "Mrs. Piggy" in *Gentlemen Prefer Blondes.* Despite the different decades in which they were produced, three film classics concerned with upclassing, *Gentlemen Prefer Blondes* (1953), *That Touch of Mink* (1964), and *Pretty Woman* (1990), carry highly charged and contradictory messages about women and work. Single working women are not quite respectable, but stay-at-home wives are sexually unattractive (*GPB*). Respectable working women are easily corrupted by the debauched lifestyle of the upper classes (*TTOM/PW*). If working women are nice enough, they may attract wealthy suitors who will rescue them from lives of near-poverty and degradation. If they are really nice, they may get really rich (*GPB/TTOM/PW*).

The higher up a woman marries relative to the social position of her family of origin, the more submissive must be her femininity, and the more techniques there are for separating women from capital (see Ostrander 1984:51–60, 65–67, 122–23).[12] As Sallie Bingham, heiress and member of a prominent Louisville, Kentucky, newspaper family, demonstrated so ably: women born into wealthy patriarchal families are paralyzed by tradition rather than taught how to manage capital. To be loved and maintain social acceptance, they must submit to powerful demands for neoteny and ignorance about finance; in other words, take on the characteristics of Barbie (Bingham 1989).[13] The very wealthiest families employ extreme measures like the family psychiatrist (Marcus 1992) to insure that women and eccentrics do not dissipate family fortunes. For women who marry into these high positions the prestige is certainly dependent and the tests for mastering the class position extraordinary. Once newcomers master the niceties of their class position, proper table manners, dress, conversation, and the like, they have rendered themselves economically impotent.[14]

Once at the top wealthy women confront another basic element of the American emotional repertoire: the horror of women with "power." This phenomenon is expressed most dramatically in media treatment of the famous rich women or media toys of the 1980s—Ivana Trump, Imelda Marcos, Leona Helmsley—as well as more serious political figures such as Geraldine Ferraro and later Hillary Clinton. There is another hitch to marrying up, however, as demonstrated both by Sarah Ferguson, the duchess of York, and Roxanne Pulitzer, a woman who grew up in Cassadaga, New York. Women who upclass dramatically are subject to equally dramatic swoops of downclassing, usually for failing to acquire adequate knowledge of the game or for buying into the myth of the power of their new status. The punishment for adopting their husband's lifestyles and sense of entitlement is divorce, impoverishment, ostracization, and loss of children (see Pulitzer 1988). Most distressing in the cases of Pulitzer and "Mayflower Madame" Sydney Biddle Barrows (1986), another media star of the 1980s, is the self-denigration that occurred through publicity seeking after the fall from grace, giving life to Gloria Steinem's observation that rich women rebel in self-destructive ways.[15] The only way Barrows and Pulitzer could obtain significant capital was through notoriety, by playing on media fascination with the decadent bourgeois woman, an option that has repeatedly presented itself to the duchess of York—at the cost of losing her children.[16]

Once women have children, they never share the same class position as men with the same "occupational" status or lifestyle. As Arlie Hochschild points out so trenchantly in *The Second Shift* (1989), women in two-career households, regardless of race or class, go to extraordinary lengths to collude with their mates in the illusion of a shared lifestyle, despite dramatic differences in household labor. Like extremely wealthy women (Ostrander 1984:40), professional women are super-servants in their own homes (Ehrenreich 1989:39–40). Their behavior maintains the leisure of their men and the fantasy that their husbands' work enables them to maintain a middle-class lifestyle for which women's work provides the "frills." If housework is shared, it is generally on their husbands' terms, not theirs. In reality shared residence has little to do with equality of lifestyle as measured by household labor, commodity consumption, leisure time, sleep, or "stress" (see Haraway 1990; and cartoonist Greg Howard's insufferable "Sally Forth.") Their households are organized according to the cultural canons of "love," yet these women know they will be devastated by divorce, professionally, emotionally, and financially.

Finally, there is a category of unmarried female executives and professionals who fulfill the occupational criterion of class but not the household definition. As a cost of maintaining an "equal" position with men in the workplace, they share their households with no one, or cats. They hold jobs in which maternity leave is equated with special privilege and pregnancy results in career derailment, demotion, or job loss (see Swiss and Walker 1993). Like domestic contracts, their civil contracts carry hidden sexual clauses. Like housewives, they must often offer sexual deference for protection. Their insistence on parity at work virtually guarantees the same result as married women's insistence on parity at home: retribution and immediate threat of downclassing (see Hochschild 1989:252). The image of Anita Hill, sweating beneath the lights of the television cameras in the U.S. Senate, comes to mind.[17]

In the final days of *thirtysomething,* Hope, the Princeton-educated housewife, has a nightmare about becoming a bag lady. In light of now familiar statistics documenting the impoverishment of middle-class women after divorce, and with a divorce rate exceeding 50 percent, this is less of an exaggeration than it might seem (cf. Weitzman 1985; Arendell 1986; Hochschild 1989:249–53). A year after *thirtysomething* went off the air, *Sixty Minutes* did a feature on bourgeois bag ladies, several of whom were from Beverly Hills. Some were permanent houseguests, and some lived out of cars, but all were desperately maintaining the total commitment to the symbolic that characterizes the bourgeoisie (Bourdieu 1984:253).[18]

The specter of the bag lady, central to the feminist sensibility, vanishes in analyses that treat race, class, and gender simultaneously. The following section considers the fate of bourgeois women in feminist anthropology of the 1980s. By then a silent player was entrenched in the American kinship system: the often conservative white male divorce court judge, champion of equality and hence significant factor in the impoverishment of women and their children (see Flax 1988).

Bourgeois Women in Feminist Anthropology

The Woman Outside the Body

Anthropologist Emily Martin's work *The Woman in the Body* (1987) is an award-winning study of class-based resistance to medical hegemony over women's bodies. In her introduction Martin acknowledges the complexities of class analysis and notes that the problem with an "anthropology of the familiar" is that one fails to see the contradictions in one's own culture. Indeed, as natives we happily, or necessarily, suppress them. Since her goal is to compare class attitudes toward medical care, Martin selected her subjects from neighborhoods of widely varying socioeconomic conditions in Baltimore, a plan that allowed her to determine, "at the level of crude differences," if class positions matter. She characterizes her subjects as "mostly white working-class women," middle- or upper-middle-class women (no race specified), and black working-class women (5). Martin's discussion of class opens with a feminist inspired description of what women have in common, biologically and otherwise: subordination in jobs, families, and/or "in general cultural imagery and language" (4). Martin acknowledges the difficulties of class analysis with regard to making clear-cut distinctions between working class and middle class, but not to gender, then discusses class by occupation (i.e., as difference).

Drawing on apparently nonfeminist work by sociologists Beneson (1980), Rothman (1978), and Braverman (1974), Martin lists as middle class: self-employed businesspeople, white-collar or blue-collar salaried professionals and managers, salaried administrative sales and clerical employees, supervisory employees, firefighters, and police. These are occupations that, for the most part, "give workers greater autonomy, responsibility, security, mobility, and prestige than working-class occupations" (1987:5). She designates as working-class: skilled craft workers, clerical office workers, retail sales clerks, factory laborers, and service workers. These occupations all "suffered increasingly the same loss of workers' autonomy and control as factory jobs have" (6).

Martin's discussion of class as occupation is crystal clear, but it makes absolutely no sense for women. First, like Marx and most Marxists, she views occupation/labor in terms of wage labor in public, a designation that does not pertain to many of her subjects. Second, many of the middle-class occupations she lists, such as firefighter, are obviously male or male dominated. Third, her discussion assumes that occupations have fixed characteristics such as autonomy, mobility, prestige, etc., regardless of the race or sex of the people who pursue them: This is capitalist ideology, not practice. Fourth, although many of her subjects are divorced or are the offspring of divorce (1987:7), and divorce clearly had a powerful psychological and economic effect on them, she does not systematically discuss divorce or its effects on household organization, resources, leisure, health, or class position.[19] For many of us this is the "anthropology of the too familiar."

Although Martin defines class mainly in terms of occupation, she does not identify her subjects by occupation in the main body of the text, nor does she question whether experience in the workplace might affect women's ability to resist established medical procedures. It is unclear whether *middle class* refers to the occupations of her female subjects or their fathers and/or husbands. If the class designation is based on the occupation of husbands, then the occupation, the labor, of the married middle-class housewife informants is similar to that of the blue-collar worker: maid, cook, nanny, chauffeur. If class designation is based on the occupation of her subjects, then a slippage factor is in effect, which makes the class designation inaccurate: women are second-class citizens within their professions, at least a half-step down the class ladder in terms of rank and income from male counterparts with similar training and experience. When women pursue middle-class occupations, they do so as a subclass within it, rarely as fire chiefs, CEO's of major companies, or tenured professors in universities. In fact, given the antagonism toward maternity leave and state-supported child care in capitalist society, middle-class occupations for women have the characteristics that Martin identifies with working-class occupations (i.e., lack of autonomy and control).

In some of the occupations to which she refers, like businessperson, sex discrimination is so severe as to make the designation almost meaningless. For instance, throughout most of its history the Small Business Association has given few loans to women, nor has it allowed women to receive loans under minority entitlements (Emshwiller 1991). How does one designate capitalists who are denied access to capital because of their sex or marital status?

Martin acknowledges the limitations of defining class by occupation and supplements her discussion with Rayna Rapp's (1982) description of class traits by household organization. According to Rapp,[20] middle-class households can count on a stable resource base and spend some resources on recreation or luxuries. In emergencies, Martin thus argues middle-class households call on institutions outside the family: banks, pensions, or credit accounts. Their greater geographic mobility (by choice or as a requirement for keeping the job) means that *families* must rely on purchased services rather than kinship or community help on a day-to-day basis and especially when in transition. Marriages are expected to involve communication and companionship between spouses, and women are *expected to choose* whether to fill only the roles of housewife and mother or to also find a job outside the home for self-fulfillment or additional income. Because resources are largely accumulated to be passed on to the next generation, families emphasize lineal kinship links from parents to children to grandchildren. People look to friends for affective ties outside the family, but they do not usually share significant resources with friends, to avoid diverting funds laterally instead of lineally. (Martin 1987:6)

Martin describes working-class households, in contrast, as relying on a more tenuous resource base and tending to develop many forms of pooling and sharing within neighborhoods and extended families. "Of course, the reality of dependence on wage labor often sends women out of the home for work, primarily into the sex-segregated lowest-paid sectors of the economy" (1987:6).

Definitions of class by household organization compound rather than clarify the ambiguities that occur when class is defined by occupation. First, both Rapp's article and Martin's synopsis refer to compound usages—"resources," "people," and "families"—that totally erase household gender dynamics. Second, Martin appears to use household and family interchangeably; this glosses over critical information, whether women are single, married, divorced, and/or mothers. Third, it is unclear whether Martin (or Rapp) is discussing the ideology or the practice of American family life (see Collier et al. 1982; Ehrenreich 1989:4). Fourth, although this is clearly neither Rapp's (1982:170) nor Martin's intention, descriptions of middle-class households in *The Woman in the Body* evoke the nuclear family of American television, "Ozzie and Harriet," a figment of the American imagination.

In the source article Rapp acknowledges the actualities of unstable working-class households—domestic violence, alcoholism, desertion, divorce, etc. (1982:174; see Rubin 1976)—but not those of middle- or upper-class households (Rapp 1982:180–83; see Ehrenreich 1989:5). Thus, Martin/Rapp's portrayal of middle- and upper-class families seems implic-

itly to accept them as unified interest groups and centers of love and cooperation, rather than as "comfortable concentration camps" for women
(Friedan 1963), "sinkholes of consumerism" (Ehrenreich 1989:41),
domains permeated by money and power (Fraser 1991:259), or centers of
exploitation and abuse. Given the Marxist and feminist stance of *The
Woman in the Body,* feminist-economist Heidi Hartmann's (1981b) analysis of families as the locus of exploitation of women and struggle over
inequities in the division of labor would seem more relevant (see
Chodorow 1979; Ostrander 1984), especially in light of situations presented in Hochschild's *Second Shift,* which were prevalent in American
society during the time of Rapp's and Martin's writing. Thus, although
Rapp's description of class by household organization may "feel right," it
simply does not make sense in light of the realities of contemporary American life.

Why would a feminist study present an "Ozzie and Harriet" version of
middle-class existence? How does one describe the class of single female
heads of households who are by culture and education bourgeois but lack
a secure resource base (see MacKinnon 1989:48)? If, as Martin's work
assumes, capitalist society is oppressive to women of all classes, why
would she ignore the family, particularly the patriarchal household, as the
primary agent of socialization for this oppression? Why rely heavily on
Marxist concepts of ideology and alienation to describe women's lives but
ignore the labor theory of value?

Let us consider how the individual propositions in Rapp's class description apply to women. First, the "stable resource base" of a middle-class
household exists primarily for the husband/father by virtue of his occupation and remains for him regardless of marital status. According to Weitzman's *Divorce Revolution* (1985), women on average experience a 73 percent loss in standard of living in the first year of divorce, whereas men
experience a 42 percent gain.[21]

Second, what of the much-vaunted recreation or luxuries for middle-
class women, particularly the free time necessary to pursue leisure activity?
One commonsense insight of feminist scholarship is that women rank last
in the allocation of household resources and that "working" women put in
an additional six-hour shift of domestic labor with all that it entails:
exhaustion, resentment, and the "emotion work" of repressing that resentment. In the last century the discrepancy in labor time between husbands
and wives was naturalized by such aphorisms as "Men work from sun to
sun, but women's work is never done." Now couples in two-career house-

holds find myriad ways to collude in the myth of shared lifestyle, pointing to shared residence and ownership of luxury items such as video cameras, sports equipment, health club memberships, exotic vacations, etc.

The meaning of *holiday* for bourgeois women provides one clue about the level of mystification at work. As the daughter of a respected small-town doctor pointed out, Sunday was a "day of rest" for her father only. It was one of the hardest days of work for her mother, who nonetheless steadfastly colluded in the myth of leisure. And let us not even get into the sexual division of labor on such holidays as Thanksgiving, with its football games, the point being that the first thing to get lost in a comparative class analysis is attention to the distribution of household resources, leaving bourgeois women, the most repressed members of their class, as mistaken symbols of its privilege.

Third, Rapp/Martin's analysis ignores the class-specific dimensions of women's roles as members of the reserve labor force and loses sight of the fact that all women are paid less than men who do comparable work, regardless of their class (Hartsock 1981:110). Like working-class women, married middle-class women, especially those who work on a part-time basis, tend to work in the "sex-segregated lowest-paid sectors of the economy," whereas wealthy married women who "don't need to work" are channeled into nonpaid volunteer work (i.e., into different, highly trivialized, and equally powerless segments of the economy). Wealthy women who take up demanding professional work might upset the tranquillity of their homes (see Ostrander 1984:61–64). Doctors' wives who decide to go "back to work" after raising children do not suddenly become partners in law firms or CEO's of major companies. Thus, rationales for women as members of the reserve labor force differ by socioeconomic circumstances, but their cumulative effect is to keep women of all classes, as a group, economically powerless.

What I find most disturbing, however, is Martin/Rapp's seemingly benign statement that women in middle-class marriages are "expected to choose whether to fill only the roles of housewife and mother or to also find a job outside the home for self-fulfillment or additional income" (Martin 1987:6). Despite their strong feminist orientation, this statement, unchallenged, seems to support the myth that bourgeois women choose to work for "meaning" in their lives, rather than to "put food on the table for their children" (the culturally accepted male rationale for work), or that they work for the same reasons that men work. The myth that women work for meaning is a central tenet of patriarchy and a fundamental assumption of pro-lifers, who assume that work is an option rather than a necessity for women. This is the single most important myth for establishing women's place in the reserve labor force. Even more curious is the silence on divorce. Why would this type of knowledge be systematically set aside in feminist class-based analyses?

One has only to see illustrations of historical "state-of-the-art" birth technology in *The Woman in the Body* to know that these instruments of torture and intrusion were meant primarily for rich or bourgeois women, yet Martin's use of class is based on one central assumption, that women's positions unambiguously improve as they ascend the social scale. This assumption is counterindicated by Martin's data (105–7, 149–50) and her conclusion that working-class women may be better equipped to resist medical hegemony (chap. 11). Instead, her data suggest that women make serious economic and psychological trade-offs as they ascend the class ladder and that higher-class positions contain hidden disadvantages that cancel out supposed advantages in ways that we accept as "natural."

The problem is in the way Martin frames her conclusion: she celebrates the strengths of working-class women while ignoring the implications for their more "privileged" bourgeois counterparts. If repression is bad and unhealthy, the premise underlying arguments that celebrate the strengths of working-class women, then middle-class women are damaged in this and possibly other respects, and the damage is powerful enough to offset their supposed greater wealth, education, and prestige. What are the assumptions that underlie these silences?

Sacks: A Unified Theory of Class, Race, and Gender?

A similar subtext runs through Karen Sacks's influential review article in *American Ethnologist*, "Toward a Unified Theory of Class, Race, and Gender" (1989). Sacks, a Marxist-feminist, explores the problem of how to conceptualize class and theorize the interrelation of class, race, and gender, drawing mostly from examples in U.S. society. Her goal is to retain Marx's notion of class and modify it so that it becomes both gendered and racially specific. Sacks briefly questions the salience of race and gender for social analysis but never class, and her article alternates between popular and analytic uses of class. Like Martin, Sacks makes frequent references to feminist work and commonsense insights of feminism—for example, that women experience class differently than men—but these insights are not integrated into her analysis.

Sacks lauds the work of "black, Asian, and Latina feminists" in theorizing the waged and unwaged domestic labor of women (of color) (1989:537). She lauds the work of "feminists of color" and "black feminists" in developing voices and theoretical frameworks built from their experiences (539–40). She praises studies that argue that African-American communities and families reject occupational bases for status, thereby resisting negative ways that white society defines black women and men based on low-status occupations "and hence class positions."

In one confusing passage, Sacks commends black, Latina, and Asian women's distinctly different perspective on and critique of domestic labor from that developed by "white feminists." She then seems to equate the positions of mostly white "madams" who act as adversaries of their domestic workers of color with those of white feminists, quoting Phyllis Palmer's statement that (unnamed) white feminists have a history of "cutting off their nose to spite their face" in denying support to black women's struggles "because of fear of confronting the fact that their class/race status is contingent on and mediated by a subordinate domestic relationship to white men" (as qtd. in Sacks 1989: 540).[22] I can think of no feminist, white or otherwise, who is not perfectly clear about the fact that middle-class women's status is contingent on and mediated by a subordinate domestic relationship to white men.

The good guys and bad guys in this script are marked by Sacks's shifting use of race and class labels. Although the article is presented as a dialogue with nonfeminist Marxism, the real protagonists appear to be the bourgeois feminists and/or "essentialist bourgeois feminists" she addresses in previous work (see Sacks 1984). Sacks has little or no praise for studies that she identifies as being done by white feminists, and she never identifies feminists of color as being bourgeois or middle class. When she discusses studies that cite women's gains in the workforce and slippage in the professions, she does not mention the race or class of the authors, many of whom are clearly white and middle class, as if this were somehow anathema to her argument (1989:542), certainly to its spirit. Sacks likewise suspends the use of class labels when discussing Latina, black, and lesbian feminists and feminists of color. Are minority women free of class characteristics, or is class, by nature, something that can be canceled out by the proper, self-selected ideological stance? The most powerful message in the article is epistemological: the only legitimate sources of insight about capitalist hegemony and resistance are working-class men and women, feminists of color, and Marxists.

Like Martin, Sacks was writing at a time of increasing impoverishment of middle-class women and children through divorce, but she, too, is curiously silent on the topic. Like Martin and Rapp, she notes that kin networks are important sources of support for working-class women in times of economic adversity, but she does not consider the implications of the absence of such networks for middle-class women. Without identifying Martin as a white feminist, Sacks cites her "wonderful" exploration showing that middle-class women tend to accept the dominant, medicalized views of women as ruled by their reproductive organs, "while working-class, especially black working-class women, do not see these as ruling events" (1989:543–44).

Again, what are the assumptions that underlie the silences? Capitalism oppresses people by dividing and isolating them. Capitalist ideology trivializes bourgeois women, exaggerates their leisure and power, erases their labor, and endorses their alienation. It assigns them primary responsibility for the characteristics of their class, caricatures them as amoral and insensitive to the suffering of others, thereby setting them up as legitimate targets of class and race hostility (see Stoler 1991). This is precisely what Sacks does, only at the end of this Marxist-feminist version of *High Noon* Helen Ramirez (Mexican actress Katy Jurado), the fiercely independent Hispanic businesswoman, triumphs morally, while Amy Cain (Grace Kelly / Barbie), the white bourgeois heroine who abandons her religious beliefs to stand by her man, cravenly takes the train out of Hadleyville.

Sacks argues in her conclusion for an expanded analytical definition of *working class* to encompass both waged and unwaged laborers who are members of a community that is dependent upon waged labor but that is unable to reproduce itself on those wages alone. She suggests that women's gender identities are not analytically separable from their racial and class identities. (What, then, is the author's gender identity?) She defines *class* as a relation to the means of production that is collective rather than individual, as a relation of communities to the capitalist state more than of employees or employers, but it is totally unclear where unwaged middle-class housewives who live isolated lives as a price of their "secure resource base" and impoverished divorcees, members of the new urban peasantry (see Hochschild 1989:249–53), stand in this equation. All of which leads to the conclusion that one should not expect to find any generic worker or essential worker or, for that matter, working-class consciousness; that not only is class experienced in historically specific ways, but it is also experienced in racially specific, gender-specific, and kinship-specific ways (Sacks 1989: 540).

Taken as a whole, Sacks's work seems to constitute more of a loyal opposition to male Marxism than a full-blown attack on it. She may indeed have attempted to comprehend class, race, and gender oppression as part of a unitary system, but she did so at a cost of ignoring fundamental feminist insights, by failing to explore ways in which capitalism oppresses bourgeois women and by disparaging the intellectual contributions of white, middle-class feminists.

How could these authors make their case without reference to those "strawmen" of capitalist society, white bourgeois women? I suggest that their theoretical differences stem, at least in part, from their working conditions. What these three authors have in common is that they are exceptionally talented white middle-class feminists, members of a first wave of American women to systematically strive for and achieve tenured university positions. All appear to be seeking to escape the designation *middle-class* or *bourgeois feminist,* by implication, self-centered woman, in university systems that are not safe or congenial places for women of any race, class, or sexual or ideological orientation (see Russell 1981; Obermiller 1992).

There are several strategies to avoid being labeled middle class or bourgeois feminist in anthropology: to attach oneself to a grand male theorist, be it Lévi-Strauss, Marx, Gramsci, Lyotard, or Bourdieu; to attach oneself to powerful white male mentors within the university system; and/or to identify oneself as Marxist, postmodernist,[23] or nonheterosexual. (Note that these subdesignations immediately put women at risk for other reasons.) A curious double standard is also at work here, one by which bourgeois women are deemed selfish and narrow-minded if they theorize about their own experience. In order to be legitimate they must look after the needs of people "less fortunate" (more enlightened?) than them, which then becomes the basis for their flawed universalizing tendencies. (The reverse does not hold true, however. Feminists of color are not expected to theorize the suffering or degradation of white middle-class matrons.)[24] Finally, in contrast to the earlier waves of feminist work that inspired *Woman, Culture, and Society,* one senses considerable "emotion work" in repressing contradictions between scholarship and personal circumstances. As R. Rosaldo notes, these practices—using the "detached observer" to make ourselves invisible to ourselves—are debilitating (1989:198).

Perhaps ladies only express anger over the circumstances of those less fortunate—the emotional aesthetic of one domain creeping into the next. Or perhaps there are hidden limits to reflexivity in anthropology (Behar and Gordon 1995).[25]

Rethinking Race, Class, and Gender

My concern about these works is with how the contradictions and hidden scripts affect the aspirations of women of any race or class. If one attains a tenure line position in academia, one by definition has elite credentials, and female professors are by definition (occupation) middle class or bourgeois. Adopting the language of postmodernist Nicholson, let us acknowledge the "specific location" of the authors. Either they gave up having children and clean houses as a condition of "equality" in the workplace like other professional women, or someone else was rearing their children and cleaning their houses so they could keep their jobs.

Borrowing from postmodernism (and Bourdieu), we can define *bourgeois women* as women of any race or class who have attained a "space of legitimate discourse" in which the condition for speaking is silence about their own lives. In contrast to poor women, who are policed externally and worn down by poverty, and working-class women, who may be ground down by fatigue and discouraged from pursuing university degrees, middle- and upper-class women are, like Barbie, self-policed, self-paralyzed, and "media paralyzed."[26] They achieve "legitimate" discourse positions at a cost of silencing themselves, much in the way that rich women, by mastering the rules of elegant dress and conversation, render themselves economically impotent.

The bashing of bourgeois women in the university sends a fearful message to women who aspire to any position of public authority. Regardless of their "specific location"—their race, class, individual struggles, and/or personal beliefs—they, too, may be easily caricatured as ambitious, vacuous, and insensitive to the needs of others, legitimate targets of race and class antagonism. As Rapp (1982:179) and others point out, upwardly mobile black women often face considerable opposition from their own kin groups, to say nothing of the hostility faced by black feminists.[27]

What is the meaning of class in relation to women? Is it genuinely related to labor, occupation, community, or capital? Is it education? Household resources? Residence? Lineage? An aesthetic? A sentiment? Following Bourdieu (1984), we could calculate class for men in terms of various sorts of capital, and occupation, education, residence, and prestige would add up to a relatively clear-cut class position. For women, however, none of these elements necessarily implies the other.

This point is most clearly illustrated in attitudes about the reproductive chances of professional women, including university professors (see Abramson and Franklin 1986: chap. 5; Obermiller 1992). Is their seeking of financial independence so unwomanly that "inopportunity" to bear children is a just retribution? Or is this supreme alienation irrelevant because they are bourgeois and inherently trivial? Is the difference in women's reproductive chances by class really that some forms of control are *external,* exercised by the state, and others are *internal,* exercised by the individual, or is this merely a variant of capitalist gender ideology? The most significant class difference between men and women may be that upward mobility for men incurs substantial benefits, many of them hidden, with relatively little fragmentation of the self, whereas for women it incurs fatigue, hostility, and alienation up to and including childlessness.[28]

This kind of naturalized violence and contradiction in U.S. society sends a message to all women: why strive? This is not a hypothetical point. I have seen a generation of women of all races agonize over the fact that pursuit of a Ph.D. degree or professional career may result in the very real possibility that they will never have children.

These "leveling factors" suggest that class for women consists of a series of interlocking, mutually exclusive aesthetic and symbolic devices that alienate women from one another and keep them a "second sex" of servants, be they domestic or intellectual. These devices operate in at least four domains touched upon throughout this essay, as: (1) rationales for women's membership in the reserve labor force; (2) discourse positions; (3) reproductive chances; and (4) emotional repertoires.[29]

Insights about the bashing of bourgeois women are central to the construction of a theoretically adequate model of Western capitalism and its export globally: The value of bourgeois ideals of femininity to processes of capital formation is that women who adopt them are least capable of resistance. The scotoma, or "blind spots," of Martin, Rapp, and Sacks's analyses occur at precisely those points where women are emotionally paralyzed and subordinated in capitalist society in ways that seem natural to the natives. Barbie has long been an extraordinarily dense transfer point for power relations within U.S. society and between the United States and the "developing nations" of the Third World. By now there is ample evidence to suggest that she is well on her way to becoming an extraordinarily dense transfer point for power relations within so-called Third World nations as well (see Young et al. 1981; Fuentes and Ehrenreich 1983; Mies 1986: chap. 4; Ong 1987).

Bashing bourgeois women damages anthropology, feminist studies, and the aspirations of all women. How can we urge students to strive for difficult goals when their supposed role models are silenced as a condition of employment, characterized as privileged while they go childless "by choice," and risk job loss should they give birth? If this is what white upper- and middle-class women experience in positions of authority and power, what can possibly be in store for "bourgeois" minority women?

The representation of white female professors as the other in this new wave of feminist scholarship occurs when significant numbers of women have entered academia and the economy is in decline. Unless these theoretical blind spots are addressed, we risk not just the specter of anthropology against women but that of feminist anthropology against women.

Surviving Academia

From the perspective of the millennium it is probably safe to say that the university in the 1980s, like other corporate environments, was about as friendly to female authority as was the "new army"—and that it operated at about the same level of contradiction. The lives of Shelly's students, like those of the authors discussed here, were "works in progress." We were not improvising as much as pursuing "visions already defined" (Bateson 1989); for many of us those visions were inspired by Shelly's life and work. Propelled by the supposed gains of the women's movement, our mandate was not to restrict ourselves to the ghetto of "women's studies" (which, in many universities, was outlawed from "serious anthropology") but, rather, to prove ourselves equal to our chosen professions.

After years of study, surmounting hurdle after hurdle in what, in many cases, was still literally "a man's world," there was a sense of disbelief that the rules could apply so differently to us. In the years before full-blown tenure and contract disputes, incident after incident, discussed in hushed tones over lunch, behind closed doors, or over telephones at night, it dawned on us that we were subject to gender discrimination—in spades.[30] Student evaluations invariably included at least one comment on our clothing: *men act, women appear.* Operating in hierarchical work settings, usually with a single, untenured female at the bottom, we quickly acquiesced to required codes of cultural idiocy—or not. Our comments and works and ideas were subject to ceaseless erasure. Had we not spoken loudly enough? Was our diction wrong?[31] Like Grace Kelly and Katy Jurado of *High Noon,* our words and actions were overwritten by powerful cultural scripts.[32] Then there were the topsy-turvy rules on decorum, staff support,[33] and harassment. The latter left us, like female physicians, fair game for almost everyone in the system: colleagues, graduate students, fraternity members inspired by the *Playboy* advisor to protect their "rights" in the classroom.

Gradually, more serious choices, or lack thereof, became clear. We were working in institutions that had no maternity leave. The price of tenure was the risk of going childless. Domestic relations court, with its own version of the glass ceiling. Here the same cultural scripts—the image of the privileged bourgeois woman "doing it all" without mussing her hair—held sway, except now children's lives were at stake (Shipp 1987).[34] Labor that was "invisible" to spouses was also invisible to the judge and his minions.[35]

The last time I saw Shelly Rosaldo, years before I brought my own child into academia, she was nursing Manny at a potluck dinner. Earlier, at a Monday afternoon seminar at the University of Chicago, she was forced to cut off a fierce, prolonged attack of the type that characterizes this event. She loved the debate, she said later, but her breasts were leaking. Shelly's death, so inexplicable, somehow seems a retribution from the gods for having stormed those portals. The image of Shelly nursing Manny triumphs.

NOTES

1. Barbie was first marketed in 1959 as part of the onslaught of consumer culture in post–World War II America (see Ehrenreich 1989:34 ff.).

2. For a graphic example of "Barbie bashing," see Grant 1990:66. Male student reactions ranged from "Take her clothes off!" (half-kidding) to anger that she wouldn't date them (or G.I. Joe). Female reactions ranged from disdain to admiration, always with an uncurrent of comparison between themselves and the Barbie ideal. The intensity of emotion aimed at the doll, ranging from violence and mutilation to obsessive desire to supposed feminist rage, underscores Foucault's observation that sexuality constitutes "an especially dense transfer point for relations of power" (in Caplan 1987:7). These examples also suggest the obvious—that Barbie/sexuality is an extraordinarily dense transfer point for power relations in our own society.

3. Barbie's odd manifestations continue to multiply at a dizzying rate. For recent academic treatments of Barbie as a cultural phenomenon, see Benstock and Ferriss 1993; Rand 1995; and Kirkham 1996.

4. In U.S. society separation of public from domestic domains is as much a shifting marker of class/prestige as it is actuality. In the workplace an idiom of care rather than one of rights or obligations is an active marker/locus of subordination. So, too, popular sociological distinctions of "achieved" versus "ascribed" status. The idea that women are psychologically less individuated than men functions as a persistent cultural rationale for assigning them the status of "girl," with attendant loss of economic benefits and civil rights. Among other things these notions drive the plots of Hollywood movies and public legal dramas.

5. Professional Barbie is amoral because she is "selfish" in the interests of her career, nonmaternal and nonnurturing. As journalist Katha Pollitt presents the dilemma of American women, "If she works, she's neglectful; if she doesn't, she's a parasite" (*Nation* 1987).

6. Most feminists recognize that women are subordinated by patriarchal institutions (see French 1992) and subjected to men in civil society. They recognize that women are second-class citizens and are connected to the state through men (Shanley and Pateman 1991; Sachs and Wilson 1978) and that civil contracts carry hidden "sexual contracts" that require obedience for protection (Pateman 1988).

7. This is true even of Ehrenreich's work *Fear of Falling: The Inner Life of the Middle Class* (1989).

8. Debates about housework as surplus value featured in the *New Left Review* in the late 1970s concluded that housework subsidizes a privatized area that subsidizes the public sector. These insights are rarely integrated into mainstream Marxism, certainly not in anthropology.

9. Engels makes this point in *The Origin of the Family, Private Property, and the State* (1942:65–66), but it is not central to Marx's classic work on the labor theory of value.

10. For instance, black females of any class, like maids and butlers of any color, may be almost totally excluded from public discourse (see Ehrenreich 1989:5). White middle-class women may experience erasure or hostile trivialization in public settings, while wealthy or prominent white women may be the target of derision and naked hostility from the press, including the global tabloid press.

11. Barbie's first words, in 1992, were "Math class is tough."

12. For some hilarious examples of elite female socialization in Spain, see *The Spy Went Dancing* (1990:155 ff.), written by Aline, countess of Romanones, an American from Pearl River, N.Y. (see Stoler 1991).

13. See Nelson W. Aldrich Jr.'s scathing denunciation of Sallie Bingham's "meddling" in her family's business (1988:204–12).

14. Countess Aline offers some not-so-hilarious examples of this principle at work (1990:326).

15. With the curious exception of Christie Hefner, heir to the *Playboy* empire, rich women do not seem to rebel by becoming CEO's of family companies or by getting MBA degrees.

16. Uncoincidentally, Pulitzer, Barrows, and Trump (1992) wrote steamy books full of terms like *bitch, slut,* and *whore.*

17. Stoler notes that in European colonies "single professional women were

held in contempt as were European prostitutes, with surprisingly similar objections" (1991:71).

18. A colleague laughed when she read this: her mother sent Waterford crystal during a divorce crisis, when she could barely afford food, rent, or daycare.

19. Ehrenreich's (1989) otherwise nuanced and sophisticated treatment of the professional middle class displays the same myopia with regard to the effects of divorce on professional women.

20. Rapp's (1982) article deals mainly with working-class households, for which she cites extensive research. She presents her observations about middle- and upper-class households as "hunches" and does not cite extensive scholarly literature.

21. For a rather muddled treatment of the debates surrounding the economic effects of divorce on women, see Sommers 1994:236–37.

22. Palmer's (1989) more recent work indicates the extent to which such "madams" and their servants are anachronisms in contemporary U.S. society, particularly among the middle class.

23. Nicholson's *Feminism/Postmodernism* (1990) is a postmodernist version of "bourgeois bashing." Like Sacks, the argument orients itself by means of indirect, critical references to Rosaldo.

24. Frankenberg (1993), for instance, addressing the cultural construction of whiteness as a dialogue between white feminists and feminists of color, focuses on "whiteness" and "privilege" as a province of women.

25. By 1989 Renato Rosaldo, writing from the perspective of a Chicano male scholar, drawing from the insights of feminism, and working from the register of emotion, was aggressively challenging the conventions and contradictions of "objectivity" in anthropology.

26. Palmer (1983) angrily observes the paralysis of middle-class women but not how their powerlessness complements that of black women. As Ehrenreich and English point out, to say that women are powerless in relation to men does not imply that this takes the same form for every class (1973:11).

27. Sociologist Elaine Bell Kaplan points out that, rather than being characterized as "bourgeois" when they are attacked by other blacks, black feminists are often accused of being "white," a great insult, since members of the black community tend to experience class distinctions as race distinctions (pers. comm.).

28. Bourdieu inadvertently acknowledges the severity of the reproductive crisis experienced by American professional women and the extent to which it is naturalized in this society in his treatment of reproductive crises of (male) peasants (1984:108).

29. For instance, cultural images of working-class women, in the television show "Roseanne," for example, depict them as barely repressing anger on the job for fear of being fired but tapping into reserves of anger at home and in public. In the ghetto open expressions of anger are a means of survival. (A local university trainer advises minority high school students to "put their anger away" as part of the orientation process.) In contrast, ladies never lose their tempers, in public or private (see Ostrander 1984).

30. Public discussion of these topics in anthropology remained virtually taboo until the publication of Behar and Gordon's work *Women Writing Culture* (1995).

31. A tenured scholar who increasingly found herself the sole female on university committees learned never to attend a meeting without an "echo," someone who would repeat and acknowledge her points.

32. Given two female faculty members, one would be assigned the role of witch, the other madonna, depending on who was least powerful at the time.

33. A junior colleague once breezed into the copy room, handed the senior secretary a computer disk, and ordered copies of an exam while the secretary was giving me detailed instructions on operating the mimeograph. Heavy in the air was the understanding that a complaint would elicit the specter of race and class oppression.

34. Professional women who request child care expenses for long work hours are often portrayed by opposing attorneys as overly ambitious, unmaternal, and neglectful of their children.

35. My first inkling of how this particular arena was run—and the fate of my brilliant career—came at a preliminary hearing on child support when a young hearing officer asked why I could not write a book and care for an infant at the same time. His sister had just had a baby, and he knew that babies slept a lot.

REFERENCES

Abramson, Jill, and Barbara Frankli
1986   *Where They Are Now: The Story of the Women of Harvard Law.* Garden City, N.Y.: Doubleday.
Aldrich, Nelson W., Jr.
1988   *Old Money: The Mythology of America's Upper Class.* New York: Alfred A. Knopf.
Aline, Countess of Romanones
1990   *The Spy Went Dancing.* New York: Jove Books.
Arendell, Terry
1986   *Divorce: Women and Children Last.* Berkeley: University of California Press.
Barrows, Sydney, with William Novak
1986   *Mayflower Madam: The Secret Life of Sydney Biddle Barrows.* New York: Arbor House.
Bateson, Mary Catherine
1989   *Composing a Life.* New York: Plume.
Behar, Ruth, and Deborah A. Gordon, eds.
1995   *Women Writing Culture.* Berkeley: University of California Press.
Benenson, Harold Berger
1980   *The Theory of Class and Structural Developments in American Society: A Study of Occupational and Family Change, 1945–70.* Ph.D. diss., New York University.

Benstock, Shari, and Suzanne Ferriss, eds.
1993   *On Fashion.* New Brunswick, N.J.: Rutgers University Press.
Berger, John
1972   *Ways of Seeing.* London: British Broadcasting Corporation and Penguin Books.
Bernstein, Basil
1971   *Class, Codes and Control,* vol. 1: *Theoretical Studies toward a Sociology of Language.* London: Routledge and Kegan Paul.
Bingham, Sallie
1989   *Passion and Prejudice: A Family Memoir.* New York: Alfred A. Knopf.
Bourdieu, Pierre
1984   *Distinction: A Social Critique of the Judgment of Taste.* Trans. Richard Nice. Cambridge: Harvard University Press.
Braverman, Harry
1974   *Labor and Monopoly Capital.* New York: Monthly Review Press.
Caplan, Pat
1987   Introduction. In *The Cultural Construction of Sexuality,* ed. Pat Caplan, 1–30. London: Tavistock Publications.
Chodorow, Nancy
1979   "Mothering, Male Dominance, and Capitalism." In *Capitalist Patriarchy and the Case for Socialist Feminism,* ed. Zillah Eisenstein, 83–106. New York: Monthly Review Press.
Collier, Jane, Michelle Z. Rosaldo, and Sylvia Yanagisako
1982   "Is There a Family? New Anthropological Views." In *Rethinking the Family,* ed. Barrie Thorne and Marilyn Yalom, 25–39. New York: Longman.
di Leonardo, Micaela
1991   "Introduction: Gender, Culture, and Political Economy." In *Gender at the Crossroads of Knowledge: Feminist Anthropology in the Postmodern Era,* ed. Micaela di Leonardo, 1–48. Berkeley: University of California Press.
Donovan, Josephine
1991   *Feminist Theory: The Intellectual Traditions of American Feminism.* New York: Continuum.
Ehrenreich, Barbara
1989   *Fear of Falling: The Inner Life of the Middle Class.* New York: Pantheon Books.
Ehrenreich, Barbara, and Dierdre English
1973   *Complaints and Disorders: The Sexual Politics of Sickness.* Glass Mountain Pamphlet no. 2. New York: Feminist Press.
Emshwiller, John R.
1991   White Women Owning Small Businesses Seek Federal Aid for the Disadvantaged. *Wall Street Journal,* August 7, B1.
Engels, Frederick
1942   [1884] *The Origin of the Family, Private Property and the State.* New York: International.

Frankenberg, Ruth
1993   *The Social Construction of Whiteness: White Women Race Matters.* Minneapolis: University of Minnesota Press.
Flax, Jane
1981   "Do Feminists Needs Marxism?" *Building Feminist Theory,* 174–85. New York: Longman.
1988   "Are Postmodernist-Feminist Theories of Justice Possible?" MS.
Fraser, Nancy
1991   "What's Critical about Critical Theory? The Case of Habermas and Gender." In *Feminist Interpretations and Political Theory,* ed. Mary Lyndon Shanley and Carole Pateman, 253–76. Cambridge: Polity Press.
French, Marilyn
1992   *The War against Women.* New York: Summit Books.
Friedan, Betty
1963   *The Feminine Mystique.* New York: Dell Publishing.
Fuentes, Annette, and Barbara Ehrenreich
1983   *Women in the Global Factory.* Boston: South End Press.
Frye, Marilyn
1981   "Who Wants a Piece of the Pie?" In *Building Feminist Theory,* 94–100. New York: Longman.
Gilligan, Carol
1982   *In A Different Voice: Psychological Theory and Women's Development.* Cambridge: Harvard University Press.
Grant, Linda
1990   *Blind Trust.* New York: Ivy Books.
Haraway, Donna
1990   "A Manifesto for Cyborgs: Science, Technology, and Socialist Feminism in the 1980s." In *Feminism/Postmodernism,* ed. Linda Nicholson, 190–233. New York: Routledge.
Hartmann, Heidi
1981a   "The Unhappy Marriage of Marxism and Feminism: Towards a More Progressive Union." In *Women and Revolution,* ed. Lydia Sargent, 1–41. Boston: South End Press.
1981b   "The Family as the Locus of Gender, Class and Political Struggle: The Example of Housework." *Signs: Journal of Women in Culture and Society* 6 (3): 366–94.
Hartsock, Nancy
1981   "Political Change: Two Perspectives on Power." In *Building Feminist Theory: Essays from Quest, A Feminist Quarterly,* 3–19. New York: Longman.
Hochschild, Arlie, with Anne Machung
1989   *The Second Shift: Working Parents and the Revolution at Home.* New York: Viking.
Kirkham, Pat, ed.
1996   *The Gender Object.* Manchester: Manchester University Press.

Lewis, Michael
1989 *Liar's Poker: Rising through the Wreckage on Wall Street.* New York: W. W. Norton.
Lutz, Nancy
1992 "Constructing the Modern Indonesian Woman." Paper presented at the Conference on the Narrative and Practice of Gender in Southeast Asian Cultures, University of California, Berkeley, March 1.
Luxemburg, Rosa
1971 "Women's Suffrage and Class Struggle." In *Selected Political Writings,* ed. Dick Howard, 216–22. New York: Monthly Review Press.
MacKinnon, Catharine A.
1989 *Toward a Feminist Theory of the State.* Cambridge: Harvard University Press.
Marcus, George
1992 *Lives in Trust: The Fortunes of Dynastic Families in Late Twentieth Century America.* Boulder: Westview Press.
Martin, Emily
1987 *The Woman in the Body: A Cultural Analysis of Reproduction.* Boston: Beacon Press.
Marx, Karl, and Frederick Engels
1970 [1938] *The German Ideology.* Ed. C. J. Arthur. New York: International Publishers.
McLellan, David
1980 *The Thought of Karl Marx: An Introduction.* London: Macmillan.
Mies, Maria
1986 *Patriarchy and Accumulation on a World Scale: Women in the International Division of Labor.* London: Zed Books.
Mullings, Leith
1994 "Images, Ideology, and Women of Color." In *Women of Color in U.S. Society,* ed. Maxine Baca Zinn and Bonnie Thornton Dill, 265–89. Philadelphia: Temple University Press.
Nicholson, Linda J., ed.
1990 *Feminism/Postmodernism.* New York: Routledge.
Obermiller, Tim
1992 "Glass Ceilings in the Ivory Tower." In *University of Chicago Magazine* 84 (5): 16–21.
Ong, Aihwa
1987 *Spirits of Resistance and Capitalist Discipline.* Albany: State University of New York Press.
Ortner, Sherry B., and Harriet Whitehead
1981 "Introduction: Accounting for Sexual Meanings." In *Sexual Meanings: The Cultural Construction of Gender and Sexuality,* 1–27. Cambridge: Cambridge University Press.
Ostrander, Susan A.
1984 *Women of the Upper Class.* Philadelphia: Temple University Press.

Palmer, Phyllis M.
1983 "White Women / Black Women: The Dualism of Female Identity and Experience in the United States." *Feminist Studies* 9:151–70.
1989 *Domesticity and Dirt: Housewives and Domestic Servants in the United States, 1920–1945.* Philadelphia: Temple University Press.
Pateman, Carole
1988 *The Sexual Contract.* Stanford: Stanford University Press.
Plunket, Robert
1993 "Age Cannot wither Her, Nor Custom Stale." Review of *Mondo Barbie,* ed. Lucinda Ebersole and Richard Peabody. *Sunday New York Times Book Review,* April 18, 7.
Pulitzer, Roxanne, with Kathleen Maxa
1988 *The Prize Pulitzer.* New York: Villard Books.
Quest
1981 *Building Feminist Theory: Essays from Quest, A Feminist Quarterly.* New York: Longman.
Rand, Erica
1995 *Barbie's Queer Accessories.* Durham, N.C.: Duke University Press.
Rapp, Rayna
1982 "Family and Class in Contemporary America: Notes toward an Understanding of Ideology." In *Rethinking the Family,* ed. Barrie Thorne and Marilyn Yalom, 168–87. New York: Longman.
Rosaldo, Michelle Zimbalist
1974 "Woman, Culture, and Society: A Theoretical Overview." In *Woman, Culture, and Society,* ed. Michelle Rosaldo and Louise Lamphere, 17–42. Stanford: Stanford University Press.
Rosaldo, Michelle Zimbalist, and Louise Lamphere, eds.
1974 *Woman, Culture, and Society.* Stanford: Stanford University Press.
Rosaldo, Renato
1989 *Culture and Truth: The Remaking of Social Analysis.* Boston: Beacon Press.
Rothman, Robert A.
1978 *Inequality and Stratification in the United States.* Englewood Cliffs, N.J.: Prentice-Hall.
Rubin, Lillian Breslow
1976 *Worlds of Pain: Life in the Working-Class Family.* New York: Basic Books.
Russell, Michelle
1981 "An Open Letter to the Academy." *Building Feminist Theory,* 101–10. New York: Longman.
Sachs, Albie, and Joan Hoff Wilson
1978 *Sexism and the Law: A Study of Male Beliefs and Legal Bias in Britain and the United States.* New York: Free Press.

Sacks, Karen Brodkin
1984 *Sisters and Wives: The Past and Future of Sexual Equality.* Westport, Conn.: Greenwood Press, Contributions in Women's Studies, no. 10.
1989 "Toward a Unified Theory of Class, Race, and Gender." *American Ethnologist* 16 (3): 534–50.
Sargent, Lydia, ed.
1981 *Women and Revolution: A Discussion of the Unhappy Marriage of Marxism and Feminism.* Boston: South End Press.
Shanley, Mary Lyndon, and Carole Pateman, eds.
1991 *Feminist Interpretations and Political Theory.* Cambridge: Polity Press.
Shipp, E. R.
1987 "In Court, A Woman's Character Can Dictate Her Legal Fortune." *New York Times,* June 10.
Sommers, Christina Hoff
1994 *Who Stole Feminism? How Women Have Betrayed Women.* New York: Simon and Schuster.
Stoler, Ann Laura
1991 "Carnal Knowledge and Imperial Power: Gender, Race, and Morality in Colonial Asia." In *Gender at the Crossroads of Knowledge: Feminist Anthropology in the Postmodern Era,* ed. Micaela di Leonardo, 51–101. Berkeley: University of California Press.
Swiss, Deborah, and Judith Walker
1993 *Women and the Work Family Dilemma: How Professional Women Are Finding Solutions.* New York: John Wiley and Sons.
Trump, Ivana
1992 *For Love Alone.* New York: Pocket Books.
Weber, Max
1946 *From Max Weber: Essays in Sociology.* Ed. and trans. H. H. Gerth and C. Wright Mills. New York: Oxford University Press.
Weitzman, Lenore
1985 *The Divorce Revolution.* New York: Free Press.
Young, Kate, Carol Wolkowitz, and Roslyn McCullagh, eds.
1981 *Of Marriage and the Market: Women's Subordination Internationally and Its Lessons.* London: Routledge.

Afterword

The Use and Abuse of Feminist Theory: Fear, Dust, and Commensality

Ana María Alonso

The anthropological record seems to feed our *fear* that sexual asymmetry is
. . . a deep, *primordial* sort of truth . . . And so, at much the same time that
the evidence of behavioral variation suggests that gender is less a product
of our bodies than of social forms and modes of thought, it seems quite
difficult to believe that sexual inequalities are not rooted in *the dictates of a
natural order.* Minimally, it would appear that certain biological facts—
women's role in reproduction and, perhaps, male strength—have operated
in *a nonnecessary but universal* way to shape and reproduce male
dominance.
—Michelle Rosaldo, "The Use and Abuse of Anthropology"

In truth, however, *the nature of things is no more immutably given, once for
all, than is historical reality.* If woman seems to be the inessential which
never becomes the essential, it is because she herself fails to bring about
this change.
—Simone de Beauvoir, *The Second Sex*

Dust is created by any perceptual stance that hastily traverses the object
world, skims over its surface, treating it as a nullity that casts no meaning
into our bodies, or recovers no stories from the past.
—C. Nadia Seremetakis, *The Senses Still*

Fear

During 1990–1991 my membership in a Feminist Theory Group led me to
reexamine my investment in some poststructuralist ideas. I still recall a
heated exchange. A scholar new to the group stated that the shared experience of menstruation could be a point of departure for a feeling of commonality among women cross-culturally. Immediately interrupted, she
was castigated by another group member for being an "essentialist." She

responded that poststructuralism was engaged in a denial of the body. What struck me about this exchange was the aura of inadmissibility with which my colleague's remarks were endowed by the label *essentialist.* Why were fear, anger, and embarrassment evoked by the public acknowledgment of the specificity of women's physiology? Had *essentialist* become a "gatekeeping label," one that prevented the recognition that biocultural bodily processes might leak out of the safe "theoretical" container of "discourse" (to which they had been consigned by poststructuralism)?

The epigraph from Michelle Z. Rosaldo's 1980 article "The Use and Abuse of Anthropology" sheds light on what motivates the abuse of *essentialist* as a gatekeeping label employed to silence alternative voices that might link our structures of experience and our structures of knowledge in more embodied ways (cf. Maurer, this vol., on the disjunction between his felt sense of sexual identity and anti-essentialism). Many American academic feminists "fear" that any acknowledgment of a bodily basis to gender necessarily means that there is a "natural order" that "dictates" inequality. But, as Rosaldo herself pointed out decades ago, following Simone de Beauvoir, there is no greater necessity attached to nature than to history. Paradoxically, the work of at least one advocate of social revolution, Karl Marx, has taught us how difficult historical change can be.

Although frequently labeled as such, neither Rosaldo nor de Beauvoir (who had an important impact on Rosaldo's work) were essentialists. De Beauvoir wrote *The Second Sex* as a critique of the notion that a "Platonic essence," an "eternal femininity," defined women's identity, dismissing this as "a product of the philosophic imagination" (1952:xvi). Rosaldo takes a similar position in the introduction to *Woman, Culture and Society,* coauthored with Lamphere, and in her own "Theoretical Overview" (1974). She notes that her focus in trying to understand cross-cultural gender asymmetry is "human social and cultural organization," adding that, though this is the product of a "constellation of different factors," of which biology is one, "biology becomes significant only as it is interpreted by human actors and associated with characteristic modes of action" (1974:22–23). She develops the domestic/public distinction as part of a heuristic model that has more in common with a Weberian methodological strategy of ideal types than a structural functionalist empiricist search for general laws. Her goal here is not to develop a "totalizing explanation" or to "deny the heterogeneity among women;" rather, she seeks to make sense of cross-cultural variation and similarity in the forms of inequality linked to the social organization and cultural values of gender orders. A point she makes (frequently elided by those who deny any connection between "sex" and "gender") is that there are limits on variation. Drawing on the unparalleled time depth as well as spatial reach of the information provided by a holistic anthropology, Rosaldo notes that women everywhere bear children, lactate, and have the primary responsibility for child care (see Collier, this vol.). Moreover, she adds that we know of no society in which women have public authority over men. While many find this information threatening, I agree with Rosaldo (1980) that we ignore it at our peril: denying the history of women's oppression will not make it all go away.

In my fall 1997 course "Gender and Social Identity" I taught *Woman, Culture, and Society* in preparation for writing this afterword, knowing that our collection emerges from and is intended to be used in teaching (see Lugo's chap.; and Lugo and Maurer's intro.). I was surprised at the number of students who misinterpreted Rosaldo's work and considered it essentialist. As I listened to their use of the term, I came to understand that they had little knowledge of philosophy; for them *essentialist* was associated with any recognition that gender was a biocultural phenomenon and not simply a free-floating signifier. Most of them were liberal feminists who had internalized modernity's distinction between acquired and achieved statuses; for them freedom meant choice, and gender could not be chosen if it was in any way anchored in human biology—particularly in sexual reproduction. What struck me was the privilege that underpinned this stance. Paradoxically, it is only those who have benefited from successful feminist struggles against the alienation of women from their bodies who can find credible the "reverse discourse" that biology is just someone's bad idea and that "women" is a category with no referent. Privileged women today, who have access to contraception, mammograms, breast reconstructive surgery, infant formulas, breast pumps, child care alternatives, sanitary napkins, tampons, Lamaze methods, etc., tend to forget that they have access to these because of earlier generations' struggles against men's control of women's generativity, against gender bias in the medical establishment, against state regulation of women's sexuality. Less privileged women—in this country and elsewhere—are much more aware of the materiality of the body because they have to struggle with the changes brought on by their cycles, pregnancies, and illnesses in ways that carry more sensory immediacy. The links between stratified reproduction and the reproduction of stratification at global, national, regional, and local levels position women differently and entail diverse experiences of biocultural bodily processes (Ginsburg and Rapp 1995). Yet such diversity should not preclude the recognition of women's forms of commonality and commensality organized around the body and the senses (Seremetakis 1994).

Commensality and Dust

"Eat my dust!" is an Americanism that indexes the preoccupation with speed, overtaking others, and victory that is one of the embodied entailments of modernity's ideology of progress. No commensality—that sense of connection engendered through "the consumption, distribution, sharing and exchange of substances" (Seremetakis 1994:11)—is extended to those "left behind." On the American academic "fast-track" people strive to be "cutting edge" by pulverizing the past. Intellectual genealogies with either a remote ancestor/ancestress (and poorly remembered interlinkages) or shallow time depth reign. Intellectual journeys are rarely nourished by exchanges of any substance with feminists whose work is distanced by adjectives such as *classic, precursor,* or *early.* Even while Western feminists have become concerned with overcoming practices of spatial distancing of "others," they have engaged in the temporal distancing of their own ancestresses.

In her essay in this volume Christine Gray notes that, when she taught *Woman, Culture and Society* at a large, urban university, graduate students "summarily dismissed" it as "bourgeois feminist" as well as essentialist. Gray was struck by the level of antagonism that this 1970s work elicited in the 1990s. Gray mentions that her colleagues "dreaded the designation 'bourgeois feminist.'" The fear and discomfort provoked by the complexity of multifaceted power relations that cannot be reduced to binary terms is part of what produces this dread. Feminists are uneasy with the privileges they have gained, but they should not be. One of the things I have learned from studying revolt and revolution is that the most subordinated are rarely those who are able effectively to challenge inequalities and change society (pace James Scott's work on the "weapons of the weak"). Guilt about privilege is pointless. Privilege should not be abused but should instead be used as a resource in our ongoing struggles against all forms of inequality and oppression. The writings of feminists such as Michelle Z. Rosaldo are resources we can use.

I am very happy that Alejandro Lugo and Bill Maurer have put together this volume in Michelle Rosaldo's memory. The heterogeneity of the contributors' voices is highly appropriate when honoring a scholar such as Rosaldo, who was in many ways a "colporteur," someone whose work glued "moments of the past and the different . . . onto the experience of the present" (Seremetakis 1994:32, 33). Colportage "brings the past into the present as a transformative and interruptive force" (31), disturbing the repression and displacement of sensory horizons and memories that have characterized modernity and postmodernity.

I congratulate the editors for producing a fine volume but cannot endorse all of the future directions they suggest for extending Michelle Rosaldo's legacy. More specifically, I strongly oppose "the shift from a focus on practice theory (somewhat positivist in nature) to Judith Butler's conceptualization of performativity." I have chosen to read this volume as well as reflect on Rosaldo's legacy through the lens of Seremetakis's work precisely to avoid the reductionisms of both realism and idealism. I seek to bring the perspective of a politicized anthropology of the senses to our analysis of gender, sexuality, and other dimensions of social relations, identities, and experience, without losing the contributions of "practice theory" to our understanding of society. Consequently, I disagree with the editors' call to "make an analytical departure from sentimental notions of feeling and emotion to a conceptual (though not necessarily purely cere-bral) discussion of the interiority or, rather, 'inwardness' of the person" (Lugo and Maurer, intro.). I am uncomfortable with the denigration of sentiment and the privileging of the conceptual that is expressed here, par-ticularly as the authors' invoke Varela to claim that emotions are "expres-sive indices of speech acts." Where is the body in this? It seems to have been turned into "dust." In this respect I find Seremetakis's anthropology of the senses to be more compatible with Rosaldo's holistic perspective and her emphasis on the centrality of the social to the formation of "feel-ing selves":

> The points of the body . . . are not merely marks on the surface but an active capacity. Awakening these points as sensate is opening the body to semiosis. The senses, the "points" (*semía*) of the body, are the sites where matter is subjected to signification. Semiosis here is inseparable from interpersonal exchange. (Seremetakis 1994:27)[1]

The other points of the editors' agenda, however, bring the past into the present in ways that recuperate aspects of Rosaldo's work that have been largely repressed. I fully agree with their insistence that we "go beyond exclusive studies of 'masculinity' and 'femininity' and into more rigorous studies of gender—of both men and women." This insight is further developed in Lugo's chapter and supported by his rich ethnographic work on the maquiladora industry and on men's expressions of emotions in a "domesticated public space." Defending Rosaldo against her critics, Lugo makes the excellent observation that one of her more radical suggestions was that men be integrated in new ways into the domestic sphere and that anthropologists study men as well as women. Contrasting the position of bourgeois men and women in the domestic and public spheres, Gray problematizes how we should determine, for analytical and political purposes, women's class positions given their unwaged work in the home. Here she contrasts the hidden entitlements of bourgeois men with the hidden exploitation and insecurity of bourgeois women. I disagree with her definition of class (Weber's distinction between class and status might be a good point of departure for addressing some of the issues Gray raises). I am also not convinced by her claim that bourgeois women may face "more severe" problems than working-class women. Yet I think that her points about "bourgeois feminist bashing" in the academy and the scapegoating of white professional women in the United States are valid and deserve our full consideration. Gutmann's chapter contributes the insight that forms of paternity are central to varying perceptions of manhood in Mexico City; patriarchy is not monolithic. Studying gender in relation to other dimensions of social identity, Gutmann notes, was anticipated by Rosaldo; this is a move endorsed but also problematized—by Gray.

Understanding gender in relation to ethnicity, class, age, and national identity is especially difficult because, as Rosaldo stressed in her 1980 piece, it entails a self-reflexive awareness of our own ideologies and how they might impact our definition of analytical categories and units. This difficulty is illustrated by Gutmann's otherwise fine piece: though he is rightly critical of earlier work that equates "machismo with Mexican culture as a whole," he himself uses "Mexico" as a unit of analysis without fully recognizing how different regional histories have shaped diverse forms of manhood in Mexico (e.g., see Alonso 1995; Nugent 1989; and Nuñez Noriega 1994; O'Malley 1986 provides an in-depth look at state formation, masculinities, and the cinema).

Another item of the editors' agenda I strongly endorse is their suggestion that the public/domestic distinction, though still important analytically, needs to be rethought in the light of more recent work on capitalism, state formation, and biopower. It is to a fuller discussion of this suggestion that I now turn.

Modernity, the Public, and the Domestic

Feminist anthropology in its consideration of male bias in scholarship anticipated the more general concern with self-reflexiveness that became integrated into mainstream anthropology in the 1980s. Michelle Rosaldo went further and examined how Victorian ideology regarding domestic versus public spheres might have impacted her own work and that of other feminists. Her exploration of the influence that Victorian thinking had on social theory and feminist theory is discussed in Jane Collier's fascinating piece in this volume. What Collier clarifies is that Rosaldo wanted to develop a social explanation for cross-cultural asymmetries in public authority between men and women and in the cultural value accorded to their respective activities. The "structural" explanation that Rosaldo developed with Collier advanced the important insight that holding authority in a society is linked to the possibility of producing public culture (an insight that shares something with Gramsci's theory of hegemony).

Rosaldo came to realize that her own version of the domestic/public contrast had been influenced by Victorian assumptions. This does not discount, however, the importance of two insights that she and Collier developed and which the editors of this book support. First, as Collier points out, it is important to realize that many cultures "make a domestic/public cultural contrast" but that the articulation between these domains varies both historically and cross-culturally. This is because they are not static givens but the product of people's actions and struggles (see Díaz Barriga's chapter in this volume on domestic/public in scholarly work on popular movements in Mexico and Latin America). Second, as Collier states, the legacy of the Enlightenment "imagined domestic spheres based on emotion in contrast to public spheres based on self-interested political contracts"; this separation of spheres was shaped by capitalism and the distinction it created between waged and unwaged work (see Gray, this vol.). In this connection Lugo's article is particularly interesting. How are the forms of contemporary, global capitalism changing domestic/public articulations? The connections between capitalism, the reification of the public/domestic dichotomy, and the devaluation of women's work and sexuality are brilliantly demonstrated by Bill Maurer's essay in this volume. By "using the dichotomy critically" rather than taking "it as a handy way to reflect the lived realities" he observed, Maurer is able to uncover a key paradox: "Many women's activities, the purpose of which is to maintain the household, are performed in the public arena. This public performance often has far-reaching public effects . . . Women's economic activities, for instance, not only affect the public sphere but partially constitute it." Maurer's insight raises a key issue for political strategy: if women's activities partly constitute the public sphere, then they can also change oppressive forms of domestic/public articulation. Anthony Giddens has made just this point, arguing that, by transforming the terms of intimacy in Western societies, feminists have spearheaded the "democratising of the interpersonal domain" (1992:3). He adds (perhaps too optimistically from Gray's point of view) that

the transformation of intimacy might be a subversive influence upon modern institutions as a whole. For a social world in which emotional fulfillment replaced the maximising of economic growth would be very different from that which we know at present. The changes now affecting sexuality are indeed revolutionary, and in a very profound way. (1992:3)

Although the editors note that the state has played an important role in organizing social life in terms of a domestic/public split and in producing the ideology that legitimates state production of this "hegemonic construct" (see intro., this volume), there is relatively little in the book that develops this notion. A large interdisciplinary body of literature exists on the subject. Recent anthropological works on the topic include Krause 1994, articles in Yanagisako and Delaney 1995, articles in Ginsburg and Rapp 1995, articles in *Identities* 2(1–2) 1995, and Brian McVeigh's work on the Japanese state's formation of subjectivities. One of his fascinating articles shows how junior colleges in Japan produce "office flowers," women who constitute about one-third of the female labor force and who "perform low-salaried, secretarial, hostess, and housekeeping tasks for businesses of all sizes" (1995:29). Like Maurer and Gray, McVeigh demonstrates how women's public work is trivialized by being "domesticated." The introduction to this volume stresses the importance of understanding how domestic/public comes to have meaning for people. In this connection McVeigh argues that subjectivity cannot be reduced to language. He demonstrates in rich ethnographic detail that "the body does more than just represent meanings through gesture, dress, and deportment: belief, through felt experience, is reified through the body itself" (1995:34). In order to understand this process of reification, we need to go beyond a performance theory of subjectivity to one that fully recognizes the materiality of the body in society and the importance of the senses in social life.

Mud

When I asked the students of one graduate seminar to define *theory,* one of them wrote:

> Mostly I think theory is what we use to keep our feet out of the mud. Still, I think it is important to understand theory in order to remove our galoshes and feel the mud squish up between our toes.

If dust is relatively common in universities, mud is not. The linguistic and aesthetic reductionism that characterizes many poststructuralist and postmodernist positions "creates dust" and keeps "our feet out of the mud." Trends such as the alienation from the body, the privileging of reason as the only source of truth, the political naïveté of a social constructionism that assumes that social life is continuously in flux and that all inequalities are "negotiated," the extreme nominalism that ignores the phenomenon of linguistic reference—all are troubling. Much contemporary work seems to be lacking concepts appropriate to an analysis of social relations that focuses on more than discourse. The work done in the 1970s by Michelle Rosaldo, Carol MacCormack, and others was more holistic. Rosaldo's work stands out for its insistence on the importance of the social and not just the cultural. For Rosaldo there was a "subject of feminism"—women. In this respect I have found teaching and writing about her work refreshing. I no longer think that the deconstruction of the "subject of feminism" (e.g., Butler 1990) is useful, either intellectually or politically. A feminism without "a subject" has little to offer to women outside the academy or to activists working in battered women's shelters, legal aid, and numerous women's health, social and political organizations. A crippling split has emerged between feminists who believe in women and those who do not.

230 / *Gender Matters*

NOTES

Profound thanks to Virginia Nazarea, who introduced me to the work of C. Nadia
Seremetakis. Thanks also to David Killick for his helpful comments. I am very
grateful to the editors of this volume, Alejandro Lugo and Bill Maurer, for invit-
ing me to write this afterword and for their patience.

1. See Seremetakis 1994:7–12, for her critique of performance studies grounded
in theatrical metaphors.

REFERENCES

Alonso, Ana María
1995   *Thread of Blood: Colonialism, Revolution, and Gender on Mexico's Northern Frontier.* Tucson: University of Arizona Press.
Butler, Judith
1990   *Gender Trouble: Feminism and the Subversion of Identity.* New York:
Routledge.
Collier, Jane, and Bill Maurer, eds.
1995   Special issue: "Sanctioned Identities." *Identities* 2 (1–2).
de Beauvoir, Simone
1952   *The Second Sex.* New York: Vintage Books.
Giddens, Anthony
1992   *The Transformation of Intimacy: Sexuality, Love and Eroticism in Modern
Societies.* Stanford: Stanford University Press.
Ginsburg, Faye D., and Rayna Rapp
1995   *Conceiving the New World Order.* Berkeley: University of California
Press.
Krause, Elizabeth L.
1994   "Forward vs. Reverse Gear: Politics of Proliferation and Resistance in
the Italian Fascist State." *Journal of Historical Sociology* 7 (3): 261–88.
McVeigh, Brian
1995   "The Feminization of Body, Behavior, and Belief: The Cultivation of
'Office Flowers' at a Japanese Women's Junior College." *American Asian
Review* 13 (2): 29–67.
Nugent, Daniel
1989   "'Are We Not [Civilized] Men?' The Formation and Devolution of Com-
munity in Northern Mexico." *Journal of Historical Sociology* 2 (3):
206–39.
Nuñez Noriega, Guillermo
1994   *Sexo entre varones: poder y resistencia en el campo sexual.* Hermosillo: El
Colegio de Sonora, Universidad de Sonora.
O'Malley, Ilene
1986   *The Myth of the Revolution: Hero Cults and the Institutionalization of the
Mexican State 1920–1940.* London: Greenwood Press.

Rosaldo, Michelle Z.
1980   "The Use and Abuse of Anthropology: Reflections on Feminism and Cross-Cultural Understanding." *Signs* 5 (3): 389–417.
Rosaldo, Michelle Z., and Louise Lamphere
1974   *Woman, Culture and Society.* Stanford: Stanford University Press.
Seremetakis, C. Nadia
1994   *The Senses Still: Perception and Memory as Material Culture in Modernity.* Chicago: University of Chicago Press.
Yanagisako, Sylvia, and Carol Delaney
1995   *Naturalizing Power: Essays in Feminist Cultural Analysis.* New York: Routledge.

Contributors

Ana María Alonso is Associate Professor, Department of Anthropology, University of Arizona.

Jane F. Collier is Professor, Department of Anthropology, Stanford University.

Miguel Diaz Barriga is Associate Professor, Department of Sociology and Anthropology, Swarthmore College.

Christine E. Gray is Research Associate, South and Southeast Asia Studies, University of California at Berkeley.

Matthew C. Gutmann is Assistant Professor, Department of Anthropology, Brown University.

Louise Lamphere is Professor, Department of Anthropology, University of New Mexico.

Alejandro Lugo is Assistant Professor, Department of Anthropology, University of Illinois at Urbana-Champaign.

Carol MacCormack was Professor, Department of Anthropology, Bryn Mawr College.

Bill Maurer is Assistant Professor, Department of Anthropology, University of California at Irvine.

Author Index

Subject Index

AAA (American Anthropological
  Association) meetings
  1971, 5, 8
  1991, x
  1992, x, 83
AFA (Association of Feminist Anthropologists), xiii
Algeria (Kabylian society), 61
Alienation, 103, 105, 106
  of bourgeois women, 204, 207
  of women from their bodies, 223
American
  academic "fast track," 224
  cultural images of working-class
    women in *Roseanne,* 211n. 29
  emotional repertoire, 195
Anthropologist(s)
  and creation of Mexican Machismo
    (section), 163–65
  ethnographic authority of, 173
  French, tend to neglect feminism, 39
  important female, 1
  moving away from universal expla-
    nations of gender inequality,
    117
  searching for universals in 1970s, 56
  use and abuse of *machismo,* 175
Anthropology
  criticized as colonial discipline, 13
  emphasis in feminist, has been on
    women, 60
  and emphasis on historical context,
    2
  "of the familiar," 197
  and feminism, 17
  feminist, 12, 16, 18

bourgeois women in, 197
  lack of training in, 72
  and hope for reconsideration of
    Rosaldo's ideas, x, 17
  los hombres (men) and *los machos*
    are valid categories in, 162
  Marxist, 72
  as politicized, 225
  privileging social structure over feel-
    ing, 70
  and a "quotable sound bite defining
    Mexican masculinity/
    machismo," 170
  and section on Mexican *machismo,*
    175–78
  and self-reflexiveness (1980s), 227
  use and abuse of, (essay), 63

Barbie
  the "Barbie attack" (trivialization of
    bourgeois women), 185, 204
  Bashing Barbie (section), 186–89
  bashing is okay, 188, 209n. 2
  the dark side of, 186–87
  the doll, 29
    as an example of American com-
      modity fetishism, 186
  doll as *the* bimbo of American cul-
    ture, 186
  and middle- and upper-class women,
    206
Barra (piece of iron or "lazy"), 73–74,
  77
Bourgeois women
  bashing of, in universities, 206, 207,
    208, 226

dreaded label of "bourgeois feminism," 187
French anthropologists neglect, 39
literature of, 54, 60
(on urban movements), 116
Feminist(s), 54
Bread and Roses (feminist organization), 4
Feminist Studies (Stanford), 10
film classic, *Rosie the Riveter* (1980), 193
lack of training in critical feminist anthropology, 72
Marxist-feminists not free from Victorian gender conceptions, 154–55
and they reproduce Victorian oppositions, 155
object to universal male dominance, 151
reclaim foremothers, 1
Ruskin's antifeminist sentiments, 148
scholarship and commonsense insight, 200
sensibility—bag lady is spectre of, 196
study presenting an "Ozzie and Harriet" version of middle-class American existence, 200
theory, the use and abuse of (whole essay), 221–29

Gambia, *Mandinka* villages in the, 41
Ghana, 45
Gender, 17
analysis and modes of production, 47
appeal for rigorous studies of, 31
assumptions as rhetorical strategies, 28
assymmetry as universal, 151
bias in medical establishment, 223
Caribbean studies of, 92–94
constructed on natural substrate of sex, 93

differences in Latin America, 74
failure of social sciences to address issues of, 24
"genderless" distinctions, 150
Gender Politics in Latin America (book), 135
groups (four male), 174
identities and aggressiveness neither masculine nor feminine, 79
identity and reified images (Mexico), 162
identity and theoretical issues, 55
inversions in gender relations, 82
issues about production of gender identity, 55
refocusing of, 65
relations and aura of authority, 27
and destabilizing aura, 65, 81, 82
relations as power, 78
roles as natural, 147
solidarity, 39
studies on women by women and men by men too narrow, 55, 81
theoretical issues redefining conception of, 81
understanding of, is especially difficult, 226

Ilongot(s), 3, 9, 12, 38, 40, 44, 60, 61, 108, 109
lack developed concept of femininity, 155
men *and* women work in domestic spaces, 38
men's hunting, 38
"self" as foil to Western "self," 108
women speak with confidence, 38
India
jajmani system in, 39
north, 45
south, 44
Inuit, 40
Israel (kibbutz), 62
Ivory Coast (Gouro), 38

Marxist opposition between production and reproduction, 93
easy to map Marxist notion onto male/female, 150
oversimplification of concept, 43
from reproduction to production (essay), 38
as stratified, 223
Reproductive
behavior, socialization of, 104
chances of professional women, 207
cycle and rationales for academic hiring, 193
new technologies, 61
and state-of-the-art birth technology, 202
Rosaldo, Michelle ["Shelly"]
against documenting sexism as social fact, 50
agenda, 63
articulation of theory and practice, 64–65, 80
and aura of authority, 54–74, 80
challenged nineteenth-century evolutionary theorists, 149
command of Marxist theory, 38
and consciousness-raising, 4
critique of Victorian ideology, 63
and discussion of "the private" and "the family" in nineteenth century, 104
distinguished power from authority, 154
and cross-cultural asymmetries in public authority, 227
and failure of social sciences to address issues, 24
and Feminist Studies (Stanford), 10
fieldwork, 3, 7
first book attempt, 5–7
focus on unequal values, 58
and Foucault, 20, 30, 104
and guilt and shame, 109
insights were beyond identity politics, 18
intellectual style, 11

legacy, xi, xiii, 1, 12–13, 16, 18, 25
disagreement about legacy, 18
never argued that women were confined to home or lacked access to public sphere, 153
her "1980s position," 116
as useful point of departure, 135
and our own cultural assumptions, 28
political agenda, 56
and Renato Rosaldo, 3–4, 6, 7, 9
said understanding women meant relating them to men, 17, 60
saw problem of women emerging from role in child-rearing, 19, 59, 93
school background, 2–3
and search for sources of power, 50, 58, 59
and "selves," 22
and the *Signs* article, 10, 11, 155
social "lens" of, 56
and Stanford University, 8–9, 16
(Press), 6
and course at S.U., 1978–79, 145
study of emotion and feeling, 23
as theorist 1, 10–12, 31
and work as theoretical rendition of capitalist gender ideologies, 30
work and de Beauvoir's impact, 222
work as inspiration, 208
and lasting influence of, 17
and resource, 204

Sex
Foucault's identification of unities centering on, 104
"games of truth" and, 105
and gender identities are products of social relations, 27
as natural substrate on which gender is culturally constructed, 93
people of both sexes make choices that count, 17

Women (*continued*)
not midwives, 40
muy hombre (term for courageous
women during Mexican Revolution), 165
are psychologically less individuated
than men (note), 210
rarely articulators of community
decisions, 57
as "rebellious" in Mexico City, 124
Rosaldo wanted them to enter public world, 60
spoke with confidence (Ilongot), 38
as *streetwalker* 107–8
and *wife, maquel,* and *malnom,*
(Dominica), 100, 110, 111
are subject to shifting forms of
incompetence and cultural
idiocy, 193, 208
subordination of (Latin America)
tied to patriarchal family, 119
sustain internal economy and maintain social networks
(Dominica), 95
trivialization of bourgeois, 185
vulnerability of middle class, 29
who are "postliberation" (1980s),
186
who dominate and *mandilones* (section), 170–73
as *zami* (Dominica), 99, 100, 107
Women's
activities performed in public arena
(key paradox), 228
biology as destiny? 169
history and the denial of, 223
motherhood highly valued, but less
prestigious, 153
participation in UMs is struggle for
citizenship, 121
place results from acquired meanings, 12
and debates over place intersect
with debates on democracy,
science, and capitalism, 148

poor, narratives, 27
symbolic presence is inherently
ambiguous, 192
work and status, 39
Work
and accidents, 133
assumptions about, are rhetorical
strategies, 28
conceptual vocabularies of, and sex
are similarly structured,
100
as a domestic (see *María*), 127–28
of men and banana cultivation
(Dominica), 94
and myth of leisure for women,
201
for wages and development of "real
selves," 103
for wages counts as "real," 96
of women not "real" (Dominica), 96
Workers
domestic, in Mexico City, 127–28,
131
men and women as factory workers
(see *maquiladoras*)
men as wage-workers (Dominica),
91, 95

Yanomamo
confusion of culture with masculinities, 69
ethnography of revisited, 55
men and masculine heroics, 68
men as aggressive/violent, 67
men as vulnerable, 82
men's fierceness as writer's masculine imagination, 71–73
public demonstrations of domesticated feelings, 71
women are present but rarely discussed, 72
younger men afraid of injury,
71

Zaire, entrepreneurship in, 39, 45